A BREAKTHROUGH IN VOCATIONAL AND TECHNICAL EDUCATION

The Singapore Story

Law Song Seng

Lee Kuan Yew School of Public Policy
National University of Singapore

Institute of Policy Studies

World Scientific

Published by

World Scientific Publishing Co. Pte. Ltd.
5 Toh Tuck Link, Singapore 596224
USA office: 27 Warren Street, Suite 401-402, Hackensack, NJ 07601
UK office: 57 Shelton Street, Covent Garden, London WC2H 9HE

Library of Congress Cataloging-in-Publication Data
Law, Song Seng.
A breakthrough in vocational and technical education : the Singapore story / Song Seng Law.
pages cm
Includes bibliographical references and index.
ISBN 978-9814616416 (hardcover) -- ISBN 9814616419 (hardcover)
1. Vocational education--Singapore. 2. Technical education--Singapore. 3. Education--Singapore--Aims and objectives. 4. Education--Economic aspects--Singapore. 5. Singapore--Economic conditions. I. Title.
LC1047.S55L38 2014
370.113095957--dc23

2014028096

British Library Cataloguing-in-Publication Data
A catalogue record for this book is available from the British Library.

In-house Editor: Li Hongyan

Typeset by Stallion Press
Email: enquiries@stallionpress.com

Printed in Singapore

To my wife and family
and
to all pioneers and supporters of vocational and technical education

Contents

Foreword

The Singapore success story is remarkable. It probably went from Third World to First World faster than any other nation in human history. This was a result of several factors, including exceptional leadership, a culture of honesty, thoughtful long-term planning, a dedicated civil service and pragmatic public policies, many of which now serve as models for other developing countries.

One unusually successful pragmatic public policy deserves careful study by the world. This has been Singapore's policy on Vocational and Technical Education (VTE). When many former European colonies became independent, the newly independent countries focussed their attention on universities. As Dr Law Song Seng notes in his introduction, VTE "does not carry the prestige naturally associated with a university".

Singapore's wise decision to focus on VTE led to many benefits. Unlike many other developing countries which had to deal with the problem of unemployed university graduates, Singapore could provide full employment to its VTE graduates who were trained with skills that the marketplace demanded. The economic benefits of VTE are clear. Few however have noted the social and individual benefits. Full employment has enabled Singaporean workers to purchase their own homes, educate their children and experience a significant improvement in their standard of living. Equally important, VTE has also enhanced both the self-esteem and personal self-confidence of its graduates.

The extraordinary success of Singapore's VTE has led to many countries coming to Singapore to learn from it. Many are curious to find out how it started. This is why this book by Dr Law is so valuable. He was the first chief executive officer of the Institute of Technical Education (ITE). The story of ITE's journey of transformation is compelling. His book provides rich insights into the fundamental principles for building a strong and sustainable VTE system. The lessons he has drawn from Singapore's experience should also prove valuable for many other countries. This is a book that should be read by all key education policymakers.

We are truly pleased that Dr Law agreed to write this volume for the Institute of Policy Studies, Singapore at the Lee Kuan Yew School of Public Policy (NUS) and we thank him for it. We hope it will spur even deeper and more critical studies on the development of VTE and the crucial role it played in Singapore's remarkable transformation from third world to first.

Prof Kishore Mahbubani
Dean
Professor in the Practice of Public Policy
Lee Kuan Yew School of Public Policy
National University of Singapore

About the Author

Dr Law Song Seng was the founding Director and Chief Executive Officer (1992–2007) of the Institute of Technical Education (ITE) in Singapore. Dubbed as "Mr ITE", his visionary leadership and team have been instrumental in the transformation of ITE. Dr Law continues to share this remarkable Singapore story in vocational and technical education with the international community.

Dr Law previously served as Senior Advisor and Chairman & CEO of ITE Education Services Pte Ltd (2007–2012); Director & CEO of Vocational & Industrial Training Board (1981–1992); Lecturer, Associate Professor and Head of Industrial & Systems Engineering at the National University of Singapore (1973–1983); Visiting Lecturer at the University of Auckland, New Zealand (1980); Manufacturing Development Engineer with the Ford Motor Company in the United States (1972–1973); and Assistant Lecturer in the Singapore Polytechnic (1968–1973).

Currently, Dr Law is Senior Advisor to the Ministry of Education, Brunei Darussalam, Advisor to Temasek Foundation and Member of the Education Sub-Commission in the Singapore National Commission for UNESCO.

Dr Law was educated at Bukit Panjang Government High School and Victoria School in Singapore. A Colombo Plan Scholar, he graduated with First Class Honours in Mechanical Engineering from University of Auckland, New Zealand in 1968, and MSc (1971) and PhD (1972) from University of Wisconsin, USA, under a Ford Foundation Scholarship. He is the recipient of several awards: The National Day Public Administration Medal (Gold)(1984), Education Award (1994) by the Japanese Chamber of Commerce & Industry Singapore Foundation, Center on Education and Training (1997) Distinguished Service Award, Ohio State University, USA, Medal of Commendation (2001) by National Trades Union Congress and Public Administration Medal (Gold)(Bar)(2006) in recognition of his national and international contributions in vocational and technical education.

Acknowledgements

After my retirement in 2007, former colleagues and friends often suggested that I write a book on the transformation of ITE. I had the intention but nothing serious happened for the next few years. Instead, I was helping to strengthen the private consultancy arm of ITE, the ITE Education Services (ITEES) and sharing the Singapore ITE experience. Then, in the later part of 2010, I was encouraged to explore the subject with the Institute of Policy Studies (IPS) under the Lee Kuan Yew School of Public Policy (LKYSPP) at the National University of Singapore (NUS). IPS liked the idea and commissioned this book.

Writing a book is a collective effort. There was much ground to cover in preparing the manuscript. I reviewed the materials and relived the events that had transpired over a 25-year period. In the process, many organisations and individuals have given their support, shared their time and extended assistance in various ways. I am deeply grateful to the following:

- Ms Ho Ching, whose words of encouragement turned what was only my intent into a commitment to write;

- NUS, LKYSPP and IPS for the interest and support in commissioning the book;
- Mr Ong Keng Yong, former Director of IPS, for seeing the value in and authorising this book project;
- Professor Kishore Mahbubani, Dean, LKYSPP and Mr Janadas Devan, Director of IPS, for supporting this project;
- Ministry of Education for the support and Mrs Tan Ching Yee for her words of encouragement in her former capacity as Permanent Secretary (Education);
- ITE, for the access to additional information, verification, preparation and the use of figures and photos;
- Mr Bruce Poh, Director & CEO of ITE, for his firm support of assistance rendered by ITE staff, including Tan Seng Hua, Sabrina Loi, Yek Tiew Ming, Chcang Wcc Kok Shang, Tham Mei Leng, Chua Ai Lian, Lim Hui Ling, Jenny Ang, Teo Keng Mwi and Lee Siew Kheng;
- Ms Chang Li Lin and Dr Gillian Koh of IPS, whose invaluable advice and guidance helped to shape the structure of the book and proposal;
- Ms Tan Jee Peng and the late Mr Wong Chai Kee who have been most generous with their time in reviewing all chapters of the book. Their perceptive critiques, comments and suggestions have helped to add clarity and readability;
- Dr Jean-Etienne Berset and Dr Yaw Ansu for giving helpful comments on some chapters of the book;
- Mr Bahari Abdul of ITE for preparing the figures and photo images;
- Ms Leong Wen Shan for her very helpful copy-editing assistance;
- Ms Li Hongyan for her meticulous editing of the final manuscript; and
- The publishers and editors for reviewing the manuscript and getting the book into print.

While I have received useful critiques, comments and suggestions, the final writing and interpretation reflect my personal experience and views. They do not in any way represent the position or views of the VITB, ITE or the Singapore government, for which I had previously worked. The responsibility for any shortcomings is mine.

Introduction

"Dr Law is new VITB director". This was the title of a short and inconspicuous article in *The Business Times* in June 1981. It was the only news announcing a change in leadership in the day's papers. With some anticipation, the article reported:

> Dr Law, who is in his mid-30s, has been with the Department of Industrial & Systems Engineering of the NUS (National University of Singapore) for the past eight years. A Colombo Plan scholar, he did his first degree in mechanical engineering at the University of Auckland. He obtained his Masters and doctorate from the University of Wisconsin (Madison). Better known for his contribution to university education, Dr Law has yet to establish his standing in industrial circles. His appointment as VITB (Vocational and Industrial Training Board) director will offer ample opportunities for him to prove his calibre as vocational and industrial training is becoming more important with the current emphasis on the

> upgrading of skills and the establishment of high-technology industries.

It further added:

> At the end of last month, the government announced that Dr Tay Eng Soon, Minister of State for Education, would take charge of Singapore's three industrial and vocational training institutes (VITB, Singapore Polytechnic and Ngee Ann Polytechnic). Industry sources say changes in policy with regard to the running of VITB programmes may be in the offing with the change of men at the helm. ("Dr Law," 1981)

That was not considered "exciting" news back in June 1981. Not many in the educational or business world had paid much attention to the changes taking place. This is natural as, looking back, even I did not know much about the world of VTE (Vocational and Technical Education). As it turned out, the anticipation and expectation of changes to come and opportunities afforded by my role were to be quite prophetic.

ABOUT THIS BOOK

Governments and policymakers the world over often pronounce the importance of Vocational and Technical Education for social and economic development. However, despite the many efforts of international organisations and donor countries to provide help in the development of VTE systems in less developed countries, the quality, standards and outcomes often remain elusive.

In addition, VTE is a sector of the educational system that does not normally attract much public attention. It does not carry the prestige naturally associated with a university. When it does attract attention, it is often for the wrong reasons, not least of which is the poor image associated with academic failures in schools. Students of vocational institutes are often assumed to be low-achievers and shunned by their peers. That was our experience too in VTE in Singapore, until a breakthrough in organisational excellence, innovation and ingenuity helped change its image in the early 2000s.

Singapore's experience as documented in this book outlines the sort of leadership, policy choices, governance system, expertise, capabilities and investments that helped achieve that breakthrough in creating an effective system of vocational training.

This book is written in three parts. Part I provides the historical background to the VTE sector in Singapore, a systems view of the dynamics and challenges faced by the VTE system and propounds the fundamental importance of aligning education with economic development goals.

The key focus in Part II is the three waves of transformation from the former Vocational and Industrial Training Board (VITB) to ITE in Singapore that was motivated by an early interest in moving towards organisational excellence and supported by a consistent use of strategic planning. Part of the process was about changing the image of vocational training and creating a unique brand of a world-class ITE education and training model that ITE is today.

In Part III is a reflection on what it takes to build a sustainable high-quality VTE system in the light of Singapore's experience, the international context and changing policy environment. I also share my thoughts on how the Singapore ITE story may be an inspiration to others facing similar challenges in VTE.

This book should be of interest to a wide audience. It sets out how governments and policymakers need to make difficult decisions on policy choices and investment priorities in VTE and training. To researchers and academics, the Singapore ITE experience could be an excellent practical model of what is achievable in vocational training and its impact on social development and mobility. International development and donor aid agencies may find some useful practical lessons in considering the applicability of the strategic policies and fundamental principles in building sustainable high-quality VTE systems from the Singapore experience. Leaders and practitioners will hopefully find in the ITE Model, an inspiration to shape a vision that will transform VTE systems according to their own national needs.

TWENTY-FIVE YEARS LATER

Twenty-five years later, in a world that had changed dramatically, not just in VTE, but the whole of Singapore society, the media headlines read: "Man who made ITE world class calls it a day" and "Thank you, Mr ITE". *The Straits Times* reported on 13 February 2007 "At the helm for 25 years, Dr Law Song Seng has given vocational training a new image and its students a sense of pride" (Ho, 2007), while *The New Paper* reported, "Once under-achievers, they are now lecturers and alma mater.... Former students grateful to ex-CEO for encouraging them" (Mathavan, 2007).

I had officially retired from ITE that month. The former VITB had been replaced by ITE in 1992. Parents, teachers and the public could see that a breakthrough in vocational training under the ITE had taken place. This time round, the news of my retirement was widely reported. There was much media interest and the press wanted to know how we had managed to transform and build ITE into a world-class institution despite the challenges. The public perception of ITE had changed significantly and society could better acknowledge the value and success of its graduates. They saw in ITE hope and opportunity for the less academically inclined students who would have otherwise been left behind in the education system without employable skills. ITE has established itself as a credible part of the post-secondary education system.

The success of ITE was never a given. The VTE system was always evolving. Against all odds, we had to win over a society that deeply reveres economic and social success through an academic education. The early signs that a major transformation had indeed taken place were confirmed when ITE won the prestigious Singapore Quality Award (SQA) for business excellence in October 2005. It was the first educational institution to do so in Singapore. Two years later, the success of the Singapore ITE story was hailed in an article "ITE wins prestigious Harvard award," in *The Straits Times* in September 2007 (Garekar, 2007). ITE had won the IBM Innovations Award in Transforming Government given by the Ash Institute for Democratic Governance and Innovation at Harvard University's Kennedy School of Government. The article reported:

> Singapore's Institute of Technical Education (ITE), once derided as a last resort for under-achieving students, received an "A" from Harvard University yesterday. The 15-year-old institute was awarded a prestigious prize that recognises the world's most transformative government programme with profound impact on citizens' lives.... In a statement, Professor Stephen Goldsmith, Director of the Innovations in American Government Program at Harvard's Kennedy School, said: "Singapore's ITE has created a highly sustainable model for transforming poorly performing educational institutions worldwide". (Garekar, 2007)

This was indeed a breakthrough endorsed by the international community. Commenting on this special honour, Prime Minister Lee Hsien Loong said, "We are all very proud of ITE. ITE has developed a unique brand of education, to train students with 'thinking hands' who excel in technical vocations" (ITE, 2009). Once dubbed "It's The End" in local filmmaker Jack Neo's comedy *I Not Stupid* in 2002, ITE is now "a jewel" of the educational system. Far from being a "place of last resort", it has become "a place of choice" for 25 per cent of school leavers in Singapore.

THREE STEPS IN EDUCATION

Looking back, I have had the privilege to serve and enjoy a journey of 39 years at various levels of the education system in the Singapore Polytechnic, National University of Singapore, VITB and ITE. However, the last 25 years addressing the unique challenges in VITB and leading the transformation of ITE have been most meaningful, rewarding and fulfilling. Twenty-five years is a long time in any organisation. Then again, education is a long-term commitment. Its mission calls for people with commitment, passion, leadership and a heart for students. The media, understandably, were interested to know what I did as the Director and CEO of VITB and ITE from 1981 to 2007. In particular, they wanted to know how I first got started with VITB. What were some of the what, when, how and whys in terms of challenges, policy decisions, strategies and initiatives? What were some of my thoughts for the future?

To begin with not many people knew that I did not choose to serve in the education service. In particular, my association with vocational training came later. It was not that I had carefully planned and charted the steps towards a career in education. And certainly not for 39 years. In fact, if I had my choice, I would have begun my career as a Mechanical Engineer with the Public Utilities Board (PUB). That would have been the natural step to acquire the necessary practical experience to qualify as a professional engineer. The aspiration among engineering graduates then was to be a Chartered Professional Engineer and in my case, it was to become a member of the UK-based Institute of Mechanical Engineers (IMechE).

However, that was not going to be. If it had been so, I wonder how different a career path mine would have been. When I shared this fact with former Minister for Education, Mr Tharman Shanmugaratnam, on the occasion of my retirement, that education was not my first choice, he responded most graciously, saying, "I suspect the best and most lasting contributions in one's career are rarely an outcome of choice." These are words worth reflecting upon. Philosophically, I tell myself that we are not always the authors of our career or life (Law, 2007).

What was the first prophetic step? It was the Public Service Commission (PSC), who saw the urgent needs and so "directed" that, as a recently returned Colombo Plan Scholar, I should be posted to the Singapore Polytechnic. I had received my degree in Mechanical Engineering from the University of Auckland, where I graduated with first-class honours and received the following compliment from the former Prime Minister of New Zealand, the late Sir Keith Holyoake, as reported in the *New Zealand Herald* on 29 December 1967: "Law Song Seng, an engineering student from Singapore, graduated from Ardmore Engineering School with first-class honours after only three years of study and gained the highest marks in his branch of engineering" ("Achievements," 1967). I was quickly hired as an Assistant Lecturer in the School of Engineering at Singapore Polytechnic in February 1968.

The next step was equally prophetic. Within a year, I was presented with an opportunity to take up post-graduate studies under a Ford Foundation Scholarship at the University of Wisconsin-Madison in the United States. At the time, I did not know nor was I told that this scholarship was an integral part of a Ford Foundation-Singapore Polytechnic Development Programme. One of the objectives of the programme was to help prepare a pool of Singaporeans for the first Faculty of Engineering in the then University of Singapore. I applied for the scholarship, was accepted and granted study leave to pursue my post-graduate studies.

EXPERIENCE IN THE UNITED STATES

The trip to Madison, the capital of Wisconsin, in the midst of winter in January 1969 will forever remain in my memory. The flight on the now defunct Pan American airline from Singapore to San Francisco was uneventful, but the domestic flight en route from San Francisco to Chicago was diverted to Pittsburgh in the Northeast for a night due to severe snow storms. Flying in the next day from Chicago to Madison, I could only see a sea of white. Upon landing, the temperature on the ground was freezing. For the first time, I was walking on snow and ice! The University of Wisconsin, one of the "big ten" state universities in the Mid-west, was already popular with foreign students, especially those from Taiwan and India. I enrolled in the Production Engineering Division at the university, which was well known for its pioneering work on the application of statistical methodologies towards solving production engineering problems. As a graduate student, I had to take a minimum of two years of required coursework before presenting myself as a PhD candidate. My research work on "Grinding Process Modelling and Analysis" involved an extensive use of statistics and computer simulation. I successfully defended my PhD thesis and graduated from the University of Wisconsin in June 1972.

I wanted to gain some industrial experience and started to explore employment opportunities. The nature of my PhD training in engineering and statistics at Wisconsin was instrumental in my securing a job with the Ford Motor Company in Dearborn, Michigan. It was not easy as the United States was in deep recession then and the automotive industry was facing stiff competition from Japanese automakers. Working as a Manufacturing Development Engineer in the Metal Stamping Division, I was tasked to initiate research in the relatively new area of manufacturing system reliability. The objective was to develop a programme to improve the design methodology, reliability and productivity of mass production systems. In this case, the underlying application was the optimisation of the total cost of production in stamping and assembly lines with the use of in-process buffers. The stamping and assembly lines produced the roofs, doors, hoods, fenders and other metal parts that went into the manufacture of the cars and trucks. I reported to the Manager of Assembly Engineering Department, which was responsible for the planning, production, tooling, equipment and overall productivity of assembly lines. This one year of working experience gave me a better appreciation of the engineering applications, real production systems and the industrial working environment.

I returned to Singapore in June 1973 after a year of work with Ford Motor Company. In view of my interest and work experience, I was invited to join the newly established Industrial & Systems Engineering (ISE) Department at the then University of Singapore, which eventually became the National University of Singapore (NUS) in 1980. ISE was a new discipline of engineering in Singapore. It uses a multitude of tools such as operational research and statistics to improve quality, productivity and optimisation of processes and systems. Adopting a broad-based interdisciplinary approach in finding solutions to Man-Machine-Materials problems, it was viewed as an important discipline in meeting the needs of Singapore's rapidly increasing manufacturing industry. The first Head of the ISE Department was Professor Donald E. Morgan from the California Polytechnic State University at San Luis Obispo. I taught undergraduate and graduate courses and supervised research projects in subjects ranging from Engineering Systems Analysis to Quality Assurance & Reliability,

Materials & Manufacturing Processes and Engineering Statistics. I was appointed Head of the ISE Department in 1975 and promoted to Associate Professor in 1983.

A CALL TO SERVE IN VOCATIONAL TRAINING

That "unexpected" phone call from the late Dr Tay Eng Soon[1] came in May 1981. A few months earlier, I had returned from sabbatical leave on a Visiting Lectureship at my alma mater, the University of Auckland, New Zealand, in 1980. Dr Tay had just entered politics and was appointed Minister of State for Education and Minister-in-charge of polytechnic and vocational education. We were former colleagues at the Faculty of

---

[1] The late Dr Tay Eng Soon was a minister of state and senior minister of state for education from 1981 to 1993. During this period, he was in charge of technical education and also Chairman of the VITB and ITE. He played a pivotal role in the expansion of polytechnic education, shaping the VITB and laying the early foundation for the establishment of ITE as a post-secondary educational institution in 1992. Under his chairmanship, the vocational training system was greatly expanded in response to the New Education System (NES), which was introduced by the government in 1981. In championing the cause of vocational training, he took a personal interest in driving major national initiatives such as BEST (Basic Education for Skills Training) and WISE (Worker Improvement through Secondary Education) under VITB's Continuing Education and Training (CET) system to upgrade the educational level of the workforce.

Dr Tay was an exceptional man. I remember him most for his selflessness, dedication and commitment to work. Whatever the project he was involved in, you could be sure that everything was done to ensure its success. He was a true champion of vocational and technical education. His humility and concern for the less able and disadvantaged in society had touched the lives and hearts of many students, working adults and Singaporeans.

Honoured by Temasek Education Foundation as the "Father of Singapore's technical and polytechnic education system," part of the citation in *The Straits Times* on 6 August 2010 reads:

> A passionate believer in education, Dr Tay Eng Soon was instrumental in shaping the science and technical education system here, and laying the groundwork for the development of polytechnics. An alumnus of University College London where he obtained a PhD in microwave engineering, Dr Tay started his academic career as a research associate at the Culham Laboratory in Britain, before becoming an associate professor in the engineering faculty of the then University of Singapore from 1970 to 1978. Dr Tay died in 1993. (Wong & Lim, 2010)

Engineering at NUS but had been teaching in different departments. I did not know him well at the time except for his chairing of a "Practical Training Committee," of which I was a member. This was the committee that coordinated the placement of engineering students in industry as partial requirement for the completion of their courses. I accepted his invitation for lunch at the former restaurant run by students of VITB's Hotel & Catering School at Nassim Hill.

Over lunch, Dr Tay explained that with the changes in leadership, he needed someone to take charge of VITB. Explaining the importance of vocational training in the social and economic development of Singapore, he asked if I would consider taking up the appointment as Director of VITB. Among the persuasive reasons was this, "Doing research at the university can be lonely. Your contribution in VITB will be more significant and satisfying." As vocational training was an area for which I knew very little, I did not show much enthusiasm, but neither did I turn down the possibility. I asked for some time to reflect on the matter. Personally, I was not too concerned with the low prestige of VITB at the time, but the people I consulted with strongly advised against venturing into this sector of the education system. The general perception was that VITB was a large institution that was very difficult to manage in view of its scope, diversity and complexity. I, too, had mixed feelings.

After two weeks of due consideration, I said "no". However, the late Dr Tay would not take "no" for an answer. He called again to convince me to take up the challenge. By then, I knew that if I had kept saying "no," he would have kept on asking! And so, I accepted.

SWITCH FROM ACADEMIA TO VOCATIONAL TRAINING

I was a relatively young 36-year-old academic in industrial and systems engineering in 1981. I had just returned after a year of sabbatical at the University of Auckland. There was no compelling reason to leave the university. Although I had some administrative experience as head of department, there was no assurance that I would succeed in leading a much larger institution whose mission was focused on helping the less academically inclined in the educational system. The students who take up vocational training tend to also come from the lower socio-economic strata of society. On the contrary, the challenges were unique with no clear solutions. So, what was it that eventually persuaded me to make the switch from teaching at the university to taking charge of VITB?

The personal character of Dr Tay had made a difference. Equally important, I believe, was our shared beliefs in the value of education that persuaded me to take up the appointment. We believed in the need to create more opportunities for school leavers to acquire the relevant vocational skills to support the skilled manpower needs of a rapidly expanding economy. Besides, it was important for a society to recognise the different aptitudes and interests of students and motivate them to develop their potential. Although I was an academic, I had experienced the earlier years of Singapore's independence as a third-world country. Access to education and jobs was limited and life was not easy. It was therefore not too difficult for me to appreciate these national challenges. In this respect, I saw the special contribution VITB could make in the social and economic development of the people and nation.

Was this call to serve in VITB the third prophetic step? Or, was it the sense of obligation as a public servant? Whatever the reason it was a turning point for me. A crucial decision had to be made; there was a mission to be fulfilled. Perhaps, it was all these and an act of faith on my part in accepting the new challenge.

MY FIRST IMPRESSIONS

The VITB headquarters was located within the former Ayer Rajah campus vacated by the Singapore Polytechnic in 1979. Housed in an old and temporary two-storey building, there was nothing notable about the offices. Despite the efforts in maintaining the premises, water would occasionally leak into my office whenever there was heavy rain. The Ayer Rajah campus itself was in no better condition. The classrooms and training workshops were housed in "Nissan Hut" style accommodation with semi-circular zinc roofs used by the British army during colonial times. There were very limited sports facilities. The level of vocational training was basic as many students only had a primary education. The facilities reflected what was then dominant in the trades — filing, shaping, grinding and sheet-metal work. The image was poor as vocational training was viewed as a last resort for those who did not do well in school.

Do I have any regrets? The switch from academia to VITB was a life-changing decision. I would never know what my career path at the university could have been. But I have no regrets. To me it was a challenge, a commitment and an opportunity. I had simply followed my heart and given my best in making a difference in an area that, although not of my choice, has become a hallmark of my contribution to Singapore's social development. The satisfaction is in the journey. In this light, I hope that this Singapore ITE story can be an inspiration for others in taking up similar challenges that come their way.

"The final test of a leader is that he leaves behind in other men the conviction and will to carry on," so said American intellectual and writer Walter Lippmann. I hope that I have done just that.

Part I

The Early Beginnings

Chapter 1

Historical Perspectives

Learning a trade had long been associated with acquiring practical hands-on skills through on-the-job training. In this learning process, vocational knowledge and skills was transferred from a master craftsman to an apprentice. Historically, this was the prevailing mode of skills development leading up to the early stages of industrialisation in the 1900s. Its evolution into a more formal and structured system of apprenticeship is best exemplified by the dual system of apprenticeship still practised in Germany, Switzerland and the Nordic countries today. Under this system, an apprentice undertakes practical training in a company, which is supplemented by theoretical lessons in a vocational school. Such a system, long established by tradition and strongly supported by unions and chambers of commerce and industry, has proven to be a highly successful model in developing a quality and professional workforce.

The concept of extending formal education to include vocational training within the school system as preparation for work was a more recent development in modern society. It was largely driven by a new demand for vocational and technical skills arising from emerging technologies in an industrial economy. Basic education was no longer sufficient as a transition from school to the world of work. As such, vocational education was instituted as an option in the school system to better prepare students with employable skills. In the process, vocational schools, technical institutes and community colleges evolved and are now a common feature in many educational systems.

VOCATIONAL AND TECHNICAL EDUCATION

What is "Vocational and Technical Education" (VTE)? VTE does not stand alone. It is a subsystem of the larger national education and training system, including training institutes, schools, polytechnics and universities. As a system, it is shaped by local conditions and the wider political, social and economic environment. As such, while the missions and challenges may be the same, the systems do vary across countries. In short, there is no one "universal" model that characterises all VTE systems. Other terminologies commonly used include "Vocational Education", "Vocational Training",

"Technical Education" or "Technical and Vocational Education and Training" (TVET). In Singapore, the term "VTE" (Box 1.1) is broadly used to include the Institute of Technical Education (ITE) and polytechnics. As post-secondary education institutions, they provide VTE for about 65 per cent of a school cohort in Singapore.[1]

However, ITE is not a polytechnic. Its focus is the lower end of VTE in terms of levels of vocational and technical qualifications. It provides a vocationally oriented education that equips its graduates with skills and standards for occupations in major sectors of business and industry. ITE graduates work as technicians and skilled personnel. They are certified under the National ITE Certificate (Nitec) competency-based system of certification. As such, they do not have to undertake further public trade tests, as may be the case in other national education systems. The kind of VTE offered by ITE is therefore not the same as vocational education generally associated with vocational high schools. Since 1973, Singapore decided to phase out vocational education in schools and replace it with pre-employment VTE in a specialised institution outside the school system. With further adaptation, this full-time institution-based model has evolved into the present-day ITE and proven to serve Singapore well in a globally competitive knowledge economy.

According to a Six-Nation Research Study (Metzger et al., 2001), there are "core attributes" that help define VTE:

- What: VTE is typically that part of a student's school-to-work transition. It is education and training for employment. It enables students to acquire knowledge and practical skills for specific jobs or occupations. VTE is traditionally not a university or polytechnic education.
- Who: VTE is primarily focused on young people aged 16 to 20, although it can apply to older working adults who undertake VTE on a part-time Continuing Education and Training (CET) basis.

[1]This is based on the primary school cohort, i.e., 65 per cent of every Primary One class receives some form of VTE post-secondary education.

- Why: Economic and social reasons require that a country sustain a high quality VTE system. VTE's importance rests in a country's responsibility to members of its younger generations who, for various reasons, do not engage in higher education as a first step in their professional careers. Failure to meet this responsibility can result in increased social costs and worse still, high youth unemployment. Second, VTE can play an important role in the process of socialisation for young people. Third, VTE has an effect on a country's economic system; in particular, the quality, productivity and competitiveness of the workforce. Finally, VTE is an important long-term investment in human capital development for individuals, companies and country.

However, certain "attributes" vary substantially across national settings:

- Where: VTE can take place entirely in school or in the workplace, as well as in dual settings that integrate formal schooling and the workplace.
- When: VTE can take place at different stages of the educational system. Typically, it occurs either during the later part of secondary education or at the post-secondary level. This is a policy choice depending on the preference for the duration of general education and shared responsibility with business and industry for VTE.
- How: VTE can vary according to the extent to which the learning is formalised. Typically, school-based VTE appears to be as formalised as general education, while VTE in the workplace can be as structured as school-based learning or as informal as learning on the job.

BEGINNINGS OF VTE PRIOR TO 1960

Singapore was founded by Sir Stamford Raffles as a British colony in 1819 (Box 1.2). The first Government Trade School in Singapore was established in 1930 (Chiang, 1998; Law, 1984). Pre-apprenticeship courses were offered to primary school leavers in electrical, radio, plumbing, automotive mechanics, fitting and turning. Originally located at Newton Circus on Scotts Road, it relocated to larger premises at Balestier Road

BOX 1.1 FACTSHEET ON VTE IN SINGAPORE

In the Singapore context, the term "Vocational and Technical Education (VTE)" is broadly used to include the vocational and career-orientated technical education and training provided by the Institute of Technical Education (ITE) and polytechnics. Both are post-secondary educational institutions with ITE focusing on the lower end of the VTE system for the less academically inclined students. The United Nations Educational, Scientific and Cultural Organization (UNESCO) term covering this broad scope of education and training activities, including VTE, is "Technical and Vocational Education and Training" (TVET). The term "TVET" was first adopted by participants at the TVET World Congress in 1999. It is an all-encompassing term comprising formal and non-formal vocational education, technical training and skills development at various levels for school leavers, out-of-school youth and adult learners.

Polytechnics in Singapore offer a wide range of three-year diploma courses in preparing school leavers with the General Certificate of Education "Ordinary" or GCE "O" level qualification for jobs as technologists, supervisors and other para-professionals. On the other hand, ITE's two-year national certificate courses are more hands-on, competency-based and aimed at training technicians and personnel in skilled occupations for major sectors of the economy in manufacturing, finance and business, technical support and services. The minimum entry requirement for ITE is a successful completion of ten years of general education.

ITE operates as a statutory board under the purview of the Ministry of Education. Viewed as an integral part of the national system of education and training, ITE addresses the needs of the less academically inclined cohort.

The Vocational and Industrial Training Board (VITB) was the predecessor to the present-day ITE. Initially offered as vocational education in secondary schools in the 1960s, VTE soon evolved into a system separate from the schools — first under the Industrial Training Board (1973), then VITB (1979) and ITE (1992).

BOX 1.2 FACTSHEET ON SINGAPORE

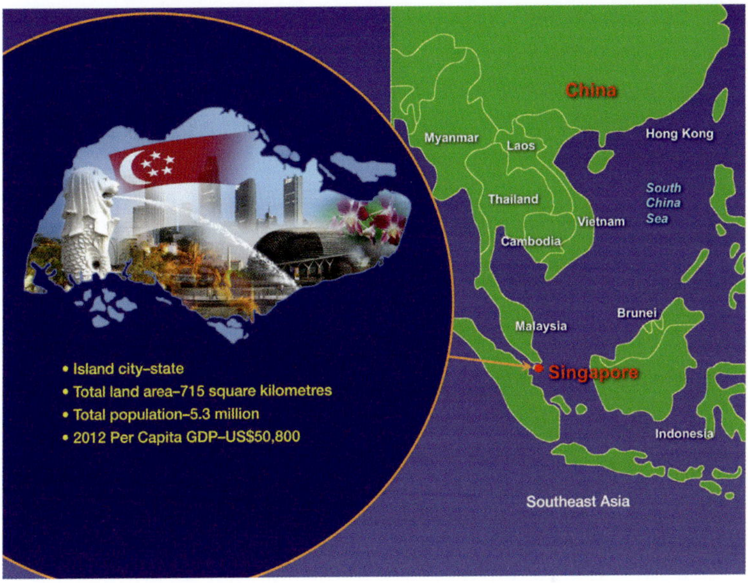

A former British colony founded by Sir Stamford Raffles in 1819, Singapore is today a modern city-state strategically located in Southeast Asia. It became an independent nation in 1965 through separation from Malaysia.

The story of its transformation, *From Third World To First — The Singapore Story 1965–2000*, as told by first Prime Minister Lee Kuan Yew (Lee, 2000) was equally dramatic. In the preface to the book, Mr Lee said,

> "The years after 1965 were hectic and filled with anxiety, as we struggled to find our feet. We were relieved when we found in 1971 that we had created enough jobs to avoid heavy unemployment even though the British withdrew their forces from Singapore… Our climb from per capital GDP of US$400 in 1959 (when I took office as prime minister) to more than US$12,000 in 1990 (when I stepped down) and US$22,000 in 1999 took place at a time of immense political and economic changes in the world…"

(*Continued*)

BOX 1.2 (CONTINUED)

This was a multi-racial society with over five million people living on a small island of 715 square kilometres, and per capital GDP was US$50,800 in 2012. Singapore is today a global centre for business, finance, industry and services. As people are its only resource, Singapore places the highest priority on the education, training and skills development of its people.

in 1940. Reflecting the uncertainty of the time, it was renamed Balestier Technical (Trade) School in 1947, Junior Technical School in 1951 and Balestier Junior Trade School in 1956. Separately, another trade school for boys, the St Joseph's Trade School, was established by the Roman Catholic Church in 1938. Located in Upper Bukit Timah, it was rebuilt in 1970 and the name changed to Boys' Town Vocational Institute. These were the humble beginnings of VTE in Singapore prior to 1960. The interest in education was very much limited to the colonial government's schools that used English as their medium of instruction, and ethnic associations' vernacular schools that conducted classes in Chinese, Malay and Tamil. From the economic perspective, there was no real reason to pay more attention than was necessary, as the economy then did not demand a highly skilled workforce.

Three notable developments, however, began to shape the directions for change. The first was the formation of the Singapore Council of Adult Education (CAE) in 1950, which later became the Adult Education Board (AEB) in 1960. The principal activities of the Board were to provide opportunities in language learning, academic education and further education for out-of-school youth and working adults in the evenings and weekends on a part-time basis.

The second major development was the Dobby Report (Dobby, 1953), which recommended the establishment of Singapore's first polytechnic, the Singapore Polytechnic in 1954. The report also highlighted the need for technical education in schools. This resulted in the government opening the first two secondary technical schools, namely, the Tanjong Katong Secondary Technical School and Queenstown Secondary Technical School in 1956. These were positioned as premier schools to promote the value of technical education and to attract the best students to take up this course of study. The third was the establishment in 1956 of the Joint Advisory Council for Apprenticeship Training, which led to the formulation of apprenticeship training schemes in conjunction with the Ministry of Labour.

BUILD-UP IN THE 1960s

A slow pace and state of affairs with respect to VTE was to continue until 1959 when Singapore attained self-government from the British. There was a sense of urgency in pushing for social and economic development with a new leadership in power under the People's Action Party (PAP). It became apparent that the commercial and service sectors alone could not expand sufficiently to provide jobs for the growing number of school leavers. In search for a solution, the government soon adopted a policy of diversification through industrialisation to accelerate economic growth. With the lack of natural resources, education and training became a top priority and vehicle in maximising the potential of its people. In tandem with this change, an increasing emphasis was placed on a parallel development of vocational and technical education in schools.

As a trading port, Singapore did not have the benefits of tradition or the experience of a culture in manufacturing knowledge and values. There was no ready supply of vocational and technical skills. The government needed to learn, and learn quickly, from the best practices in the developed world. The significant step was the establishment of the first vocational institute, the Singapore Vocational Institute (SVI), in 1964 under the Ministry of Education. The result of a recommendation from the Commission of Inquiry into Vocational and Technical Education (Chan, 1961), the SVI was a reorganisation of the former Balestier Trade School. It took over the full-time two-year craft courses run by the Singapore Polytechnic.

School leavers with at least two years of secondary education took courses ranging from carpentry to plumbing and joinery, refrigeration and air-conditioning, mechanical engineering practice, electrical fitting, motor vehicle mechanics, engineering drawing, machine woodworking, reinforced concrete and brickwork.

As was the practice at the time, day-release — where employers allow employees to attend courses by taking the same day or days off work each week — and evening courses were conducted for working adults who were employed in related technical occupations. Graduates received the Craft or Advanced Craft Certificates awarded by the Ministry of Education. Another recommendation of the Commission was the establishment of two-year secondary vocational schools for primary school leavers who failed to qualify for the more prestigious academic or technical streams leading to the General Certificate of Education "Ordinary" or GCE "O" level examination. Students who completed secondary vocational education could progress for further craft training at the SVI.

With the increasing pace of industrialisation, there was growing concern on how best to expeditiously expand the vocational training capacity so as to meet the manpower requirements of the emerging industries. This task was undertaken by the National Industrial Council in 1968. As a result, the Technical Education Department (TED) was set up within the Ministry of Education to administer and oversee the development of technical schools, vocational and technical institutes, industrial training centres and technical teacher training. The secondary vocational schools, which only provided basic technical skills, were phased out and some were converted into Industrial Training Centres. This was a clear response to the national task in skills development. During this rapid pace of rationalisation and development, the apprenticeship schemes were transferred from the Ministry of Labour to the TED in 1969.

In 1969, the Singapore Technical Institute (STI), an institute dedicated to the training of industrial technicians, was established. In response to the needs of industry, these technicians represented the bridges and worked at a level between the graduates of vocational institutes and the diploma holders of the polytechnics. STI graduates received the Industrial Technician Certificate (ITC) after two years of full-time training. Employment surveys of graduates and feedback from employers had shown that these graduates who had the GCE "O" level qualification and practical skills training were versatile and successful in employment and further career development. In view of their technical training, the graduates were also seen as an ideal pool of potential teachers in technical schools. A highly valued qualification, the ITC has since been replaced by the Higher National ITE Certificate, or Higher Nitec, under ITE's current system of certification in 2002.

FORMALISATION OF VOCATIONAL TRAINING SYSTEM IN THE 1970s

By 1973, TED had developed a training infrastructure that was ready for the next major phase of development. The number of graduates had increased more than 10-fold from 324 in 1968 to over 4,000 in 1972. A new governance structure under a separate authority with greater autonomy and adaptability was deemed necessary to better respond to the needs of a rapidly changing economy. Thus, the Industrial Training Board (ITB) was created in 1973 to centralise, coordinate and intensify industrial training. The late Mr Sng Yew Chong, who was formerly a science teacher and Director of TED, became the first Director of ITB. In policy terms, it meant that for the first time, the system of vocational training was taken outside the school system and placed under a statutory board.

A quasi-autonomous agency created through an Act of Parliament with specific provisions, rights and accountability for industrial training, the ITB had greater autonomy and flexibility in performing its functions. In contrast, training under the TED was administered as a regular civil service department with its more hierarchical governance structure. The ITB, on the other hand, was constituted as a tripartite board with representation from the government, unions and employers. Funded by the government, the ITB took direct responsibility for its administration, staffing, planning, development and operation. Decision-making and implementation could be expedited. In terms of oversight, the Board was still accountable to the Parliament through the Minister for Education. This governance structure encouraged the full participation of industry and unions while safeguarding national interests in industrial training. It was envisaged that this close partnership would enable the Board to better assess the skilled manpower needs and respond in the educational sector, where lack of timeliness could result in high training wastage on the one hand and critical skills shortages on the other. It would otherwise have been difficult to create a training environment that could address the different needs of students within the school system. The autonomy and flexibility as a statutory board had enabled the training system to evolve and realign its mission and goals with changing social and economic needs.

Moving along with developments in vocational training, the previously mentioned AEB was undergoing rapid changes in the character of its operations. As educational opportunities for youth of school-going age in the formal school system had increased, the need for its language and academic education courses diminished. The growth of community centres also reduced the demand for its recreational and community-based programmes. As such, AEB's activities began to extend towards more basic vocational-oriented programmes. It started to offer pre-vocational classes for primary school leavers and training such as office skills, sewing and hairdressing.

It soon became apparent that the domains of the AEB and ITB were inseparable components of a system for the training of school leavers and upgrading the occupational skills and productivity of adult workers. It was therefore decided that the two statutory boards should be merged to rationalise their functions and optimise the use of resources to achieve greater effectiveness. The Vocational and Industrial Training Board (VITB) was therefore established on 1 April 1979 with Dr Ahmad Mattar as the Minister-in-charge and Chairman. Mr Lim Jit Poh was appointed the first Director of VITB and served in this role until 1 June 1981. VITB was to become the single national authority responsible for the promotion, development and provision of vocational training for the industrial, commercial and service sectors of the economy. The primary functions were to provide vocational and industrial training and related continuing education and training (CET) at appropriate levels and forms so that the skilled manpower requirements of Singapore could be met as far as possible by Singaporeans who were trained to the highest level of competence.

LATEST PHASES OF DEVELOPMENT: 1980s AND BEYOND

A training system is constantly shaped by the forces driving change in the social, educational and economic environment. It was therefore not unexpected that the ITB was subsequently restructured and replaced by VITB in 1979 as mentioned earlier, thus paving the way for the second phase of expansion and consolidation. In fact, it is this ability of a system to periodically restructure and adapt that will ensure its relevance and sustainability. The challenges faced by VITB and its response to a New Education System (NES) and high economic growth strategy in the 1980s will be shared in later chapters.

The third phase began with the journey of transformation under the Institute of Technical Education (ITE) when it replaced VITB in 1992. The story of ITE is the modern history of vocational and technical education in Singapore. Its establishment in 1992 was the result of a policy decision by the Ministry of Education to reposition vocational training as an integral part of the post-secondary educational system. With the intake of students targeted at school leavers, who have completed at least 10 years of basic education in schools, this policy shift opened up new challenges and opportunities for the dramatic transformation of ITE into a world-class institution. The key milestones in the evolution of Singapore's vocational training system from 1960 to 2007 are shown in Box 1.3.

BOX 1.3 KEY MILESTONES IN VTE IN SINGAPORE

1960	• Adult Education Board (AEB) was established.
1964	• First vocational institute, Singapore Vocational Institute (SVI), was set up under Ministry of Education (MOE).
1968	• Technical Education Department (TED) was set up in MOE to administer and operate vocational schools and institutes.
1973	• Industrial Training Board (ITB) was established as a statutory board under MOE to replace TED, when vocational training was first formalised outside the school system. • A three-tier National Trade Certificate (NTC) System for skills certification was introduced. • Public Trade Test (PTT) System for those with prior skills experience was introduced.
1979	• Vocational and Industrial Training Board (VITB) was formed through an amalgamation of AEB and ITB.
1980	• Approved Training Centre (ATC) Scheme for companies and associations with the capabilities and resources to run NTC courses was introduced.
1981	• Business Studies Courses leading to Certificate in Business Studies (CBS) and Certificate in Office Skills (COS) were implemented.
1982	• Full-time NTC-2 Courses were first introduced for secondary school leavers.
1983	• Basic Education for Skills Training (BEST) Programme for adult learners to acquire literacy and numeracy skills up to Primary Six level was launched.
1986	• Modular Skills Training (MOST) Programme for adult learners was launched.
1987	• Worker Improvement through Secondary Education (WISE) Programme for adult learners to acquire literacy and numeracy skills up to Secondary Four level was launched.

(Continued)

BOX 1.3 (CONTINUED)

1990	• New Apprenticeship System (NAS) modelled after Germany was introduced for school leavers.
1991	• Training Initiative for Mature Employees (TIME) with choice of instruction in English, Mandarin, Malay or Tamil was launched.
1992	• Institute of Technical Education (ITE) was established as a post-secondary institution to replace the VITB, thus repositioning vocational training to post-secondary level.
1994	• Certified On-the-Job Training Centre (COJTC) system launched to promote and upgrade quality of OJT in companies.
1995	• ITE new headquarters at Dover Drive was completed. • ITE's first five-year strategic plan (1995–1999) entitled *ITE 2000* was launched.
1997	• First Corporate Rebranding Programme to enhance the profile and public image of ITE was rolled out.
2000	• ITE's second five-year strategic plan (2000–2004) entitled *ITE Breakthrough* was launched.
2002	• ISO 9001:2000 Certification for ITE's Quality Management System was attained. • e-Tutor Learning System (e-Tutor) was implemented. • e-Student Administration System (e-Student) was implemented. • New National ITE Certification System (Nitec) was introduced to replace the NTC System and streamline ITE's certifications.
2003	• ITE Education Services Pte Ltd (ITEES), the consultancy arm of ITE, was formed to share ITE's expertise with the international community.
2005	• ITE's third five-year strategic plan (2005–2009) entitled *ITE Advantage* was launched. • First comprehensive Regional Campus, ITE College East, was completed.

(*Continued*)

BOX 1.3 (CONTINUED)

	• ITE's brand of *"Hands-on, Minds-on, Hearts-on"* education was articulated. • ITE won the Singapore Quality Award (SQA) for overall business excellence.
2006	• First Triennial International Conference on Vocational and Technical Education was organised by ITE.
2007	• ITE won the Harvard-IBM Innovations in Transforming Government Award conferred by the Ash Institute at Harvard Kennedy School.
2008	• First Technical Engineer Diploma in Machine Technology was developed in collaboration with Ministry of Education, Youth and Sports, Baden-Württemberg, Germany.
2010	• ITE's fourth five-year strategic plan (2010–2014) entitled *ITE Innovate* was launched. • The second Regional Campus, ITE College West, was completed. • Second Technical Engineer Diploma in Automotive Engineering introduced, in collaboration with the Ministry of Education, Youth and Sports, Baden-Württemberg, Germany.
2011	• ITE won the Singapore Quality Award (SQA) with Special Commendation — first and only education institution to win this pinnacle award. • The Technical Diploma in Culinary Arts was launched in collaboration with the renowned Institut Paul Bocuse, France.

Chapter 2

Dynamics and Challenges

VTE systems are dynamic. As systems, they are subject to the forces driving change in an economic environment that is increasingly global and competitive. Playing a crucial role in social and economic development, they constitute an important sector of the education and training system. The dynamics and challenges are complex and unique.

An outcome of the interplay of dynamics and challenges is a VTE system or model that reflects the political leadership, economic goals and social aspirations of the people. No two systems are exactly the same. There is no one ideal universal system for all. The challenges and goals may be the same but the responses would vary depending on the kinds of policies adopted in education, skills training and economic development. On a continuum of possible models, the system can vary from the Singapore ITE-type of full-time institution-based training on the one hand to the dual system of apprenticeship in Germany and Switzerland on the other.

SYSTEM DYNAMICS

An analysis of the VTE operating environment in the light of Singapore's experience can illustrate the way the dynamics and challenges interact and eventually resulted in shaping the country's ITE. As shown in Figure 2.1, a VTE system is constantly subject to the external forces driving change in the political, educational, economic and social environment. The system responds to and is in turn shaped by these forces, interdependently working within a larger system (i.e., the nation) in building a more vibrant economy and socially inclusive society.

POLITICAL

Politically, it is in the interest of governments to have a VTE system capable of responding to the skilled manpower needs of the economy and at the same time maximising the potential of its people. In education, apart from universities and polytechnics, the role and success of VTE will have important political, social and economic ramifications for a nation. For these reasons, VTE is a sector of the educational system that

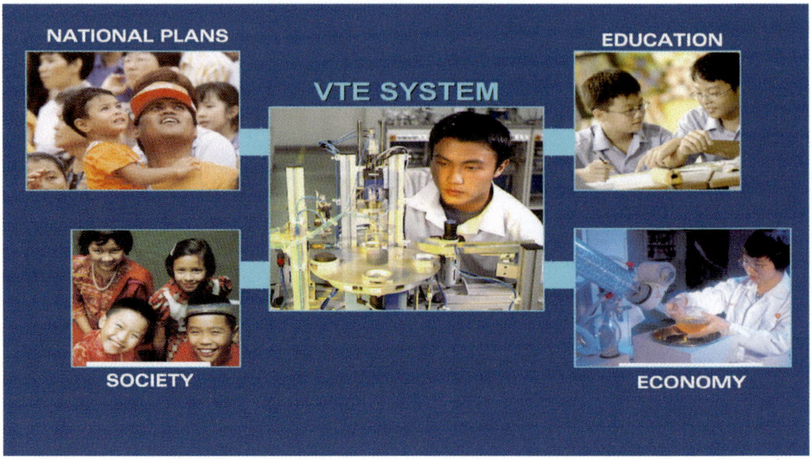

Figure 2.1 Dynamics and challenges

deserves much government attention and support; it should be a primary responsibility of the government.

Former Prime Minister of Singapore, Lee Kuan Yew, after a visit to ITE College East in 2008, was quoted in *The Straits Times*, saying:

> I think it (ITE) is one of the success stories of Singapore that we are able to uplift the academically less-advantaged 25 per cent and use their other skills, hands-on skills and ability to improvise, to give them that added value so that they can make a contribution to life, to society and to make a good living. (Goh, 2008)

This is what makes Singapore's ITE unique. Its mission is "to create the opportunities for school leavers and adult learners to acquire the skills, knowledge and values for employability and lifelong learning in a global economy." Its focus is the training of technicians and skilled personnel for the major sectors of the economy. Reiterating the government's policy on moulding diverse strengths in education, former Education Minister Dr Ng Eng Hen said:

> Singapore believes that every student should be developed to his/her fullest. But this does not mean equal or similar outcomes. We accept the inherent differences in students' abilities… To achieve

> our educational goals, we build higher education institutions at varying levels to cater to a spectrum of academic ability... The Institute of Technical Education (or ITE in short) was established in 1992. It is meant for the lower quartile of our students in terms of academic ability... I say this with pride. ITE is a shining jewel in our system... It has given confidence to this group of students, provided them vocational expertise to be employed to be self-sufficient, and ignited their internal drive to upgrade themselves...(Ng, 2008 June).

Providing that alternative pathway, ITE, as a post-secondary education institution, adds diversity and robustness to the education system. VTE is not a panacea for all social and educational issues that a country may face, but it is an essential and powerful educational tool. It is an enabler that gives hope and meaning to those who may not do as well in a purely academic environment. By offering an experiential learning environment, these students can blossom with self-esteem and have the confidence to want to study hard and do well in life. Lives can be transformed. What ITE has demonstrated is that they too deserve the best in a world-class learning environment that is no less than a polytechnic or university. While the majority of graduates will enter employment and build a professional career in industry, others will continue to further their education and training or become entrepreneurs. Politically, when the young can be meaningfully engaged in education, productive work and are earning a good living, there will be a stable and inclusive society.

EDUCATION

From an educational perspective, ITE is an integral part of the national education and training system in Singapore. As such, there are good reasons for close linkages and co-ordination between the schools under the Ministry of Education (MOE) and ITE. Schools represent the initial springboard in building a strong foundation for further education and skills development. The national objective of developing each individual in accordance with his or her talent and potential would not be achieved if students were not sufficiently motivated to do their best in schools.

In this educational value chain, those who can benefit from vocational training after leaving school need to be persuaded and convinced of the value in further training. The progression from schools to VTE cannot be taken for granted.

Our experience in VITB in the 1980s had shown that in a tight labour market situation when there was shortage of manpower, it was very tempting for school leavers, especially from the lower socio-economic strata of society to seek direct employment and forgo an opportunity for skills training. In fact, even those who had already enrolled might be tempted to leave prematurely because of the need to help the family financially. Some would choose immediate gains rather than invest in the future. VTE systems must therefore be flexible and offer options such as full-time, apprenticeship or part-time training at various levels of certification, so as to attract and accommodate the abilities, interests and challenges of a diverse group of students.

ECONOMY

Another key driving force is the economy. A strong economy creates jobs and wealth for the people and nation. However, sustaining economic growth requires a ready pool of relevant and well-trained manpower, because the skills sets required at the workplace will continue to change due to new developments in knowledge and technologies, organisational structures, the internet and economic restructuring. An underlying principle is therefore to ensure that educational systems are aligned with and responsive to the needs of the economy. Vocational training today is no longer limited to the acquisition of practical skills though this must remain the core foundation in skills development. Providing a more broad-based holistic training with social skills such as communications, problem-solving, independent thinking and teamwork will make for a more versatile, market-relevant and all-rounded graduate. This type of training will also be more appealing to the youth of today.

The availability of a skilled workforce is an important factor in the global competitiveness of the nation. International investors would not be attracted to commit multi-billion dollar investments in Singapore if there was no assurance of a professionally trained and skilled workforce. On the other hand, a governmental institution such as ITE does not work alone. It needs to coordinate its efforts and collaborate closely with its network of stakeholders and partners. By its very nature, vocational and skills training is incomplete without the experience that can only be acquired in the real world of work. In addition, while the government plays the dominant role in funding the education and training institutions in Singapore, it also works in close partnership with employers and unions in the continuing education and training of the workforce.

A system has many parts working interactively towards achieving common goals and objectives. At the national level, ITE, as a statutory board, operates under the purview of MOE. In actual fact, there are three key stakeholders with respect to manpower planning — the Ministry of Manpower, Ministry of Trade and Industry and Ministry of Education. Today, a National Manpower Council (NMC) chaired by the Minister of Manpower oversees overall planning and direction to ensure national coordination and alignment among the key stakeholders in manpower planning and development. The Council conducts annual reviews on the economic prospects for graduates, the medium and long-term manpower demands, and sets intake places for the educational institutions. The ITE, polytechnics and universities are represented at this Council by the MOE. Within the MOE is a platform chaired by a Minister of State in charge of technical education for consultation with the polytechnics, ITE and the industries.

At the institutional level, ITE conducts its own review, planning and development of training programmes. In particular, it works with employers in the process of curriculum development and approval of national skills standards to ensure the close linkage between training and the economy. Through its internal system of governance and operation, it reaches out and actively engages with its stakeholders and partners, including governmental ministries, agencies, schools, parents, teachers, employers, unions and the society at large.

Manpower planning is taken seriously among the stakeholders and at all levels. It works because of the coordination. There are clear objectives aligned with national social and economic goals and strategies. The projection of manpower needs and implications for training and skills development are useful guides in prioritising investment in human resources. Another key element is effective follow-through and implementation by the education and training institutions. Part of this process are the internal systems and processes for further consultation, feedback and monitoring of the targets and outcomes. The core capabilities and capacity to respond in a timely manner is crucial. Above all, a culture of working in concert across ministries and agencies within the public service to achieve national goals is essential.

UNIQUE CHALLENGES

Governments the world over often pronounce the importance of VTE. Much research, studies and analyses have been done. Despite the intent and efforts made, VTE continues to remain a "weakest" link in the total education system in many countries. Unlike the university or the polytechnic, VTE is neither glamorous nor prestigious. It suffers from a poor image. The quality, standards and outcomes often remain elusive. In contrast, parents continue to cherish the hope and aspiration that their children will make it to university. This intense desire to pursue an academic education is pervasive in Asian societies. It generates unrealistic expectations amongst parents and puts an undue amount of pressure on students in schools. Ironically, we read frequent reports of shortages in vocational and technical manpower.

A case in point is the impact of VTE on the rapid social and economic development in China. A 2003 article entitled "Harnessing China's people power" in *The Straits Times* (Chua, 2003) reported on the tremendous need for expanding basic education and vocational training in China in order to match the massive growth of the economy. Quoting a China report entitled "China's Education and Resources," released in the same year, the article explained that there were already great concerns on the education, quality of the workforce and mismatch of skills experienced by rapid industrial development and productivity improvements. As an example, it said that while there was a great shortage of skilled workers in the Suzhou Industrial Park, there were many university graduates who could not find jobs. Yet, all parents wanted was to enrol their children in academic high schools and universities, but not what they considered as "second-rate" vocational schools in a rapidly growing but developing economy. The problems and concerns highlighted are not peculiar to China. In fact, these are the same concerns and challenges faced by policymakers and educators who oversee VTE in both the developed and developing countries.

In the following year, I was invited to share our Singapore experience as a keynote speaker in an international symposium on vocational training in Suzhou, China (Law, 2004). The country was already achieving extraordinary rates of rapid economic growth. It was therefore a timely symposium for China to review and share views on how it should restructure and position its vocational and technical education and training system. While there were still policy issues regarding funding, recognition and public-private sector participation, I observed a clear interest in pursuing the qualifications of well-established overseas institutions.

On the sideline of the symposium, a reporter from trade magazine *Shanghai Business* (Lu, 2004) asked for my views on the market demand for vocational skills training in view of China fast becoming a global manufacturing centre.

Based on our experience, my view was that the demand for vocational skills to support China as a global manufacturing centre would greatly increase. The range of skilled technical workers required and their levels of skills would also increase as the manufacturing sector expands in terms of production capacity, supporting services and technological sophistication. There would be an increasing need for the government to give higher priority and focus on vocational technical education and training. The market for vocational skills training in China is expected to experience phenomenal growth in the years ahead.

As China is a big country with a huge population, the task of providing vocational skills training to support industrialisation is enormous. The challenge would be for the government and the private sector industries to collaborate and maximise their resources to ensure that vocational and technical training is relevant and delivered at the appropriate levels in meeting the needs of the growing economy.

Major Chinese cities like Shanghai, Beijing and Suzhou, which have been experiencing rapid economic growth, will become the leading education and training hubs in China. They will set the pace and act as role models for other provinces and cities. In particular, the increasing number of industrial parks in these mega cities will boost the market demand for vocational skills training throughout China.

A similar dilemma is faced even by successful and developed economies in Asia, for example, the Republic of Korea. In an article in *Time* magazine on 14 November 2005, entitled "Breaking Through," it was reported that:

> The Republic of Korea has built a modern economy through manufacturing, but has now started to see significant breakthroughs in Information Technology, Bio-technology and Life Sciences. Korea's scientists are on the cutting edge of stem-cell research. New entertainment industries like movies, music and Internet games are growing rapidly. (Spaeth & Macintyre, 2005)

By 2011, an article in *The Straits Times* reported that there were "too many graduates in South Korea":

> South Korea's government has decided that too many people are going to college... And that has to be sobering for anyone who has assumed that education will be the antidote to the downward mobility pressure of globalisation. [South Korea] is working to restore the lustre of a high school diploma as a stopping point for some and to establish a vocational track for others... More than 60 per cent of Koreans aged 25 to 34 have higher education... But South Korean officials are alarmed that many graduates are

> not finding jobs — more than 40 per cent in the past year, even though the country's economy was doing pretty well… That is why President Lee Myung Bak is promoting alternatives… "Professional footballers just need to be good at kicking footballs," Mr Lee said. "They don't need to graduate from Seoul National University…". The government also is investing in vocational schools designed to put young people on a career track without going to college. (Hiatt, 2011)

Closer to home, the Singapore society had also wrestled with the many challenges and policy issues in the course of our social and economic development since independence. There is no doubt that our priority and heavy investment has resulted in a public education system that is much admired in the world. The achievements of our students in mathematics and science are highly ranked internationally. Singapore came up tops by the International Institute for Management Development in its World Competitiveness Yearbook in 2008 (ranked third in 2014) for having an education system that met the needs of a competitive economy. However, with socio-economic progress and new challenges and opportunities in a global economy, Singaporeans are also pressing for more places in the local universities.

The Straits Times cited Singapore's Minister of State for Education Lawrence Wong in an article entitled "More new varsity places for poly grads":

> When the government expands the university sector to give places to more than 30 per cent of students from each cohort, more of these places will go to polytechnic graduates, said then Minister of State for Education Lawrence Wong. But it must ensure that the new degree programmes remain relevant to the industry and focus on hands-on practice. "We must think of providing a university pathway that will build on the strengths of their polytechnic education and allow them to maximise their potential in areas they are good at," he added. Doing so will ensure that these students enjoy good job prospects when they graduate… By 2015, Singapore's four universities, together with the Singapore Institute of Technology, which offers degrees for polytechnic

upgrades, will be able to take in 14,000 Singaporeans each year. That means 30 per cent of each Primary 1 cohort will get to go to a local university. (Davie, 2011)

Responding to the higher social aspirations of the people while trying to maintain relevance, quality and standards of the education system will be a continuing challenge for a government.

What can governments do to improve the VTE system? Recognising the importance of VTE is necessary but not enough. It will take much greater coordinated and concerted efforts and a government, willing and ready to invest in VTE, to make a real difference. What will it take to develop graduates who not only have the technical knowledge and skills but also values for employability and lifelong learning? Graduates must not only be well trained, entrepreneurial and confident, but must also be ready to contribute to the economy and serve society. Beyond these more immediate educational goals are the questions of how educational institutions should respond to the increasing expectations of stakeholders in terms of organisational excellence, systems, processes and best practices. What will it take to build a sustainable quality VTE system that is relevant and responsive to changes in a global economy?

Policymakers, administrators and educators would have reflected on these challenges and issues. Many would be looking for possible solutions. From a strategic perspective, which models of VTE may accommodate the different social, economic, educational and cultural conditions in different countries? Is the VTE system aligned with and does it help to sustain continuing economic growth? How is it positioned within the national education and training system? Does it address the needs of school leavers who are academically disadvantaged? How well is VTE accepted by school leavers, parents, industry and society? What is its public image? What are the governance, funding and educational policies and issues? How can the goals and objectives be translated into reality? What makes an effective VTE system? And how do we measure the results?

Singapore too had faced similar challenges and issues as it strove to build a high-quality sustainable system. It has been a continuous journey reflecting the challenges, opportunities and responses. Driven by the changing needs in social and economic development, the search for the appropriate system was characterised by the speed in which the vocational training system was restructured; over a period of 24 years, we saw the birth of four institutions, namely, the TED (1968), ITB (1973), VITB (1979) and ITE (1992).

AN INTERNATIONAL PERSPECTIVE: VTE IN FOUR COUNTRIES

These dynamics, challenges and issues were the subject of discussion and debate in an international education research project entitled "Different Paths, Similar Pursuits — The Economic and Personal Potential of Vocational Training and Education in an International Context", involving Switzerland, Japan, Singapore and the United States (Metzger et al, 2001). Singapore and Switzerland were relatively smaller economies while Japan and the United States were the world's largest. This specific project on VTE was one of the educational projects conducted under a broader Six-Nation Education Research framework, hosted by the University of Pennsylvania, to explore and compare the relationship between education systems and economies in six nations.

The underlying question of interest in the research, directed by Professor Christoph Metzger of University of St. Gallen in Switzerland, was "What can participating countries learn from each other's experiences in order to understand the differences and similarities among the VTE systems in each country?" The other principal members of the research team included Dr Jean-Etienne Berset of the Federal Office for Professional Education and Technology in Switzerland; Professor Hidenori Fujita of University of Tokyo; Professor Robert Zemsky of University of Pennsylvania; and me, representing ITE in Singapore.

Conducted over a period of four years, from 1996 to 2000, the main focus was the role of VTE in the changing social and economic context in the four countries. Adopting a qualitative ethnographic approach, the main observations were gathered through site visits and focus group interviews with stakeholders, including students, teachers, parents, employers and government officials. The site visits were, in reality, a mirror reflection of the differences and similarities of VTE in practice. The images of the different pathways within the national education and training systems convey powerfully the impact of global forces driving social and economic changes in the various communities. At each of the site visits in the four participating countries, the researcher from the country whose VTE system was under study would act as the host. The other members would act as visitors. In this way, the images gathered were richer as we evaluated our own VTE systems not only through our own lenses but also through the "borrowed" lenses of our colleagues in an international collaborative research setting.

After much research and deliberations, what lessons did we learn? The first was that the educational pathways in VTE may be different but the goals and concerns are the same. They represent opportunities for school leavers to prepare themselves for employment and career development through further education and training. The crux lies in the whens, whats and hows of VTE. The responses would very much depend on the economic, social and cultural conditions of the local communities. There is no one ideal universal system to suit all needs. Whereas the United States and Japan have adopted a more liberal and open-door policy in providing 12 years of general education, including vocational education in upper secondary schools, the VTE systems in Switzerland and Singapore are seen to have a more specialised focus on skills development in meeting manpower needs.

In Switzerland, private industry takes the greater responsibility of training young people through the dual system of apprenticeship. It is a system widely recognised for its quality, professionalism and comprehensiveness. It is the main system that is responsible for training 75 per cent of a school cohort (as at year 2010) after nine or 10 years of general education. Under this industry-based model of training, the apprentice acquires practical skills on-the-job in companies and receives complementary theoretical lessons in government vocational schools. Regulated by federal laws but carried out by the chambers of commerce and craft at their own costs with the support of labour unions, it is a system of formal training for young people that is unmatched in other countries.

In Japan, there is less priority on vocational training in the educational system. A high school education is the norm. There are also specialised vocational high schools. Employers prefer to recruit those with a high school education and train them in-house. The skills of employees are developed through the well-established industry practice of structured on-the-job training in companies. In this traditional mode of skills acquisition, all employees, irrespective of rank, are exposed to the inner workings of the company by rotational deployment. However, this practice — borne out of the strong Japanese culture of lifelong employment — was already beginning to change in the face of globalisation and increased business competitiveness.

As for the United States, the VTE system is one of diversity, fluidity and choice in comparison to more formal systems with common standards and clear pathways. As such, it was difficult to define a national education system. The state, local community and private sectors take primary responsibility for education and training. In general, VTE is offered as a "vocational technical" track within a senior high school programme. While students in this track would attend academic classes with other students at school, they would travel to a regional vocational high school for their practical workshop lessons. In such a social setting, the poor image and stigmatisation of "vocational technical" students and the association with low ability was visible and accentuated. In a loosely coupled system of education and employment, students who are not college bound often wander in and out of a variety of job experiences before settling on a career. They may then consider returning to a community college to earn a two-year associate degree or enrol in an academic programme with transfer credits to a four-year college or university.

In the case of Singapore, VTE is largely provided by the polytechnics and ITE. Based on full-time institution-based training, these post-secondary institutions are an integral part of the formal educational system. Heavily funded by government, their missions are strongly aligned towards supporting social and economic goals. The efforts of the government in investing and developing people with the relevant vocational and technical skills have been a strategic incentive in attracting foreign direct investments for economic development. With national manpower planning, student intake targets were set and measures taken to influence career choices towards science and engineering in order to support the needs of industry. Within the efficiency-driven education system, special attention is paid to the different needs of students. The less academic students in schools would undertake a technically oriented track, the Normal (Technical), before progressing to ITE.

Unlike the apprenticeship model, which focuses more on the specific needs of individual employers in industry, the success of ITE has been its ability to build relevant skills and competencies within a more holistic educational environment. However, it was also observed that with an increasingly knowledge-based economy, VTE systems would likely converge towards greater diversity in pathways, opportunities in maximising individual potential, flexibility in curriculum development and acquisition of skills and values for lifelong learning.

Secondly, the debate was not so much about the importance and values of VTE, nor the approaches or training systems. What emerged as a more important concern was whether sufficient attention had been paid to students who were weak in academic achievements. Experience has shown that not all students will do equally well in an academic setting. Children come with different talents, abilities, interests and aptitudes. They learn and develop differently at various stages of their lives. The more technically inclined will be motivated to do well in a more experiential "hands-on" learning environment. The issue is not whether institutional-based training, apprenticeship or on-the-job training offers a better option; each system has its place and values. What is important is that programmes are relevant and of high quality in meeting the needs of the students, industry and society. VTE is an expensive but a necessary investment, whether funded by the government, industry or individuals.

The third lesson is one that has continued to be a key challenge in many countries. We call this the "college mania" phenomenon or "paper chase". This intense desire to pursue a university degree was found to be pervasive in all four participating countries. The reasons are understandable. Traditionally, in most cultures, scholars had been held in high esteem in societies, perhaps more so in Asia. Scholarship was the path to a successful career cherished by many. To do well academically in school was therefore of utmost importance. However, despite the wider choices in education and careers, parents continue to cherish the hope and aspiration that their children will make it to university. This unrealistic expectation from parents and sometimes, teachers, generates intense competition and pressure in the school system.

The fallout of this undue focus on the university degree is the "college mania" phenomenon. The consequence is a prejudice against and poor image of VTE and all its negative associations with those who do not do well in schools. The distinction between the scholar and a mechanic with low-level vocational education will only perpetuate the poor image. The negative perception is more likely to be felt when academically weaker students are not viewed as a part of the educational mainstream. For example, in the United States, the image of vocational education students being bussed from their home schools to a regional training centre reinforced the problem of stigmatisation. This was not a problem in Switzerland because the majority of school leavers undertake the dual system of apprenticeship, which is viewed as an integral part of the education and training system. In Singapore, the former VITB was looked down upon as a place of last resort because it was positioned for those at the lower end of the educational system. The repositioning of vocational training at the post-secondary level under ITE in 1992 provided opportunities for its transformation and change of image.

If an education system is to maximise the potential of all students, then this negative perception and old mindset must change. Every individual needs to be developed. Different pathways of education and training are important in building a strong and robust educational system. The diversity in the system will bring out the best in each individual.

Accepting vocational training as an integral part of the mainstream education and training system is an important step towards shaping a more inclusive society.

PERSONAL INSIGHTS

The opportunity to participate in the above international research project, albeit in education and not engineering, was too attractive to pass up. Unlike my earlier tenure in industrial and systems engineering at the National University of Singapore, being the Director and CEO of ITE did not ordinarily encourage me to undertake or allow much time for research. What then was my interest and motivation? On reflection, part of the answer could be found in the project title "Different Paths, Similar Pursuits", which aptly defines in an overall sense what VTE is all about.

VTE students generally represent the lower socio-economic strata of society. As such, giving these students a system that they can be proud of is even more crucial in enhancing social development and mobility. In view of its mission, the success of ITE and its graduates is a significant factor in the wider context of building a more inclusive society in Singapore.

I had shared some of my views with the late Dr Tay Eng Soon, Senior Minister of State for Education. I drew his attention to an article entitled "The Training Trap" published on 21 April 1990 in *The Economist*. The article was quite critical of a new initiative of the British government at the time in establishing training and enterprise councils to tackle the problem of skills shortage. In forwarding the article to him, I wrote that "the article raises many doubts and concerns on the setting up of Training & Enterprise Councils (TECs)." His reply was crisp and to the point: "Basic problem in the UK (United Kingdom) is their class system and disdain for blue-collar skills. No matter what schemes they try out, if skills are looked down upon, they will have great difficulty. Are we in similar danger in Singapore?"

The question he posed was taken seriously enough to elicit my response below:

Chairman/VITB, 2 May 1990:

1. I will try to address the question you posed with reference to the article, "The Training Trap," in *The Economist*.
2. The question is "Are we in similar danger in Singapore?" The question has profound implications on the type of society we expect to see in Singapore in the long run. There is no real danger at this time.
3. My feeling is that we do not today have a class system highly entrenched in the working system as in the UK. The Singapore society is much more egalitarian in that we value equal opportunities rather than given rights. The people who run the government and private sectors have risen from the rank and file of society based on merit and performance. The majority of our people share a common background of a hardworking immigrant population.
4. However, the question needs close attention of our leaders because of the dangers of a class society. And the government has in fact helped diminish these dangers through a number of its policies on education, healthcare and housing.
5. Opportunities for education and training must be made available to the people depending on their own abilities and choice. Singaporeans have the drive and are fundamentally achievement-oriented. Rewards must be seen to be commensurate at all levels of the workforce. In due course, workers at the lower ranks need to be paid more because they must also be rewarded for the hard and socially less desirable jobs. If there is going to be any significant discontent, it is likely to come from the less successful, lowly paid strata of society.
6. The success of moral education in our schools is crucial. Children at a younger age are more amendable to concepts of right and wrong, ethical values, responsibilities and obligations in society. They can imbibe these through good examples of teachers and others. The right values, once accepted, will help make a more cohesive society. There will then be less danger of a class society developing.

7. In this connection, our project on VITB image building and promoting the value of vocational training in schools and subsequently the public, have an important bearing on the question you posed.

Dr Law Song Seng
Director/VITB

In his response on the following month, Dr Tay replied, "Thank you for your response. The way to even upwards *[sic]* for the lower paid is to improve their productivity through job enlargement and increase their pay, e.g., I believe we use too many people as clerks and assistants as compared with offices in the West. Our training should aim at *job enlargement.* I agree with the points you have made."

With the impact of even more rapid economic restructuring and changes in technologies in a globally competitive economy, these social issues had generated great interest among policymakers and researchers. There were growing concerns on the role of VTE systems in social and economic development in both the developing and developed economies.

Singapore too was facing the challenges of economic restructuring, worker upgrading and improving productivity in a knowledge economy. Meanwhile, the ITE had started its journey of transformation with its first five-year strategic plan "ITE 2000" in 1995, to develop ITE into an established post-secondary technical institution by year 2000.

Personally, I was glad that I had taken part in this international research project. I was also curious to see what university professors would be looking for in an international academic research setting. It had given me new perspectives and a deeper understanding of the dynamics and challenges at a more strategic and international level. While there are more differences in approach and delivery, the underlying challenges, goals and concerns are the same. Shaped by the local conditions and community, the different systems have successfully served the needs of the four respective economies.

Before embarking on the project, I was already of the view that it would be futile if one were to search for the "ideal" system, as if it could be simply transplanted across countries. In a letter to Professor Metzger in 1996, I wrote, "... the research intent should not be focused on proving that one system is better than another, i.e., that there is a universal 'best' model. In view of the increasing need for greater flexibility and responsiveness to meet changing needs at the workplace, a national system of training will more likely be a 'mixed' model comprising various approaches and options. On the other hand, an in-depth comparative study can help to identify the relative strengths and understand how the different systems have contributed to the social and economic goals of the participating countries."

With new insights from the international research project, it was clear that ITE was heading towards and transforming in the right direction. In 2000, we formulated an ambitious second strategic plan "ITE Breakthrough", to develop a world-class technical education institution for a knowledge-based economy. In particular, the following were the perspectives that arose from the project that shaped the efforts to strengthen the ITE system:

- *Preparing graduates for a knowledge-based economy:*
  The pedagogy and curriculum models must extend beyond the delivery of core knowledge and technical skills. Employability skills, including communications, Information Technology (IT) and problem-solving, provide a foundation for lifelong learning. An IT-based teaching and learning environment will also help to further promote independent learning, collaboration, creativity and innovation. Students will be empowered to be active learners, develop with greater confidence and self-esteem and become better prepared for the working world. To achieve these educational outcomes, a system of regular curriculum reviews must be put in place to ensure that ITE as an institution stays relevant and responsive to the changing needs of the students and economy.

- *Positioning ITE in the mainstream of education and training:*
  The image of vocational training will continue to be an issue especially when it is focused on meeting the needs of the lower end of a school cohort. This means that while staying focused in its mission, ITE must

continue to build on its strengths and promote its value and importance to society and the economy. In this respect, the standards of world-class facilities, quality programmes and career success for graduates that society has come to expect of a university or polytechnic should also be available for ITE. At the same time, the ready acceptance of vocational training cannot be taken for granted. There is a continuing need to promote the image of ITE as a post-secondary institution within the mainstream of education and training.

- *Importance of linking VTE with work experience:*
  Making work an integral part of VTE will strengthen the school-to-work transition for young people. Although the "first-school-then-work" institution-based training may seem more compatible with the needs of a knowledge-based economy, there is value to retain and further enhance apprenticeship as an option for school leavers. Employers, as interested partners, could play a more supportive role in ITE's apprenticeship system, which is modelled after the German's "dual" system of training. Besides the more formal and structured apprenticeship, other schemes that can provide real work on campus to ITE students during their training should be explored.

- *VTE meeting the needs of lifelong learning:*
  The primary role of ITE has been the formal preparation of young people for immediate entry-level employment. Yet, there was increasing recognition of the need for more non-formal Continuing Education and Training (CET) in a knowledge-based economy. Working adults would need to be re-skilled as the economy experiences more frequent restructuring. Meeting the increasing needs of working adults and returning (ITE) students require a national rethinking in the approach and delivery in terms of accessibility, flexibility, recognition, relevance and responsiveness. Pre-employment training, on-the-job training and CET should be viewed as a seamless journey in lifelong learning. Whether full-time or part-time, school leavers or working adults, the formal and non-formal training systems must respond to needs of all learners.

Chapter 3

Aligning Education with Economic Development

A VTE system is an integral part of the national education system. As previously discussed, it is a subsystem of the larger political, economic and social environment. As such, a VTE system does not stand alone. Its relevance and sustainability derive from and are dependent on the support of partner organisations, employers, individuals and society.

Why is this so? One reason has to do with its mission, which in the case of ITE is clearly focused on "the acquisition of skills, knowledge and values for employability and lifelong learning". Training must be purposeful and relevant to the skilled manpower needs of the economy. A fundamental principle for education and training is therefore its close alignment with economic development (Law, 2009, 2010). The second reason has to do with the attractiveness of the VTE system itself. This is especially true for ITE whose specific mission is to address the needs of the less academically inclined among the cohort of school leavers. While many of these students see ITE as a pathway towards higher education, high employability is what makes VTE attractive. The ability of a young ITE graduate to secure a job with skills relevant to the market is the strongest testimony in building a foundation for the individual and society.

The third reason stems from the oft-repeated assertion that vocational training is too heavy an investment. One way of thinking is that governments cannot afford such investment and should look towards industry-funded schemes and private education providers. It is true that a high quality and sustainable VTE system is a heavy investment; it is certainly not a cheap option in skills development. However, what would be the political, social and economic costs to the nation when there is a wide mismatch between the jobs available and supply of skills? The costs to the economy due to the shortage of skills and graduates who are unemployed because they do not have relevant skills are even higher. In fact, rising unemployment due to economic restructuring is a growing concern globally.

Who then should take the responsibility for vocational training and provide the necessary resources? I hold the view that it is the primary responsibility of the government. My contention is that the government plays the central role in education. The training of young people is too important a social enabler not to be taken seriously. VTE, in particular the pre-employment training of school leavers, should be an integral part of the formal national education and training system. It is an important pathway for school leavers who require a vocationally oriented qualification for employment. Adequate funding by the government is necessary and a wise policy for long-term human capital development. No doubt, there will be competing priorities and resources have to be deployed to achieve optimal results in line with national social and economic goals. In the case of Singapore, investing in people has been the basis for national survival. Private sector education providers can and are encouraged to play a complementary role. Nonetheless, as business institutions, they are not likely to want to invest in the competency-based skills and technical training that incurs heavy investment. The issue of funding is a hard policy decision that developing countries need to review carefully as they look for appropriate models in vocational education and training.

Where and how then are the required financial resources going to be created? Jobs must be created in a growing economy for which vocational and technical skills are in demand. Ultimately, it is the economy that will create the jobs and wealth for the nation. The close alignment between VTE and economic development represents the "closed loop" in a sustainable system. Viewed as a part of the larger educational, social and economic system, VTE provides graduates with relevant skills for the economy, which in turn, creates wealth for the nation. With the right policies and prioritisation, resources so created can then be reinvested in sustaining a quality VTE system. This is why a VTE system must remain relevant and responsive to the changing manpower needs of the economy.

In this respect, the Singapore government believes in and has invested heavily in education and training, not only in the universities and polytechnics but also in vocational and technical education under the ITE.

The cost of ITE education is almost fully subsidised by the government, with capital development and annual operating budgets both heavily funded. The government continues to be committed to investing in ITE, with an estimated investment of two billion dollars over five years starting from 2011. ITE remains an integral pillar in Singapore's education system and, as was the case in its predecessor institutions, has been restructured and repositioned in line with the dynamics of Singapore's social and economic development.

PHASES OF ECONOMIC DEVELOPMENT AND VTE STRATEGIES

In the early days of independence, it became clear that the traditional trading, commerce and service sectors alone could not provide sufficient jobs for the number of school leavers in a growing population. Industrialisation in Singapore started without the tradition or benefit of a manufacturing base or culture in vocational skills. The overall strategic plan of the Singapore government then was to diversify and accelerate economic growth through manufacturing. During this early phase of economic development, from the 1960s to 1970s, the educational priority was to provide and expand primary and secondary education, including vocational education and training, so as to lay the necessary foundation for the acquisition of basic vocational and technical skills. It was only in the 1980s onwards that an increasing emphasis was placed on improving the level of skills and quality of the entire education and training system, including the schools, universities, polytechnics and VITB.

The economic development of Singapore may be characterised in three phases as shown in Figure 3.1. A "Factor-Driven" economy involving intensive labour in the 1960s and 1970s progressed to an "Investment-Driven" economy, which is capital intensive, in the 1980s and 1990s; and then to the "Innovation-Driven" economy powered by the needs of knowledge-intensive industries in the 2000s. Through these three phases over a short period of about 45 years, Singapore has also evolved from an early industrialising economy to a newly industrialised economy and to the globalised and diversified economy it is today. In tandem with the changing economic landscape, the VTE system was restructured several times in response to the changing manpower needs. The education and training system ensured that graduates from the various educational

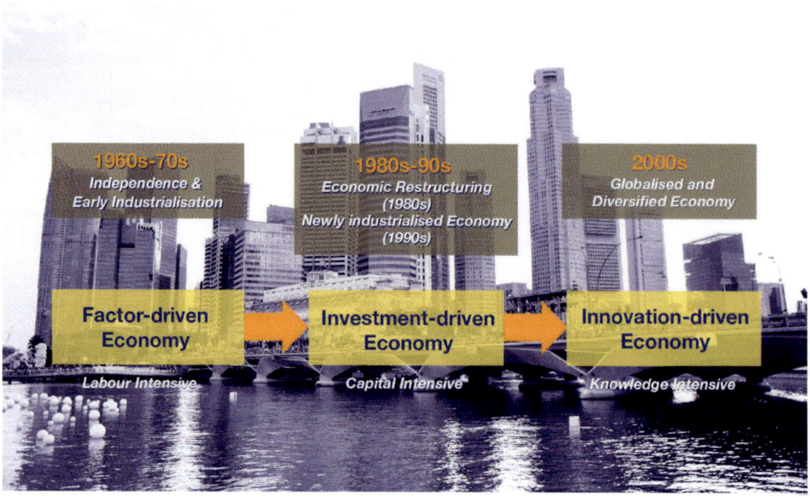

Figure 3.1 Phases of Singapore's economic development

institutions had the necessary skills and knowledge for the many new jobs that were created in a rapidly growing economy.

LABOUR-INTENSIVE ECONOMY (1960s–1970s)

In these early days of industrialisation, after Singapore's independence, the main challenge was to create enough jobs. The high unemployment situation was compounded by the sudden decision of the British government to pull out its naval bases in Singapore. The economic strategy shifted in 1968 from one of import substitution to one of rapid industrialisation by attracting foreign investment for export-oriented and labour-intensive manufacturing. From the manpower development perspective, the immediate task was to ensure that the workforce had the basic vocational and technical skills to support the labour-intensive manufacturing and repair activities in areas such as ship repair, turning and fitting, sheet metalwork, plumbing and radio maintenance and repair.

The priority in the 1960s was to expand the educational system, especially primary and secondary education. The government embarked on an accelerated school building programme. Large numbers of teachers were recruited and trained to meet the dramatic increase in student enrolment. In this so-called "survival-driven" education system, the goal was nation building and preparing Singapore for economic survival. With respect to VTE, the first vocational institute, the Singapore Vocational Institute (SVI), was established within the school system in 1964. With the increasing pace of industrialisation, there was growing concern on how best to expedite and expand to meet the technical and skilled manpower needs of new emerging industries. Mainstream education remained largely academic. In 1968, 84 per cent of students in schools were enrolled in the academic stream with only 8 per cent in the technical stream, 7 per cent vocational and 1 per cent commercial (Law, 1984).

In 1968, the Technical Education Department (TED) was established within the Ministry of Education to oversee the development of technical secondary education, industrial training and technical teacher training. Beyond the general subjects taken in the first two years of secondary schooling, basic workshop practice in metalwork, woodwork, technical drawing and basic electricity was made compulsory for all boys and 50 per cent of the girls. The remaining 50 per cent of girls took a home economics course. The secondary vocational schools were first converted into industrial training centres and soon after, phased out in favour of vocational institutes. This change reflected the shift from basic skills in the various crafts to the kind of technical skills required by the emerging industries.

In 1969, the apprenticeship schemes were transferred from the Ministry of Labour to the TED so as to merge the training of young persons under one authority. As an incentive, apprentices were given a deferment of their national service obligations for selected trade areas. This consideration shows how serious the national intent was in skills development. The number of vocational institutes increased in line with a rapidly expanding economy. In 1973, the first Industrial Training Board (ITB) was established as a statutory board through an Act of Parliament. This significant step marked the formalisation of the system of vocational training outside the school system.

Even at this early phase of development, it was abundantly clear that to remain market-relevant and responsive, there must be strong links and collaboration between the VTE system and industry. There were three important aspects to that relationship. The first was in the area of curriculum development. Delivery of theory and knowledge in VTE in the classroom was insufficient. In order to equip graduates with the required competencies for the job market, the skills standards for the various occupations had to be developed in partnership with employers and industry. This was done by establishing an extensive system of training advisory committees with industry-wide participation and supported by a rigorous curriculum development process.

The second aspect was tapping into the wealth of technologies and capabilities of industry leaders to supplement training that was otherwise too costly or impractical to replicate in vocational institutions. The specific sectors identified included printing, ship repairing and aircraft maintenance. Consequently, various industry-based training schemes were developed and administered by ITB so that companies were able to support apprenticeship and on-the-job training, which directly responded to their manpower needs.

The third aspect of industry partnership was the exchange of technology and sharing of learning resources through the signing of memoranda of understanding (MOUs). These MOUs with partners such as Mitsubishi Electric Asia, Robert Bosch (SEA), Siemens, IBM, Cisco System and Sun Microsystems, helped teaching staff to keep abreast of technology developments in the industry and equipped students with up-to-date knowledge and skills. MOUs are expressions of intent in collaboration among partners but may also include provisions for contributions in kind or monetary terms. These MOUs were signed at the ITB or training institute levels. Today, this tradition of a strong culture of collaboration with industry partners is embedded as a key feature of the ITE system.

A new three-tier system of skills certification was introduced in 1973 to define the different levels of skills competencies and standards required by industry. Called the National Trade Certificate or NTC system, the three levels were defined as semi-skilled (NTC-3), skilled (NTC-2) and highly skilled (NTC-1). The NTC system was specifically designed for the trade courses offered by ITB and not part of any national qualification framework. The NTC-1 was modelled after the "Meister" (master craftsman) from the German apprenticeship system. A wide range of courses were introduced starting at the NTC-3 level in areas such as electrical and electronics, metal and mechanical engineering, wood and building construction and heavy-duty diesel and motor vehicle mechanics. The unique feature of this system was that the same competency standards for full-time institutional training courses could also be used for the public trade testing system for working adults who had acquired the skills through relevant job experience. The NTC was further consolidated with other certifications and subsumed under the present unified National ITE Certificate or Nitec system of certification under ITE in 2002.

In the early 1970s, another government agency, the Economic Development Board (EDB), whose mission is to promote foreign investment into Singapore, played a strategic role in strengthening the industrial training system (Chan, 2002). Under a Joint Industrial Training Scheme, training centres were jointly established by EDB and multinational corporations (MNCs) such as Tata of India, Rollei of Germany and Philips of the Netherlands. The objective was to assure potential investors of a ready pool of specialised technical manpower for targeted industries. Between 1972 and 1979, four such centres were set up for the metal precision engineering trades and the camera industry. This unique approach in partnering with overseas investors was later extended to the establishment of joint technical institutes in partnership with foreign governments, such as the German-Singapore Technical Institute (1982), Japan-Singapore Technical Institute (1982) and French-Singapore Institute (1983). The technical institutes provided training up to the diploma level. Jointly financed by the Singapore government, MNCs and foreign governments, the training centres and technical institutes served an important phase in contributing to Singapore's skilled manpower development.

The educational requirement for admission in the joint training centres was a secondary education or NTC-3 qualification. Training was modelled as a four-year apprenticeship scheme whereby the first two years was spent in the training centres undergoing full-time workshop practice and theoretical instruction under factory-like conditions. The apprentices continued their skills development while acquiring work experience for another two years on attachment to MNCs and other companies. These centres were the first to pioneer the NTC-2 skilled level of training and the NTC-1 master craftsman. These training centres and technical institutes were subsequently subsumed within Nanyang Polytechnic and ITE in 1993 as part of the further expansion and consolidation of the national system of post-secondary education and training. In the process, different training approaches and practices were infused into the local systems. In particular, the "teaching factory" model (Chiang, 1998), where students and staff work on real-life industrial projects on campus, continues to be a hallmark of the Nanyang Polytechnic and the NTC-2 precision machining courses in ITE.

The EDB continues to take the initiative in facilitating specialised skills development when the need arises. In this respect, a new S$52 million government initiative to train 2,800 "master craftsmen" in the precision engineering sector was announced in a joint statement with SPRING Singapore in 2011. SPRING Singapore is a government agency whose mission is to help the growth of small and medium-sized enterprises (SMEs). As reported in an article in *The Straits Times*, "Master craftsmen represent the peak of manufacturing talent in countries such as Germany and Japan... highly skilled craftsmen are critical to Singapore as we move into the design, development and manufacturing of technology-intensive components and complex equipment..." (Tan, 2011).

CAPITAL-INTENSIVE ECONOMY (1980s–1990s)

As a result of effective industrialisation and manpower development policies, full employment was achieved by the early 1970s. In 1979, the government embarked on a major restructuring of the economy towards higher value-added, high technology and more capital-intensive industries. The restructuring was driven by a decline in domestic labour supply, increasing competition from resource-abundant neighbouring countries and rising trade protectionism from the industrialised world.

The new strategy was focused on the development of new industries such as petrochemicals, biotechnology, aerospace, information technology as well as manufacturing services in testing, financing, warehousing and purchasing.

To achieve competitiveness through higher productivity, mechanisation, automation and computerisation were promoted. A Council on Professional and Technical Education (CPTE) was established to coordinate national efforts in manpower planning. The objective was to ensure that there was a ready supply of professionals, technicians and skilled manpower to match the jobs that were being created. The Council, chaired by the Minister of Trade and Industry, would review manpower needs in the light of economic development strategies and endorse student intake targets and the corresponding staffing and financial requirements for universities, polytechnics and the vocational and training institutes managed by ITB and EDB. During this phase, the education and training institutions were called upon to respond to the manpower needs of more capital-intensive industries. The role of the CPTE was subsequently taken over by the present National Manpower Council, chaired by the Minister of Manpower. Such manpower planning worked when, as stakeholders, the ministries and educational institutions viewed the task of developing a professionally qualified and skilled workforce as a common area of national interests. While the CPTE endorsed the intake targets, the educational institutions were accountable for the results in numbers and quality of graduates, thereby meeting the needs of employers.

In the area of vocational training, a new stage was set in 1979 with the establishment of the Vocational and Industrial Training Board (VITB) by amalgamating the ITB and Adult Education Board (AEB). The AEB was established in 1960 to meet the educational needs of working adults, including general education and some basic vocational training. With increasing educational and training opportunities, it became apparent that the domains of AEB and ITB were complementary components of the same system of training for school leavers and working adults. With the formation of VITB, efforts were directed towards expanding the training system, developing new programmes and improving the quality of vocational training. In particular, the higher NTC-2 skilled level of certification was extended to include electrical, electronics, mechatronics, mechanical engineering, precision engineering, automotive technology and printing.

A new Certificate in Business Studies (CBS) was introduced in Accounting and Secretarial Practice in 1981. In line with the shift towards higher value-added industries and skills, the concept of a NTC-1 level training was approved in 1986. This master craftsman qualification was targeted at NTC-2 graduates with several years of working experience. Formal training was deemed necessary and the curriculum emphasised the further development of advanced technical and pedagogic skills. The first NTC-1 course in Precision Engineering (Tool & Die-Making) was conducted by the Brown Boveri Government Training Centre in 1987. For the first time, a Centre of Vocational Training was set up within VITB to develop professional capabilities in areas such as curriculum development, training of trainers and instructional media development. These areas of expertise had subsequently proven to be essential core capabilities in building quality and sustainability in the vocational training system.

Economic restructuring has direct implications on the skills and capabilities of the existing workforce. It is not just the young school leavers that need to be trained. Working adults also need to stay relevant and responsive to changing manpower needs. In moving up the economic ladder, it was necessary to develop a more educated and skilled workforce. In this respect, the VITB was called upon to develop a more comprehensive and integrated Continuing Education and Training (CET) system to upgrade the education and skills of the workforce, especially those with a lower education and skills. Many of these were older workers who had missed the opportunities of a formal education or training. So, between 1983 and 1987, the VITB responded by launching three national CET projects, namely — the Basic Education for Skills Training (BEST), Work Improvement through Secondary Education (WISE) and Modular Skills Training (MOST).

Focusing on adult literacy (English language) and numeracy (mathematics), BEST and WISE were conceived as mass adult education programmes to enable workers to acquire a basic education for skills upgrading. The challenge was in contextualising the programmes to adult Singaporeans and delivering these through an extensive network of education centres in VITB, unions, schools and companies. Each programme had four modules. Well received by working adults and supported by employers, the programmes contributed to upgrading the quality of the workforce. More importantly, whether it was mastering a module in English or Mathematics, many Singaporean working adults learned how to resume learning. They demonstrated that age was not a barrier in lifelong learning. A unique national experience, it was a major effort in marshalling the support and resources to reach to a potential pool of 225,000 workers for the BEST and 112,000 for the WISE. Eventually, an estimated 296,380 workers participated in and received at least one module certificate in either of these programmes. It was a significant achievement in worker education. MOST, on the other hand, provided the incentive for working adults to upgrade and acquire a formal skills qualification on a part-time modular basis. As an incentive, modular certificates were awarded to those who successfully completed individual modules.

In 1990, a new national framework was launched to upgrade and expand the scope of the apprenticeship system in Singapore. It was recognised that apprenticeship provided an important alternative pathway for some school leavers to learn a skill through training in companies. Exemplified by the highly successful dual system of apprenticeship in Germany and Switzerland and the structured on-the-job training in Japan, companies with the necessary in-house capabilities could help to train workers in areas which were too costly to provide in the full-time institution-based system or by nature lend themselves to apprenticeship training. Thus, the VITB, in partnership with the Skills Development Fund (SDF) and Singapore Manufacturers Association (SMA), extended the apprenticeship scheme to aerospace, retail sales, healthcare, travel and tourism and computer operations. Beyond the acquisition of skills and knowledge, an inherent feature of an apprenticeship is the value in cultivating a long-term bond between the apprentice and the company. As an "earn-as-you-learn" training scheme, the apprenticeship also served to attract school leavers who needed the additional income due to strained financial circumstances.

To leverage on the experience of Germany in the field of vocational training (Federal Ministry, 2003), an MOU was signed between VITB and the Ministry of Education, Youth and Sports of Baden-Württemberg, Germany, in June 1991. This laid the foundation for what was to become a most successful bilateral collaboration that still continues today. The assistance from Germany was timely in the early phase of helping VITB to enhance the apprenticeship training system, instructor training and teaching pedagogy. In particular, we borrowed the concept of technical, methodological and social skills from the German system of apprenticeship. The "soft" skills competencies such as planning, organising and decision-making were eventually adapted into our own ITE process-based curriculum model for an institution-based training system. With respect to pedagogic competencies, we adopted the mentoring approach of developing teachers who in turn acted as mentors in providing guidance and support to new colleagues undergoing the "train-the-trainer" programme. In recent years, the German partners assisted ITE in the development and launching of the first two "Technical Engineer Diploma" programmes in machine tool technology and automotive engineering in 2008 and 2010, respectively.

Some 16 years later, Hartmut Mattes, Government Director of Education at Ministry of Education, Baden-Württemberg, Germany, was interviewed by ITE on the occasion of my retirement in 2007, where he said, "We send best wishes from the Minister for Education, Youth and Sports, Mr Helmut Rau, whom he [Dr Law] knows personally. We started in the early days as helping partners for vocational training in Singapore. But now we are equal partners. In many of these fields in vocational education, Dr Law and his ITE have actually overtaken us, we must admit this." The importance of sharing and learning through this partnership between ITE and Germany was reiterated during the third renewal of the MOU in Singapore in October 2002 (Box 3.1).

BOX 3.1 COLLABORATION WITH GERMANY IN VOCATIONAL TRAINING

The ITE and Ministry of Education, Youth and Sports (or KM, for short), Baden-Württemberg, Germany, have enjoyed a close and longstanding partnership established through a MOU in 1991. In the renewal of the third consecutive MOU in 2002 in Singapore, the importance and value of this collaboration in vocational training was reiterated by both partners.

On 29 October 2002, speaking on behalf of ITE and the Ministry of Education, Singapore, Dr Ng Eng Hen, then Minister of State for Education and Manpower, said, "Singapore and the Federal Republic of Germany share a similar philosophy and approach towards education. Both our countries are dependent on a skilled labour force and therefore invest heavily in education... Today's renewal of the MOU for the third consecutive term since the initial signing in 1991 is testimony of both ITE and KM's commitment to their long standing bilateral co-operation. It reaffirms ITE's commitment in continuing and forging even closer ties with KM, a ministry that is responsible for an education and training system, which produces one of the best skilled workforces in the world. In particular, the strength of the dual system of vocational training through apprenticeship in Germany is well-known internationally."

On his part, Helmut Rau, then Secretary of State for Education, Youth and Sports, Baden-Württemberg, Germany, said, "For the positive development of a modern industrial society, permanent and lifelong training of skilled and technical specialists is indispensable because they strengthen a country's economic power in order to survive in the world market... I am therefore particularly pleased about the continuation of our benchmarking efforts with ITE... I have the honour of inviting you [Director & CEO/ITE] to share your achievements at an International Symposium on Quality Management, which will take place at the Academy for Teachers at Esslingen in Autumn 2003... We have witnessed ITE's many great transformations and innovations in one short decade. We note that ITE has already established a very comprehensive and robust Organisational Excellence and Quality System for Vocational Training that is global class and mature. ITE's VTE system is comparable with or even better than the world's best in advanced countries like Germany, Switzerland, Japan and the United States." (Rau, 2002).

In 1991, the Singapore government published a new Strategic Economic Plan to chart the next phase of Singapore's development. The goal was to turn Singapore into a first-league developed nation within the next 30 to 40 years. The new direction focused on building the manufacturing and service sectors as the twin engines of economic growth. Companies were encouraged to diversify, upgrade and develop into strong export-oriented companies and invest in the regional economies. To stay relevant and competitive, a more qualified workforce was required. The stage was set for a critical review of the post-secondary education system, including the universities, polytechnics and VITB, to ensure the availability of well-trained and professionally qualified manpower in the high-technology, knowledge-intensive and service sectors.

In the same year, a review of primary school education and vocational training by the Ministry of Education led to a restructuring of the education system. The government decided on a new policy to provide at least 10 years of general education to all students before progressing to further education and training. At the secondary level, a differentiated curriculum is offered according to three tracks. A technically oriented track known as the Secondary Normal (Technical) course was introduced for the less academically inclined to better prepare them for training in VITB. The other two tracks are the Express and Normal (Academic). The Express stream is a rigorously academic track where students prepare for the GCE "O" level qualification in four years. Students in the Normal (Academic) track will do so in a slower pace in five years. There are provisions for mobility across tracks depending on the academic progress of the students.

On vocational training, the policy was to reposition the system at the post-secondary level. The vocational training system was to be improved, upgraded and made attractive to school leavers. The VITB was thus replaced by the present day ITE in 1992. It became clear that to meet the skilled manpower needs of Singapore's future economic development, a primary school education was no longer sufficient for those who enrolled in the VITB. Employers were asking for vocational graduates who had a secondary education and higher-level NTC-2 skills to respond and adapt in a changing global economy.

As the Minister-in-charge and Chairman of the VITB and ITE from 1981 to 1993, the late Dr Tay Eng Soon played a pivotal role in the policy review leading to the establishment of ITE as a post-secondary technical institution in 1992. In celebrating the inauguration of ITE, Dr Tay's message was:

> The establishment of ITE marks a new chapter in technical education and training in Singapore. ITE will further strengthen our system of training for school leavers and workers. ITE will offer a wide range of full-time and apprenticeship courses in engineering, business and service trades. New initiatives will also be introduced to further upgrade the quality of the workforce through part-time courses. Our tradition of partnership in training involving government, unions and industries is growing. The apprenticeship approach, as practised in Germany and Switzerland, will enable this partnership to reach many more companies, including small and medium-sized enterprises. ITE will play a significant role in the training of our workforce. Many challenges lie ahead. With the support of employers, unions and the public, I am confident that ITE will succeed in helping to develop a better-educated and trained workforce for Singapore. (ITE, 1992)

In retrospect, Dr Tay's words more than manifested themselves in how ITE has changed since 1992. Passionate for what he truly believed in, the late Dr Tay would have been the first to endorse the breakthrough we see in the ITE today. ITE is an institution he would have been proud of. It should be noted that the education system in Singapore is largely based on a "6–4–2" structure, that is, six years of primary education, four or five years of secondary education and two years of pre-university education. In comparison, a post-secondary education in ITE would mean the last two years of a high school or upper secondary education in many other countries. ITE replaced the former VITB. It was an example of the forces driving change in the schools and the rising expectations of industry and society. It was a challenge but also an opportunity for ITE in building a world-class institution.

KNOWLEDGE-INTENSIVE ECONOMY (2000s)

Moving forward into the 2000s, Singapore saw the need to increasingly develop into a global, entrepreneurial and diversified economy. While continuing to strengthen the higher-end manufacturing activities, there was a clearer recognition of the importance of the service sector as the second engine of economic growth. Concerted plans were formulated to attract and nurture new growth sectors such as the biomedical sciences, info-communications technology, integrated resorts, high-value engineering and research & development. The response in the educational sphere was to position Singapore as an education hub by attracting foreign students and internationally renowned institutions to Singapore. Local institutions would continue to seek quality and excellence in developing a first-class education at all levels. This would also indirectly help to enlarge the talent pool in view of Singapore's limited human resources.

Meanwhile, the ITE in Singapore was well on its journey of transformation. By 2007, ITE was recognised as a world-class institution and global leader in technical education. This was also the year of my official retirement from public service after having served as Director and CEO of ITE and the former VITB from 1981 to 2007. The story of ITE's transformation has since continued under new stewardship with Bob Tan Beng Hai as Chairman of the ITE Board of Governors and Bruce Poh Geok Huat, the Director and CEO, respectively. New goals, strategies and programmes are being pursued with continuing passion under the current fourth five-year strategic plan, the "ITE Innovate" (2010–2014). The plan seeks to provide a wider range of courses, introduce more e-learning platforms, enhance progression pathways and expand collaboration with foreign institutions.

Chapter 4

Vocational Training under the former VITB

The former Vocational and Industrial Training Board (VITB) was an iconic institution in its own right in the evolution of vocational training in Singapore. Established in 1979 through an amalgamation of two predecessor Boards, namely, the Industrial Training Board (ITB) and Adult Education Board (AEB), the VITB represented the second phase of development — the consolidation and expansion of the vocational training system. (The first phase was the beginning of vocational education in the school system and the search for a more relevant training model to serve the economic needs in the 1960s and 1970s.) Inextricably linked with the dynamics of economic transformation, VITB played a significant role from 1979 to 1992. The economy was booming and there was a shortage of local labour. Driven by a New Economic Policy, companies were encouraged to move from low-skilled labour-intensive manufacturing activities to higher technology and more value-added products and services. The Skills Development Fund (SDF) was established in 1979 to encourage companies to upgrade the skills and improve the productivity of the workforce through a mandatory contribution from companies to a fund that promotes skills development. The SDF continues to be a valuable instrument in promoting employer participation in worker education and skills development. As a result of these efforts, Singapore emerged as a newly industrialised economy.

On the educational front, there was the urgency to improve the quality of education and vocational skills training (Lee et al., 2008; Yip, 1993). With the expansion of primary and secondary education largely achieved towards the later part of 1970s, attention was redirected at the problem of high attrition rates in schools. This had a direct implication for vocational training. It was recognised that without a basic educational foundation, including language and mathematics, it would not be possible to build a skilled and competitive workforce. The linkage between general education and vocational training was therefore crucial. Vocational training should not be the place for remedial work by default because of weaknesses in the education system. The expected outcomes of schools should be clearly defined so that students are well prepared for further education and vocational training. In this respect, the schools and vocational institutions must work as partners in the interest of the students. This partnership can best be achieved with a common vision and spirit of collaboration across government ministries and agencies.

A study by a team of young systems engineers (Goh, 1979) led to the implementation of the New Education System (NES) in 1980. The key feature of system was streaming or tracking of students based on academic abilities in schools. The underlying objective was clear. It was to reduce the number of early school leavers. Using a differentiated curriculum, the goal was to enable students to better cope with their studies and pace of learning according to their aptitudes and inclinations. Progression through primary and secondary schools was strictly based on academic performance. Educational standards were maintained. There was a gradual reduction in attrition rates. The outcomes were positive. However, the negative fallout was an increased peer pressure and social stigmatisation of students. The negative perception that the academically weakest students were channelled to VITB for vocational training was further reinforced.

From a policymaking perspective, it was never a politically popular decision, but one that was necessary and pragmatic. Speaking on "Educating the Next Generation" at the 4th Anniversary Public Lecture at the Lee Kuan Yew School of Public Policy in 2008, then Minister for Education Dr Ng Eng Hen said:

> The third cornerstone of our education system is streaming. Singapore owes a great debt of gratitude to Dr Goh Keng Swee for his report in 1978, which is commonly referred to as the Goh Report. Where it would have been simpler to avoid hard truths, this report was underpinned by the fundamental belief that students had varying learning ability, and would therefore be better off being grouped together to learn at their appropriate pace. Put simply, streaming allows each child to better fulfil his inherent potential.
>
> Singapore today has reaped the benefits of that difficult transition. Before streaming, 29 % of primary school students did not

progress to secondary education either because they had dropped out or did not pass the PSLE. These high levels of attrition still occur today in other systems that attempt to wallpaper the differences… In contrast, in Singapore, with ability-based learning, 98.4 % of each cohort stay in school and receive 10 years of education… (Ng, 2008 August)

This fundamental shift in educational policy and its implications on skills development had a direct impact on the challenges impinging on the newly established VITB. It is an example of the need for periodic policy reviews and restructuring of training institutions, organisations and systems. To remain relevant and responsive to the dynamic forces driving change, it is inevitable that from time to time, a strategic repositioning is required. In this case, the VITB was called upon to respond to the need to expand, upgrade and strengthen the system in line with the goals of the New Education System and help develop a better educated and trained workforce.

THE VITB: 1979–1992

As a statutory board, VITB was established as the single national authority and agency responsible for developing, providing and regulating vocational and industrial training in Singapore (VITB, 1979/1980). The principal objectives under the VITB Act 1979 were:

- To provide for, promote, assist in and regulate the training or apprenticeship of persons employed in or intending to be employed in commerce or industry, and to upgrade the skills of such persons by providing advanced training in skilled work or otherwise;
- To establish the nature and length of the training for any employment in commerce and industry, and the further education to be associated with the training, the persons by and to whom the training ought to be given, the standards to be attained as a result of the training and the methods of ascertaining whether those standards have been attained; and

- To conduct such programmes of further education as may be required from time to time.

As provided for under the broad mandate of the Act, the overriding task of the VITB was the vocational preparation of young persons and industrial training of working adults in commerce and industry. In the context of economic development, the word "vocational" would include the wide range of skills relevant to a developing and expanding economy. At the same time, "industrial training" would broaden the scope and reinforce the importance of continuing education and part-time skills training for working adults. The birth of VITB was celebrated with much enthusiasm and optimism. While the intent was clear, its name did not augur well in society. The word "vocational" in the name "VITB" continued to be strongly associated with a poor image. In fact, for many more years, vocational training under the VITB would continue to be looked down upon as a system for failures and low achievers.

The focus of VITB was on training technicians and skilled personnel for the middle and lower-level jobs in the economy. It was about the employability of its graduates. What was perhaps not as explicitly articulated at the time was the role of an educational institution such as the VITB in social development and mobility. As mentioned in earlier chapters, the importance of vocational training goes beyond the acquisition of employable skills for the individual. It is often expected to solve a myriad of issues ranging from reducing the number of early school leavers to youth unemployment, skills gaps, economic growth and access to a post-secondary education. Its long-term value is the social impact it can make in transforming the lives of those who would otherwise be left behind in the educational system. Its success makes for a more equitable and inclusive society because it enhances social development and mobility for the less academic in the lower socio-economic strata of society.

The mission of VITB as stated in 1990 was "to develop to the maximum, the human and skills potential of Singaporeans so as to support the social and economic progress of the country while meeting the aspirations of the people." In keeping with its mission, the efforts of VITB were governed by two primary functions:

- Preparing and training school leavers for employment; and
- Providing opportunities for Continuing Education and Training (CET) to workers

By 1990, the VITB had developed an integrated and comprehensive system of full-time training for school leavers and CET for working adults. The main programmes, reflecting the system of vocational training at the time, were the following:

- Conducting pre-employment, full-time institutional training for school leavers;
- Conducting part-time Continuing Education and Training for workers;
- Promoting and supporting industry-based training by employers, including Apprenticeship Schemes and Approved Training Centres;
- Administering national adult literacy projects, i.e., Basic Education for Skills Training (BEST) and Worker Improvement through Secondary Education (WISE) to raise the educational level of workers; and
- Administering Public Trade Tests to certify the skills of workers

THE KEY CHALLENGES (1981–1985)

Appointed as the new Director of VITB in June 1981, I was a young university academic thrust into a sector of an educational system that I knew very little about. I was not familiar with the dynamics and challenges. While daunting, there was no time to worry. What I remember most was a sense of urgency and importance of the task ahead. The enormity of the challenges became more apparent when I was introduced by the Chairman of VITB, the late Dr Tay Eng Soon, at our first formal meeting with members of the VITB Directorate comprising G. F. Pillay, Anna Hee, Yip Seck Weng, Peter Seow, Victor Seah Quee Soon, Gwee Teck Yew, Peter Syddall and the late Koh Watt Seng.

The nature of work was wide-ranging and diverse. Within a week, the directorate team started to address some of the more immediate issues. These included concerns on the projected enrolment for VITB, expansion of the Diploma in Applied Arts programme in Baharuddin Vocational Institute and phasing out of the Industrial Technician Certificate courses under plans already endorsed by the Council of Professional & Technical Education. Another priority area was the need to develop new programmes for the Primary 8 Monolingual (P8M) and Primary 8 Extended (P8E) school leavers who would be coming on stream under the new education system. The P8M and P8E school leavers were academically weaker students who had taken eight years to complete their primary education. The P8M students being the weakest would only take the oral examination for the mother tongue or second language (Mandarin, Malay or Tamil). The P8M and P8E streams were phased out in 1991.

VITB was already a large organisation with a staff of 1,476 in 1981. Reflecting on my management approach, I believe my work in industrial and systems engineering and at the Ford Motor Company had brought a fresh perspective to the challenges we were facing. On leadership, I too had to learn and adapt to a new environment. Believing in keeping things simple, I would look for basic principles and develop concepts within a larger system based on fundamentals. I wanted to be strategic in thinking but also meticulous and thorough in working through the questions and issues to proffer an orderly and systematic approach in problem-solving. I saw the need to set higher standards in administrative functions, build professionalism among teaching staff and promote teamwork. To promote a spirit of commitment, openness and collaboration, I advocated the adoption of People-Centred Management (PCM) as VITB's management philosophy as early as 1983. As it turned out, this decision in embracing PCM was a fortuitous step in laying the foundation for our subsequent move towards organisational excellence.

The key challenge ahead was to further expand the training capacity, make vocational training attractive for school leavers and improve the quality and levels of skills for school leavers and working adults. As a new organisation in 1981, the VITB was positioned to respond to the skilled manpower needs of an economy that was poised for more capital-intensive industries. But, the learning environment and social climate was far from encouraging. Making do with campuses housed in old school buildings and semi-circular zinc-roofed army "Nissan Huts" was the normal practice. The various trade courses were only offered at the NTC-3 or semi-skills level. Without modern infrastructure and facilities, the campus environment was not conducive. Many of the teaching staff, who were directly recruited from industry, had the practical skills but were lowly qualified professionally.

The public image of vocational training was poor. There was a social stigma attached to and prejudice against VITB students who were viewed as academic failures. Even parents would fight shy of sending their children to VITB. Without parental and community support, the task of attracting and developing the less academic students would seem insurmountable. Unlike the university or polytechnic, the attractiveness for school leavers to enrol in vocational training was something that could not be taken for granted.

In 1980, VITB had already adopted an expansion plan to increase its training capacity from about 10,000 to 30,900 full-time training places by 1986 (VITB 1981/1982). This was based on a projected average annual demand of 11,800 VITB graduates for the 1980s. The beginning of 1981 therefore saw the Board addressing several issues on the implementation of the plan. The principal one was to confirm the availability of school leavers. The second concern was the ability of the Board to attract the projected number of school leavers under a voluntary system of education and training. The third aspect was the suitability of the Board's courses and curricula in relation to the academic attainment of the principal target groups of school leavers coming on-stream under the New Education System (NES). Another emerging issue was the opportunity to attract even the more academic students into skills training, not only to increase the skilled workforce but also to minimise the loss of a limited human resource. These concerns and issues set the scene for some of the most challenging work in VITB for the next five years (Law, 1985).

THE FIRST CHALLENGE — VERIFYING VITB'S EXPANSION PLAN

Under the 1980 expansion plan, the implicit assumption was that all school leavers, who had completed a primary or secondary education but did not qualify for pre-university or the polytechnics, would progress to VITB. We needed to build capacities at different levels of training to match the outputs from the NES. On closer scrutiny, I found that from the systems point of view, there was no provision for losses at the input-output interfaces of the system. In fact, there were early signs of declining subscription rates as new training places were being created. Historical data showed that only about 20 per cent of early school leavers (students who did not successfully complete primary or secondary education) were opting for vocational training.

The important lesson here is that the progression of school leavers to vocational training cannot be assumed. As there was no compulsory education in Singapore then, provision for losses should have been made in the transition from schooling to vocational training. Care needs to be exercised in setting national targets, especially in training and skills development. Capacity building and matching of real demands are complex issues. Creating training places may not be a problem but success in getting students to enrol is harder to assure. Yet, realistic "capture" rates at various levels of education and training had to be set as part of a more detailed and reliable planning process.

We henceforth defined the intake capture rate of a given target group of school leavers as the ratio of the number of students enrolled against the target pool available for VITB. At the time, there were several potential pools of school leavers that VITB was trying to attract for vocational training.

The expansion plan therefore had to be verified. An in-depth review was undertaken in 1981–82 of the availability of school leavers under the NES, capture rates, trainee performance in the various courses, utilisation of existing resources, and the employability of the VITB system. Besides this analysis, other factors such as the popularity of courses, age, gender, educational levels and optional choices were also considered. Adopting a systems approach, capture rates were projected for different target groups based on experience.

Targets were set to capture 70 per cent of P8M, 70 per cent of P8E and one-third of secondary school leavers. On this basis, it was projected that under the NES, VITB would in the long-run have an intake of about 15,000 to 16,000 trainees a year, which translates to 32–38 per cent of a primary one school cohort of about 40,000 to 50,000 students. As a result, the original expansion plan in student enrolment capacity earlier endorsed by the Council on Professional and Technical Education was scaled down from 30,900 places to 24,100. In practical terms, it meant a saving of three additional vocational institutes that would otherwise have been built. The capture rates set were successfully achieved in the January 1985 intake exercises. The actual rates of capture either exceeded or were close to the planned targets. They were 86 per cent for the P8M, 77 per cent for P8E and 26 per cent secondary school leavers, respectively. These were the first real outcomes that validated and boosted confidence in the expansion plan. The wrong decisions could have resulted in a waste of valuable resources, so it is necessary to exercise care and realism in target-setting.

THE SECOND CHALLENGE — DEVELOPING AN ATTRACTIVE SYSTEM

The second challenge was in making vocational training "attractive" to Singaporeans. By this, I mean developing a system that enjoys a high response rate from school leavers, is seen to provide relevant skills with high employability and has low attrition rates. In an environment where a high premium had traditionally been placed on academic success, the motivation to undertake vocational training could have been undermined. Besides, there was the poor image to overcome. We approached this challenge by introducing a more systematic and professional approach in vocational training, promoting the desirability of skills acquisition and improving the image of VITB. We soon recognised that unlike other higher educational institutions, VITB's intakes could range from those with a primary education (at the time) to lower secondary and GCE "O" holders. To be attractive, different levels of courses must be designed to match the expectations and aspirations of the different target groups of school leavers. In particular, the VITB system must be flexible and responsive in accommodating the needs of students from the NES.

The system of vocational training was thus systematically restructured. Four major changes were introduced.

The first was the introduction of full-time two-year National Trade Certificate Grade 2 (NTC-2) courses for GCE "O" level holders. This was training at the "skilled" level. Previously, these students had to undertake the one-year semi-skilled NTC-3 courses before progressing to the skilled level under an apprenticeship scheme. This scheme did not attract many applicants, as apprenticeship was not a popular choice. On the other hand, the response to the direct entry full-time NTC-2 courses was overwhelming. The NTC-2 level of qualification was better aligned with the expectation of GCE "O" school leavers in view of the higher level of skills training and technical qualification. More importantly, a potential pool of students with a higher educational qualification was successfully tapped for skills training. A new norm had been set in building a more qualified and skilled workforce in keeping with the increasing needs for higher-level skills in industry.

Secondly, a new Pre-Vocational Training (PVT) programme was identified, developed and pilot-tested. The PVT programme was conceived as an integral part of the system of vocational training so as to meet the specific needs of the P8M school leavers. As a new programme, the underlying concept of PVT was to create a learning environment that could stimulate the interests and establish the self-confidence necessary for the development of one's personal potential. PVT was an innovative programme very much built on hands-on skills, project work and experiential learning.

As a transitional but critical interface between the school environment and world of work, this one-year experiential learning would enable the young trainees to appreciate their innate abilities, aptitudes and learn some basic operative skills useful for employment in the major manufacturing, commerce, personal services and household sectors of the economy. Those who performed well and had the potential to progress would go on to attain the Certificate of Competency or National Trade Certificate Grade 3 (NTC-3) courses. It was subsequently shown that those with only a primary education had difficulty in completing NTC-3 courses successfully. For those who decided to seek employment or apprenticeship training, they would have acquired the additional maturity, work discipline and basic skills foundation for work and training.

The third change was the establishment of close linkages between the schools and VITB's system of training. Progression from school to vocational training cannot be taken for granted. The idea was that the channels of progression must be so coordinated that the parents and students would accept vocational training as a logical continuation of education before entering employment. An "automatic" registration system was introduced whereby a primary school leaver was automatically posted to a vocational institute nearest to his or her home. The primary school leaver did not have to make a conscious decision to apply for admission to VITB for training. Without compulsory education, this was essentially a "default" system of registration. As for secondary school leavers, a well-coordinated system of registration was also established with the support of principals and teachers. However, at this secondary level, an application had to be made, as there were different vocational institutes and courses to choose from, based on admission requirements. These student intake systems were further supported by promotional efforts in the schools and VITB. They proved to be highly effective and essential mechanisms as demonstrated by the achievement of the targeted capture rates in the January 1985 and subsequent intakes.

The fourth change was directed at the need to provide motivation for VITB trainees to reach their highest level of skills potential. Getting students admitted was only the first step. The next was the need to motivate them to excel and progress to further education and training. For this purpose, a system of recognition, based on the award of a Certificate of Merit for outstanding performance, was introduced in 1983. The certificate also provided a basis for progression within VITB's system of training. In schools, students had the motivation to do well, as admission eligibility to the various levels of courses in VITB would depend on the educational qualifications and academic results. Most students who took up vocational training in VITB would still aspire for a higher education. As such, they would be motivated to perform well in order to qualify for progression to the polytechnic. The certification was thus the building block for the "bridges and ladders" to other educational pathways. Such a system of progression was formally articulated and officially established between VITB and the two local polytechnics at the time, in 1984 namely, the Singapore Polytechnic and Ngee Ann Polytechnic. Today, about one in five ITE graduates progresses to polytechnics.

THE THIRD CHALLENGE — ENHANCING SYSTEM RESPONSIVENESS

The third challenge, and a continuing one, was to ensure that the system of vocational training was responsive and adaptable to the rapidly changing economy and work environment. New and relevant programmes had to be identified, developed and introduced in time and courses that had become obsolete due to new technologies and skills phased out according to plan. In short, how could one keep abreast of the ever-increasing rate of technology changes in order to maintain the relevancy of training?

A training institution is inherently limited by its speed of response. Lead-time is required in the process of curriculum review, updating workshop facilities and staff capability development before training can be effectively implemented. Training institutions, unlike research institutes or industry technology leaders, do not normally have the latest knowledge, expertise or technology to foresee emerging occupational skills required at the work place. The latest application of knowledge and technology is often accessible to and confined within the industry technology leaders. Yet, vocational training institutions must keep abreast of changing needs, which in practice means the task of bridging the gaps between training and occupational skills within the constraints of a training system. The ability of the system to anticipate and respond quickly to a changing work environment is crucial. This responsiveness is measured by the time it takes from identifying the need for a new course to the time required for curriculum development, staff training, facility set-ups and implementation.

The basic approach was to develop a close partnership with industry, for instance by establishing an extensive network of trade advisory committees with external expert representation from trade associations, educational institutions and industries. The work of such committees was supported by VITB's internal training development committees, whose members were specialists in the curriculum development process. The VITB Board of Governors would make regular visits to and have dialogues with business and industry. Follow-up surveys and assessments were conducted for trade areas that had been identified as potential for new courses. Another important step was to build up and strengthen in-house expertise and capabilities in professional core areas such as curriculum development, instructor training and instructional media development.

In this respect, we are grateful to the late Dr Robert E. Taylor who, as Director of the former National Center for Research in Vocational Education at the Ohio State University in the United States, was most supportive in the sharing of knowledge and resources with VITB. The Center, founded in 1977, was well known for its leadership in workforce development. It was renamed as the Center on Education and Training for Employment in 1987. In particular, we learned and adopted its model of "Developing a Curriculum", which is central to a rigorous curriculum development process. A well-recognised job and occupational analysis technique, the model ensures a process whereby duties, competencies and tasks are derived and documented based on the needs of industry. It was through this close association with the Center that a pool of VITB curriculum specialists was trained as facilitators of the process. The investment in equipping our professional staff with this and other core capabilities proved to be crucial in assuring the quality and standards of vocational training in Singapore. In 2003, the Center and ITE jointly conducted a workshop on the model in Singapore, so as to share the accumulated knowledge, expertise and experience in curriculum design and development with training institutions in the Asia-Pacific region.

CONTINUING CHALLENGES (1986–1992)

The task of development in vocational training is a continuing one. It is a long-term investment in human capital development for the future. So, while the system had been restructured and expanded in response to the changing policies in education and economic development, the challenges and work continued. Looking ahead then in 1986, I saw the following as major challenges:

- Quality and professionalism in training
- Efficiency in administrative and operating systems
- Maintaining relevance in a rapidly changing work environment

The challenge for better quality and professionalism reflected the need to further upgrade the system of vocational training in Singapore. As the system evolved, more was expected of our teaching staff and those who provided professional support in areas such as curriculum development, test assessments, instructor training and instructional media development. At the operational level, greater attention had to be paid to the quality of delivery and critical trainer-trainee inter-relationships in the classrooms and workshops. Teaching staff had to be professionally qualified and have the relevant working experience. In particular, it was crucial that staff had practical "hands-on" skills and a heart for the students. Keeping in view the mission of the Board, heads of departments and training managers were expected to adopt a broader leadership and professional role in the governance and management of the vocational institutes.

There was heavy investment in human and physical resources in the development and expansion of the vocational training system. The Board's training programmes had more than doubled and annual operating expenditure increased from S$32 million to S$81 million in the period between 1980 and 1987, or an average increase of S$7 million a year. There was concern about the overall cost-effectiveness and optimal utilisation of training resources. The need for better efficiency in administrative and operating systems was therefore another challenge. Maintaining relevance in a rapidly changing work environment was seen as a continuing challenge. To stay relevant, the system had to continue to sustain its ability and capacity to respond to the needs of a better-educated and trained workforce. In this respect, the extensive network of advisory committees and professional core capabilities continued to play a key role in the continual development and improvement of the vocational training system in Singapore.

THE VITB IN 1990

By 1990, VITB had developed an integrated and comprehensive system of vocational training for school leavers and working adults. Besides its primary role as a training provider, VITB was also the national authority for developing national skills standards, conducting public trade tests and certifying occupational skills. With the expansion of the system to 15 training institutes, VITB's full-time enrolment increased from 10,000 in 1980 to 16,000 in 1990 (VITB, 1990/1991). The annual intake of workers in part-time educational and skills training courses, including the BEST and WISE programmes, had exceeded 100,000 training places. The VITB and its predecessor, the ITB, had together trained an estimated 175,000 school leavers and workers with occupational skills since 1973. That was about 13 per cent of the workforce in 1990. There was no doubt that the VITB was a major player in the training of a better-educated and skilled workforce. The vocational training system, which by then had greatly expanded under VITB, was characterised by the following key features:

Full-Time Institution-Based Model

The model of vocational training was one based on pre-employment full-time institution-based training for young school leavers. Whereas it might have been sufficient for a school leaver to enter employment and learn on the job in the past, institutional training had become a necessary and critical step to meet the increasing demand for skilled manpower in a modern industrialised economy. Conducted outside the school system, vocational training was provided by VITB in vocational and technical institutes. The choice of this approach was driven by the recognition that the delivery of market-relevant skills was best undertaken by a specialised institution such as VITB. Being mission-driven, the system could better address the needs of the less academically inclined to train and prepare for a career in employment. VITB was the transitional interface between general education and the world of work. Without such a vocational training system, many would have found the school-to-work transition more haphazard and missed the opportunity to acquire the vocational and technical skills needed for employment.

This model had responded well to the skilled manpower needs of the many MNCs setting up operations in Singapore. Such training not only provided the knowledge and skills competencies, but also was an assurance of a ready pool of well-trained and skilled manpower. A strong incentive no doubt in promoting foreign direct investment into Singapore, this strategy had also helped to build a robust vocational and technical education system that was relevant and responsive to changing manpower needs. Training conducted in vocational institutes was hands-on and competency-based in line with industry standards. The students received a strong practical foundation in the occupational areas for which they would seek employment. It was a system purposefully designed to complement the school education system, attract school leavers, match their abilities and aptitudes and motivate them to maximise their individual potential through skills training.

Integral Part of Education and Training System

The role of VITB as an integral part of the total education and training system in 1990 is shown in Figure 4.1 (Law, 1990). With streaming as a key feature of the NES, primary education could take from six to eight years depending on a pupil's academic ability. The three tracks were Primary Normal, Primary Extended and Primary Monolingual. Similarly, students were tracked at the secondary level into Secondary Special (four years),

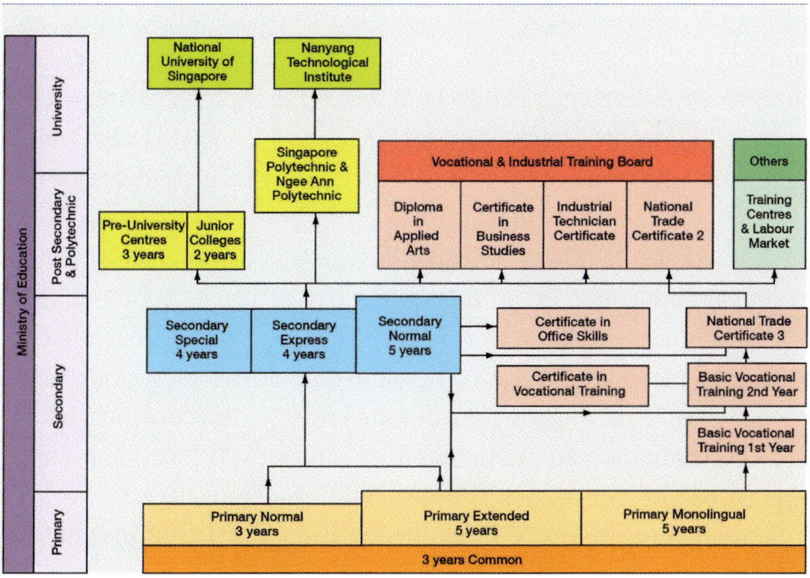

Figure 4.1 Education and training system (1990)

Secondary Express (four years) and Secondary Normal (five years). At the lower level of vocational training, school leavers who only completed primary (Primary Extended and Primary Monolingual) and post-primary (Secondary 1 Normal to Secondary 3 Normal) were the main target groups for the Basic Vocational Training courses in VITB. Those who performed well could progress to the NTC-3 (semi-skilled) and NTC-2 (skilled) levels of training under the NTC system of certification. The Secondary 4 Normal school leavers were eligible for direct admission into the one-year NTC-3 or Certificate of Office Skills courses. The Certificate of Vocational Training was a new work-based programme specially designed for girls who wished to seek employment in the service sector or the garment and electronics industries.

At the higher levels of VITB training, two-year Certificate and three-year Diploma programmes were conducted for secondary school leavers with the GCE "O" qualification. The NTC-2 courses provided an attractive direct entry for training at the skilled level. The Industrial Technician Certificate programmes trained technicians and junior supervisory staff in engineering and design. Certificate in Business Studies courses were offered to school leavers who were more inclined towards an office career, for instance as secretaries and account clerks. The Diploma in Applied Arts courses in Graphic Design, Interior design and Product Design trained graduates who would work as middle-level professionals in design.

In 1990, there was about an equal distribution of students who had a secondary education and those with only a primary education. Those with a primary education were largely from the Primary Extended and Primary Monolingual streams. The ratio of male to female students was 66 to 34 per cent. Many were from the lower socio-economic strata of society. Annual operational budget for VITB was S$101.8 million and the average cost of training was S$5,100 per full-time student each year. With 15 training institutes, VITB was offering a range of 47 full-time courses at different levels of certification as shown in Box 4.1.

Comprehensive and Integrated CET System

As part of its statutory mandate, VITB had developed a comprehensive and integrated system of continuing education and training for working adults. Often viewed as the non-formal system offering part-time and short-term courses, continuing education and training are nonetheless an essential component in the total preparation of a better-educated and skilled workforce. In fact, the upgrading and retraining of workers is a continuous process with its own unique challenges. Continuing education and training offer a framework (Law & Low, 1997) by which the government, unions, employers and workers can participate as partners in response to new demands in the types and levels of education, knowledge and skills.

In this respect, the VITB had been offering part-time and weekend general education courses leading to the GCE "N", "O" and "A" levels since its early beginnings. It administered the previously mentioned three special national projects aimed at raising the educational and skills levels of the workforce, BEST, WISE and MOST (see next section). In collaboration with unions, employers and related government agencies,

BOX 4.1 FULL-TIME COURSES IN VITB (1990)

Diploma

- Graphic Design
- Interior Design
- Product Design

Industrial Technician Certificate

- Electrical Engineering
- Electronics Engineering
- Electro-Mechanical Engineering
- Mechanical & Electrical Drafting & Design
- Mechanical Engineering

Certificate in Business Studies

- Accounting
- Secretarial Practice

Certificate in Office Skills

- Certificate in Office Skills

National Trade Certificate Grade 2

- Air-Conditioning & Refrigeration Mechanics
- Architectural Drafting
- Civil/Structural Drafting
- Dressmaking
- Electrical Fitting & Installation
- Electrical Power & Machine
- Electronics Instrumentation
- Electronics Servicing (Digital)
- Electronics Servicing (Video)
- Electro-Mechanical Servicing
- Hairdressing
- Heavy Duty Diesel Mechanics
- Maintenance Fitting
- Motor Vehicle Mechanics
- Dressmaking
- Precision Machining
- Tool & Die Making
- Tool & Die Making (Press Tool)

National Trade Certificate Grade 3

- Air-Conditioning & Refrigeration Mechanics
- Building Drafting
- Building Servicing
- Dressmaking
- Electrical Fitting & Installation
- Electronics Servicing
- Furniture Production
- General Welding
- Graphic Reproduction
- Hairdressing
- Heavy Duty Diesel Mechanics
- Maintenance Fitting
- Marine Fitting
- Metal Fabrication
- Metal Machining
- Motor Vehicle Mechanics
- Offset Printing
- Upholstery

Certificate of Vocational Training

- Certificate of Vocational Training

many other upgrading opportunities were created through initiatives such as apprenticeship and approved training centres under the Industry-based Training scheme.

Historically, the VITB and polytechnics, as government educational and training institutions, had also taken on the responsibility as major providers of CET. However, in the early 2000s, the increasing need for a greater national focus on skills development and lifelong learning led to the establishment of the Workforce Development Agency (WDA) in 2003 (Box 4.2). Operating under the purview of Ministry of Manpower, WDA is the national agency responsible for overall policies, coordination, regulation, workforce certification and funding on CET and related initiatives in lifelong learning. Promoting lifelong learning to ensure the relevance, quality and competitiveness of the Singapore workforce is a national priority. In this respect, the government's strategic approach has always been to work in close partnership with employers and unions within the spirit of tripartism.

The importance of preparing the young and need for retraining of the workforce is not new. Highlighting the challenge that Singapore was facing as a developing country, former Prime Minister Lee Kuan Yew, during his address at the Opening of the Singapore Polytechnic new campus at Dover Road in 1979, said, "To be like the industrialised societies, our young must be educated to the same high degree of literacy, knowledge, skills, and versatility in acquiring new skills through retraining as those of the industrialised countries" (Lee, 1979).

BEST, WISE and MOST

There was much media interest in the launch, development and progress of BEST and WISE. It helped that the one championing the cause of worker education and training was the late Dr Tay Eng Soon himself. As a Minister of State in charge and Chairman of VITB, he was in a good position to garner the support of political colleagues, unions and employers. A front-page headline article "Foreign help for Best teachers" in *The Straits Times*

BOX 4.2 FACTSHEET ON CET

The ITE and polytechnics are an integral part of the formal education system under the Ministry of Education. Their primary function is in providing pre-employment full-time vocational and technical education for school leavers. In this formal system, there are pre-requisites for admission and training leads to formal educational qualifications. As key public institutions, they were and continue to be major providers of part-time continuing education and training for working adults to acquire a technical qualification or upgrade their skills. In responding to the needs of adult learners, the VITB (predecessor to ITE), for example, had offered its full-time courses on a part-time modular basis. Another significant contribution was in worker education. It launched the BEST (Basic Education for Skills Training) and WISE (Worker Improvement through Secondary Education) in 1983 and 1987, respectively. These pioneering national projects in English language and Mathematics had benefited a quarter of a million workers over a period of 20 years.

With its establishment in 2003, the Workforce Development Agency (WDA) took over the direct responsibility for developing a nation-wide system of continuing education and training, as part of the lifelong learning initiative. Its mission is to enhance the employability and competitiveness of the workforce. Operating under the Ministry of Manpower, it champions the cause of worker training, administers funding policies, coordinates efforts among stakeholders and undertakes special initiatives. As part of the national continuing education and training infrastructure are the Singapore Workforce Skills Qualifications (WSQ) system, the Continuing Education and Training Master Plan, Institute of Adult Learning and Continuing Education and Training institutes. There have been wide-ranging initiatives to help working adults stay relevant and responsive in the face of changing manpower needs and economic conditions. A prime example was the two-year Skills Programme for Upgrading and Resilience (SPUR) that was launched in December 2008. SPUR leveraged on the extensive national continuing education and training system to help companies and workers manage the economic downturn by saving jobs while investing in building skills for the recovery.

(*Continued*)

BOX 4.2 (CONTINUED)

In a response to the Economic Strategies Committee's report in February 2010, a high-level National Productivity and Continuing Education Council (NPCEC) was established. Currently chaired by Deputy Prime Minister Teo Chee Hean, the goal is to galvanise national efforts to boost skills and enterprise productivity through a first-class continuing education and training system. In this respect, the NPCEC oversees the work of the different government agencies and promotes close collaboration amongst the business sector, workers and unions and the public sector.

on 23 June 1983 reported on the overwhelming response and impending plans for a daily television series and better training schemes (Ng, 1983). There was much anticipation, excitement and public interest as the programmes were making a direct impact on the lives and employability of many ordinary Singaporeans. Even non-working adults and housewives took the opportunity to improve their competency in English language. With such extensive media publicity and outreach, BEST and WISE soon became household names in Singapore.

Indeed, we enlisted the help of foreign expertise in the development of the BEST and WISE programmes. Professional expertise came from the former Alberta Vocational College in Edmonton, Canada. The college, now known as NorQuest College, was especially chosen as a partner in view of its vast experience and expertise in basic adult education programmes for new immigrants in Canada. A team of five professional staff from Alberta led by Dr Michael Andrews, the President, was deployed at different times in Singapore to work with VITB's curriculum specialists in developing the instructional materials, including text books and teacher guides between 1983 and 1988. An important consideration was the need to customise the content to the local cultural and work context for working adults. Teachers play an important part in the success of any educational programme. In this international collaboration, Alberta

Vocational College helped to train 820 BEST and 500 WISE teachers by equipping them with the basic knowledge and skills in the teaching of adult learners. Twenty local teachers were also trained as "Master Trainers" who subsequently took over the responsibility of conducting the teacher-training programme.

The task of upgrading the education and skills of workers was a crucial one. Technological changes in industry had made a significant impact on the job skills of the workforce. Without a basic education, it was difficult to adapt to the needs for new knowledge and skills. With a changing work environment, the worker in a modern industrial economy also needed to have a broader understanding of inner workings of the organisation, technology, systems and processes. The way to adapt was self-improvement through worker education and training. In effect, this was a route made possible to an estimated more than 300,000 workers who had participated in the BEST, WISE and MOST (Box 4.3).

Industry-Based Training

Apprenticeship was another important avenue for skills development and training. As the national agency responsible for the system of apprenticeship in Singapore, VITB defined the regulatory requirements and administrative processes. It developed the training programmes and provided support for the off-the-job training (Off-JT) through its full-time or continuing education and training courses in VITB institutes. The on-the-job training (OJT) was the responsibility of the sponsoring companies. Depending on the trade areas and level of training, the duration of apprenticeship could vary from two to three and a half years. Apprenticeship training also led to a formal skills qualification under the NTC system of certification. As a statutory board, besides vocational training, VITB was also empowered as the national authority for the development and certification of national occupational skills and standards.

Modelled after the German system, apprenticeship training offered an alternative pathway to the full-time institution-based system for about 5 to 10 per cent of VITB students. In general, apprentices spent four days

BOX 4.3 BEST, WISE AND MOST

Programme	**BEST (Basic Education for Skills Training)**	**WISE (Worker Improvement through Secondary Education)**	**MOST (Modular Skills Training)**
Overview	National worker education programme launched in January 1983 by the government, the National Trades Union Congress (NTUC) and employers to improve basic literacy and numeracy of workers who had less than a primary level education.	National worker education programme launched in September 1987. Built on the successful BEST model, WISE aimed to raise the competency level of workers in English language and Mathematics to the GCE "N" level.	National scheme launched in October 1986. MOST was directed at workers who lacked basic vocational skills, needed new skills or wished to upgrade their present skills.
Curriculum	Four modules each in English language and Mathematics. Each module comprised 60 hours and could be completed by workers attending classes twice a week for 20 weeks on a part-time basis.	The same modular curriculum approach as BEST was adopted for the WISE programme.	The MOST scheme offered formal NTC skills qualification. Each module was complete by itself, competency-based, took only six months on a part-time basis and led to certification in an employable skill. Initially, MOST only offered skills courses

(*Continued*)

BOX 4.3 (CONTINUED)

			at the NTC-3 (semi-skilled) level. In July 1988, the scheme was extended to the higher NTC-2 (skilled) and Certificate of Competency.
Outcome	Targeted to reach out to 225,000 workers. Over a period of six years (1983 to 1989), 127,000 persons or 56 per cent had already enrolled for at least one module. The number who had successfully completed Module 4 (the highest module) in English and/or mathematics was 28,580. Of this number, 6,530 or 23 per cent proceeded to take up skills training or further education. The interest in BEST continued to be strong with each intake averaging about 19,000 participants at the time.	A total of 11,110 places were taken up against a planned target of 7,700 in the first two pilot intakes in September 1987 and March 1988. This was 44 per cent above target. It reflected the importance workers attached to education. Of special significance was the fact that some 2,800 or 33 per cent of the participants in the two intakes were BEST Module 4 graduates. WISE was established as a regular programme in September 1988.	From 1986 to 1989, some 33,300 training places were taken up. About 22 per cent were sponsored by NTUC or employers and the rest self-sponsored.

doing OJT in industry and one day attending Off-JT in VITB institutes. A legal contract signed between the apprentice and the sponsoring company ensured that the appropriate training was provided by the employer and the apprentice was committed to the training programme. An apprentice received a wage as an employee of the company. The cost of training to the company was partially subsidised by the Skills Development Fund.

Major companies and industry groups with the necessary expertise and resources were encouraged to work with VITB in setting up their own in-house training centres. Companies and joint industry training centres that met the Board's criteria in terms of curricula, facilities and staffing were granted the "Approved Training Centre" or "ATC" status. With accreditation, the ATCs could train their own apprentices under VITB's national system of certification. There was no additional need for the apprentice to sit for the public trade tests. Other benefits to the companies were the professional support provided by VITB in the setting up of the centres, curriculum development, training materials and pedagogic training for the trainers. There were 30 ATCs with an enrolment capacity of 2,000 apprentices in 1990.

Public Trade Test System

A common feature in skills development is a national system of public trade tests. Such a system was administered by VITB, especially in the earlier stages of industrial development. The purpose was to certify workers who had acquired the necessary skills through years of relevant working experience but did not have the formal vocational qualifications. A public trade test thus defined the benchmark and skills standards for which a worker could seek certification. The skills standards and test criteria were developed by VITB in consultation with its Training Advisory Committees represented by technical experts from the industry.

Between its inception in 1972 and 1989, 83,000 workers had been tested under the system. The system was able to certify vocational skills in over 50 trades at NTC-3 and NTC-2 levels. Occupational skills that were

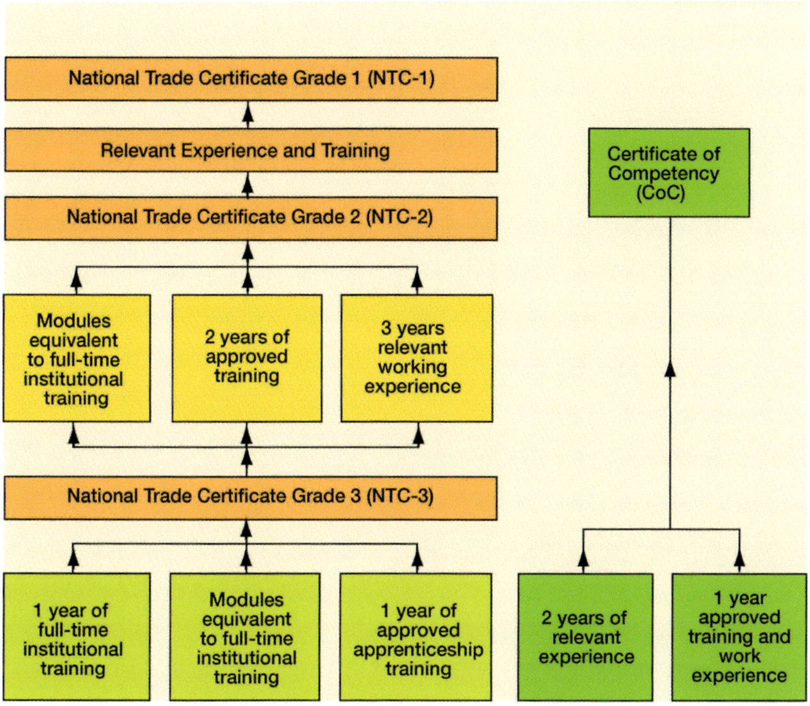

Figure 4.2 Public trade test system (1990)

narrower and specific in nature were certified under the Certificate of Competency system. The eligibility criteria for the public trade test are shown in Figure 4.2. Certification could be achieved through full-time training as in the case of school leavers who were trained under the formal full-time institution-based system. Workers who wished to prepare for the tests could do so through part-time continuing education and training programmes, apprenticeship training or relevant on-the-job working experience.

Part II

Journey of Transformation

Chapter 5

Move towards Organisational Excellence

High-performing institutions do not happen by chance. They are often founded by people who share a common mission, vision and values. A common value of successful organisations often has to do with an underlying management culture or philosophy. One such philosophy is people-centred management (PCM), a concept that former Prime Minister Lee Kuan Yew shared when he launched the National Productivity Month in November 1982. Inspired by the global competitiveness of Japanese industries to launch Singapore's first productivity drive in the 1980s, he had said, "All successful management have in common a people-centred management where care and the concerns for the workers are high in the managements' priorities." A national attitudinal survey by the former National Productivity Board (now SPRING Singapore) also revealed that the approach was a potential factor in motivating workers towards achieving higher productivity. The findings found that workers preferred a management that treated them with dignity and recognition than being provided with higher salaries or more benefits but devoid of a supportive work environment.

NATIONAL INTEREST IN PEOPLE-CENTRED MANAGEMENT

This interest in people-centred management in reinforcing productivity through better management practices was championed by National Productivity Board as part of the National Productivity Movement. With an economy that was restructuring towards more capital-intensive industries, the concerns of increasing labour costs and low productivity when compared with the developed countries were beginning to assume greater national priority. The rationale was that if Singapore was to sustain its rapid economic growth, Singaporeans must learn how to manage and work more effectively. Increasing productivity through better management practices was one way to motivate and maximise the potential of the workforce.

It is noteworthy that some 30 years later, the need to raise productivity had regained prominence in underlying the recommendations from the Economic Strategies Committee (ESC) in 2010. Higher productivity was highlighted as the way to sustain economic growth and increase real wages for the long term. When asked for his views at a dialogue with participants at a Singapore National Employers Federation's (SNEF) 30th anniversary summit in 2010, then Minister Mentor Lee Kuan Yew was reported as saying:

> We've been trying ever since… can [we] equal the Japanese? Very unlikely… Can we be competent? Yes. But, we don't have the culture… Instead, Singapore could succeed in supporting productivity growth with its more Western orientation and its openness to foreign talent… developing a 'Singapore brand'… capitalise on other strengths such as its complex manufacturing industries, its research and development infrastructure, biomedical services and water technology… It could also position itself as a base for Asian companies to expand, due to its global outlook…. (Lin, 2010)

So, what is "productivity?" In particular, what is its relevance in the context of organisational excellence? This is a complex subject of interest to governments, employers, unions, researchers and practitioners in human resource development and management. There are various definitions and perspectives. From an economic perspective, it may be viewed as the efficiency with which resources are being used in the production of goods and services. It is a measure of the relationship between the units of input and output. Viewed from a national perspective, the goal of higher productivity could be a strategic positioning to compete in a global market and create employment and improve standards of living for the people. In a socio-organisational context, "productivity" embraces the wider concept of leadership, management practices and culture in organisations. It is an attitude of the mind that seeks the continuous improvement of systems, processes and services. It is a conviction and belief that one can do better today than yesterday and that tomorrow shall be better than today. It is a motivation in striving towards better quality and standards. It is a culture that places trust and respect as core values irrespective of the roles people play in an organisation. It is an investment in education and training. It is human capital development. It is about practising people-centred management and much more.

The questions as to why the country was not achieving much in raising productivity were poignantly posed by Minister of Finance Tharman Shanmugaratnam, during a dialogue with the business community hosted by the Singapore Business Federation in 2010. Offering ideas on productivity as a member of the ESC, Shanmugaratnam (presently a Deputy Prime Minister and a former Minister of Education) was reported as saying:

> What it boils down to is a different motivation in our society... It is a bit of a puzzle as to why, with a very good education system, good schools system, first-class polytechnic and ITE (Institute of Technical Education) systems and one of the best-rated university systems in the world, why is that despite this, we're not achieving as much in the workforce in terms of skills, expertise and, therefore, productivity... There is a gap... I think it requires a different motivation: Moving beyond paper qualifications towards wanting to become an expert at the job. More of us have to be like that. Regardless of the job you're in — wanting to be the best bartender, the best graphic artist, the best lawyer, the best machinist. Wanting to be on top of your game....
>
> The second question is: How do we get that different motivation brewing... Studies have shown that some companies do much better than others... You can see it in Singapore. Some companies have workforces that are completely ripped up, excited, always looking to do something better. And it's not just about incentives, not just the promise of bonuses... that it is extremely important for employees to feel that they are individually contributing to something larger than themselves, than their immediate job, contributing to what is happening in their company as a whole... they want to feel empowered... it's not beyond us to achieve this. It requires a management revolution in Singapore. (Chan, 2010)

AN EDUCATOR'S INTEREST IN PEOPLE-CENTRED MANAGEMENT

Worker motivation and good management practices are certainly important factors. Good education and training is essential but only a part of the equation in the drive towards higher productivity. Our education and training system is well aligned with the strategic needs of Singapore. But, productivity and organisational excellence are also relevant factors and should be of interest in the working of an educational institution. In this respect, "productivity" is more than imparting the knowledge, skills and values to students. Beyond the immediate mission, strategies and goals are the issues of how educational institutions are managing the expectations of students, partners and other stakeholders. How do we measure up to the best performing organisations, be it public or private, known not only for their products and services but also leadership, people and culture?

It was this frame of mind that led me to believe that people-centred management could be the motivating force in helping to galvanise the management, staff and students through the educational system and processes. I did not, at the time, know or expect that embracing people-centred management would be laying that early foundation for our journey towards organisational excellence — a journey that was to lead to ITE winning the prestigious Singapore Quality Award in 2005.

In line with the national thrust in productivity, the National Productivity Board had invited a people-centred management practitioner and former Managing Director of General Motors (S) Pte Ltd, Ron Gill, as advisor and consultant in disseminating the people-centred management philosophy. I attended a discussion session organised by the Board for senior government and union officials in May 1983 and was personally inspired by the philosophy. I felt then that it would be good for VITB to embrace such a management philosophy and its practices. What attracted me most was that it makes good sense that showing care and concern for staff would more likely win their trust and confidence and help to create a more conducive working environment. I shared my personal views with VITB senior management at a special session in the same month. After consultation with VITB management and unions, a proposal for adopting people-centred management as VITB's management philosophy was then prepared and subsequently accepted and endorsed by the VITB Board that same year.

Why was I interested in people-centred management? My motivation was to provide an educational environment where staff would want to strive for excellence and maximise their own potential. I wanted to see VITB not just as a successful educational institution but an organisation where staff understood their roles, shared common goals and objectives and were motivated to want to do the best in serving the students, industry and community. I was in favour of a culture that would encourage open communication, mutual trust and honesty in dealing with one another. It was important that members should collaborate and work as a team. Ultimately, the way to achieve productivity and organisational excellence was to pay special care and attention to each member of the organisation.

A DEFINITION OF PEOPLE-CENTRED MANAGEMENT

What is the people-centred management philosophy? It is a management philosophy that focuses on developing people and their potential. After much learning and internal discussion, this was how we defined it:

> The people-centred management philosophy is one that recognises staff as the most important resource in an organisation and will develop them and create an environment where they are self-motivated to give their best. The belief is that if staff are treated with respect and dignity, they will reciprocate by giving their best. (VITB, 1983/1984)

The following were practices of people-centred management formulated and adopted by VITB:

- Treat staff fairly and firmly, as discipline is a major factor to the success of the philosophy. The philosophy is by no means "soft" as it relates to how management wins respect. A "soft" manager who only wants to be liked and avoids enforcing appropriate discipline will lose control and respect from his staff.
- Promote two-way communication. Management needs to inform staff of major policies, future plans and development and listen to their views, feedback and suggestions.

- Engage in consultation with staff. Encourage them to take an active part in improving their work areas and participate in the decision-making process.
- Take a genuine interest in the staff. Management demonstrates its concerns by taking time to explain and listen to them. The objective is to develop rapport and a bond of trust with the staff.
- Accord recognition to staff when due and offer constructive criticism when required. This is, however, done with sensitivity such that staff do not feel embarrassed or humiliated.
- Practise what is preached and lead by example.
- Motivate their staff through better understanding of their strengths and weaknesses. Management therefore assigns tasks and indicates their expectations clearly.
- Strive to establish good relationships and be open enough to admit mistakes.
- Ensure that management is competent in their jobs and train their staff by sharing their knowledge and experience.

Much of the extensive research into employee-centred supervision by the late Professor Rensis Likert from 1946 to 1970 was conducted at the Institute of Social Research at the University of Michigan. Professor Likert was best known as an educator and organisational psychologist for his work on management styles in industrial organisations. According to the research studies, the practices of people-centred management would promote the following results:

- Rapport, team-spirit and mutual support
- Sincerity, openness and sensitivity between management and staff
- More confidence and trust on the part of the staff
- Improved staff morale and motivation
- Better two-way communication
- Higher productivity and improvement in the work environment

PRODUCTIVITY STEERING COMMITTEE

Before people-centred management was formally adopted as VITB's central management philosophy in 1983, the institution had compatible practices that provided a suitable foundation for the new approach. First, a VITB Productivity Steering Committee had already been formed in April 1982 as part of the wider National Productivity Movement. This in-house Committee provided the overall direction for promoting, developing, reviewing and implementing policies and plans related to improving the work environment, quality and productivity. Second, Work Improvement Teams (WITs) had been set up by VITB in August 1982, again as part of the Movement. WITs were the equivalent of the better-known Quality Circles (QCs), which the Japanese very effectively adapted from the Americans for the manufacturing industries in Japan.

In a way, WITs are an application of the people-centred management philosophy in promoting employee participation in the daily workings of an organisation. The concept of WITs emphasises the development of team spirit, pride in work and good attitudes towards work and productivity. WITs are a people-centred, people-development and team-building programme. Involvement in WITs encourages staff to take the initiative in improving their work areas, thus moving towards a more participative form of management that engages staff in contributing to the overall decision-making process. WITs promote communications among and between teams, thus reinforcing confidence, trust and teamwork. The end result is a more productive and motivated staff.

To improve mutual understanding and rapport among management and staff, various channels of communications were established in reaching out to staff, training managers, union representatives and newly appointed staff. Through workshops, dialogues and meetings, staff and management were kept informed of the latest developments, future trends, policies and insights into the thinking of management. At the same time, feedback was gathered on the challenges faced by staff and management throughout the organisation. I had my CEO communication platforms in reaching out to management, staff, students and unions. These dialogues and meetings gave everyone a better sense of direction, mission, commitment and teamwork. They also gave me a better feel of the organisational climate.

Underlying these lines of communications was a special effort in building a strong and close management-union relationship. I valued and respected the role of our two unions, the Union of ITE Training Staff (UITS) and ITE Administrative and Ancillary Staff Branch (ITEAASB). It was a mutually supportive relationship built over the years through formal and informal avenues. Maintaining a climate of trust, openness, fairness and understanding with the union leaders had facilitated the process of our transformation. It had contributed significantly towards achieving our goals and effectively discharging our responsibilities to society and the community. I was honoured with a Medal of Commendation by the National Trades Union Congress (NTUC) in the 2001 May Day Award. The value of this close management-union relationship was captured in the citation of the award:

> Besides facilitating the close bonding between union officials and management staff, he [Dr Law] also assures that policies are sensitive to the needs and feelings of staff. His empathy for the staff has enabled the Union of ITE Training Staff (UITS) to resolve many sensitive issues amicably for the members. Under his able leadership, ITE has established a comprehensive framework for continuing education and training for working adults. Each year more than 82,000 training places together with the collaboration from the industries and the labour movement are offered to working adults and many have benefited from these programmes.

THE WITS MOVEMENT

Why WITs, one may ask? The simple answer is that we were committed to developing a more effective and productive workforce. As mentioned earlier, the concept of Work Improvement Teams (WITs) was adapted from the better-known Quality Circles (QCs). Originated in the United States, QCs were quickly adopted by and credited as one of the secrets of success in Japanese industries. The underlying philosophy of WITs is to draw upon the loyalty of staff towards the organisation by encouraging an active and voluntary participation in the workplace in order to identify and seek solutions to problems that may arise in the course of daily work. WITs create the opportunities for team members to contribute ideas and suggestions in improving the work environment and quality of working life. WITs are a powerful concept that, when put into practice, builds a positive mindset towards quality improvement and fosters teamwork. In the process, members also learn the tools of planning, problem-analysis and decision-making. This helps to fulfil the staff's need for a sense of belonging, achievement and recognition. As a result, the staff and organisation can look towards better cooperation, morale, team spirit and achievement of vision and goals.

In the context of an educational institution, our role in the national productivity movement goes beyond that of an employer. We also play the role of the trainer in imparting the concept and need for productivity, good work attitudes and teamwork to trainees who represent the future workforce. So, under the guidance of our VITB Productivity Steering Committee, there were much sustained and coordinated efforts in promoting WITs through working committees, in-house training, seminars and task forces.

A major movement such as WITs would obviously face challenges in reaching out to everyone and sustaining its momentum and growth. At an annual WITs Presentation Day for VITB staff in November 1985, I spoke of the need to overcome the teething problems of initiating, promoting and establishing WITs. The critical challenge I saw then was the need for a three-level commitment:

> Top management has clearly declared its commitments. At the middle-management level, we need each and every manager and supervisor to give his support to WITs. Middle managers can provide words of encouragement and take actions to facilitate WITs activities... All managers have the responsibility to promote and sustain WITs within their own environment. They are, in part, responsible for the success of WITs... At the staff level, I would like to reinforce your commitment by reiterating that WITs is a

> people-development programme... Great efforts must therefore be made by all staff to get involved and benefit from participating in WITs. (Law, 1985a)

It has been said that productivity is a like a marathon without an ending. It is a culture that is nurtured over time. After a decade of development, the participation rate in WITs grew from 10 per cent in 1983 to 44 per cent in 1992. More than 850 staff participated either as team managers, facilitators or members. More than 200 projects were completed by 113 WITs teams. The WITs teams were active participants at the National Quality Control Circle conventions and received many awards for their project presentations and contributions. As an organisation, VITB won the Newcomer Quality Control Circle Organisation of the Year Award in 1984. In 1991, VITB was one of nine statutory boards conferred the Outstanding WITs Organisations Award by the Civil Service Institute. This was presented in conjunction with the 10th WITs Anniversary and Reaffirmation Ceremony. This was followed by the Outstanding Quality Circle (QC) Organisation Award in 1996. By 1997, every ITE staff was a member of WITs, an achievement only a few organisations could claim.

With new developments and challenges, the National Productivity Movement was renamed as the Singapore Productivity & Innovation Movement. In his National Day Rally speech in 2001, then Prime Minister Goh Chok Tong cited "innovation" as one of the key thrusts in the nation's economic strategy to create a "New Singapore":

> We need to foster a culture of innovation... Efficiency is important. But it can be easily matched by others, and does not provide a sustained advantage in competitiveness. Innovation and imagination give an economy or a company the extra edge. Today, wealth is generated by new ideas more than by improving the ideas of others. The innovative spirit must permeate our whole society. (Goh, 2001)

ADOPTING THE PEOPLE-CENTRED MANAGEMENT PHILOSOPHY

With the endorsement of the VITB Board in adopting PCM, the first step was a seminar conducted by the aforementioned Ron Gill on 13 December 1983 for senior management, WITs chief facilitators, union leaders and training managers. It was the beginning of a learning journey for all of us in trying to have a better understanding of the concept and practices of the management philosophy. More importantly, as management, we needed to be convinced that its application could help in promoting productivity and enhancing the role of the trainer in an educational institution like the VITB. Embracing PCM had direct implications on the need for change in existing management practices, attitude, belief and behaviour in line with the practices of people-centred management. A series of workshops was conducted for all management staff with the participation of top senior management and union representatives. Eventually, all staff attended briefings by their respective divisional directors and managers.

The second significant step was the attitudinal and organisational climate survey as recommended by Ron Gill. The survey, called the "VITB PCM Survey," was conducted by Eliza Quek of Performa Pte Ltd in June 1984. Covering management and staff, the objective was to have a better feel of the pulse of VITB as an organisation — the people, interpretations, perceptions and managerial practices. Valuable key findings were gathered on the knowledge and attitude towards people-centred management and obstacles pertaining to policy, organisational and attitudinal issues. At this stage, a project committee was formed to evaluate, resolve issues, plan and monitor follow-up activities.

As Director of VITB, I personally undertook the effort to disseminate the survey findings to all VITB staff through a series of eight face-to-face sessions from February to April 1985. In these sessions, I took the opportunity to reiterate the Board's commitment to people-centred management and that it would be a long journey in fostering a new VITB culture. It would take many years but it would be a journey worth the effort for everyone. Reflecting on this phase of VITB's development, I have no doubt that these earlier efforts in disseminating and embracing the concept, values and practices of people-centred management had helped to build a strong culture of commitment and teamwork, which subsequently transformed ITE into a world-class educational institution.

An important outcome of the people-centred management action plan was the development of a "Management Leadership Development Programme" for VITB and later on ITE managers and supervisory staff. A five-module comprehensive programme, the overall objective was to share the Board's mission and corporate values, foster team spirit and commitment and develop managerial skills. In particular, a one-day module on "Management of Training in VITB" was focused on a better understanding of the corporate philosophy, productivity framework, professional roles of managers and heads of departments and key issues in the management of training institutes. In keeping with the spirit of "walking the talk" under the people-centred management philosophy, my deputy directors and I took responsibility in conducting this module which continued into its 15th series in 1995. Thereafter, with the repositioning of ITE as a post-secondary institution, I offered a revised module called "Management Philosophy and Policies" which continued until 1999.

As a result of these in-house courses, we were able to develop and agree on the respective roles and attributes of our managers for training and non-training functions as shown in Boxes 5.1 and 5.2. A manager (training) refers to a professional head responsible for teaching staff in the technical and vocational institutes. A non-training manager would be an administrative or support staff with non-teaching functions. This practice of engaging senior management in leadership development had helped to foster a closer bond, trust, team spirit and commitment among management and staff within the organisation.

EVOLUTION IN FRAMEWORK FOR ORGANISATIONAL EXCELLENCE

The interest in laying a foundation for organisational excellence started with the participation of VITB in the national WITs movement launched by

BOX 5.1 ROLE AND ATTRIBUTES OF A MANAGER (TRAINING)

- All-round Professional
  Technically qualified, pedagogically trained, an effective manager, a learner and enthusiastically in-tuned in the training environment.
- A leader to staff
  A mentor, a source of motivation and inspiration, well respected, takes initiatives, articulates his/her views and philosophy, a team builder and people developer.
- A counsellor to students
  Understanding students and expectations of society, has empathy, provides guidance and motivation, selfless to the tasks.
- A communicator and believer
  Sharing ITE's vision and goals with staff and students, articulates views, policies and regulations with clarity and understanding.
- A team member on board
  Always seeking improvement in administration or in training, generating ideas and suggestions, providing constructive feedback and committed to safeguarding the interest of students and ITE.

the National Productivity Board in 1982. Next was the conscious decision to embrace people-centred management as the VITB management philosophy in 1983. Whereas people-centred management as a philosophy represented the "approach" and WITs provided the "platform" for engaging staff, the VITB Productivity Steering Committee guided the "direction" towards organisational excellence. These three factors then constituted the cornerstones in nurturing VITB's management philosophy and care culture with an operational focus on staff development and WITs. With the establishment of ITE in 1992, the VITB Productivity Steering Committee was renamed the ITE Productivity Steering Committee.

BOX 5.2 ROLE AND ATTRIBUTES OF A MANAGER (NON-TRAINING)

- An administrator
  Knowledgeable and up-to-date on regulations and procedures. Reliable and independent in executing instructions. Known for efficiency and thoroughness.

- An expert
  Respected for his/her expertise and specialisation in area of responsibility. Well-informed and commanding a professional standing in the field, he/she provides critical support to higher management.

- A decision-maker
  Rational in decision-making. Good at problem-solving. Having the ability to clarify issues, analyse and synthesise, to make sensible, objective and realistic decisions.

- A leader
  A mentor, a source of motivation and inspiration, well respected for his/her views, takes initiatives and a team builder.

- A communicator
  Sharing ITE's vision and goals with staff, articulates views and policies with clarity and understanding.

- A team member on board
  Always seeking improvement in administration. Generating ideas and suggestions, providing constructive feedback and committed to safeguarding the interest of students and ITE.

In 1994, a new national quality award framework for business excellence called the Singapore Quality Award (SQA) was established by the Singapore Productivity and Standards Board (now SPRING Singapore). Shown in Figure 5.1, the award is a comprehensive framework modelled after the American Malcolm Baldrige National Quality Award and the European Quality and Australian Quality Awards for business excellence.

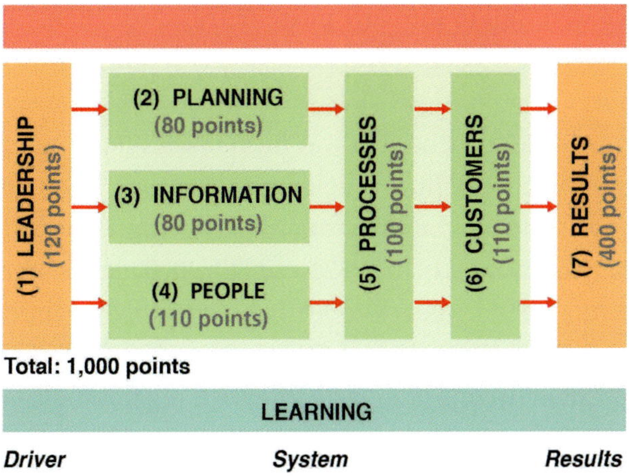

Figure 5.1 Singapore quality award framework

As a framework, the SQA is built upon a set of core values and concepts comprising the seven criteria of leadership, people, planning, information, processes, customers and results. These criteria are broad and inter-related areas of work critical to the success of an organisation. Organisations are assessed according to a point system with a maximum possible score of 1,000 points. Those aspiring to compete for the SQA are expected to score 700 points and more. As a model of business excellence, it has helped ITE to align its systems, processes and practices with its mission, vision and values and benchmark against the best in the world in its journey of transformation.

In May 1995, a "Public Service for the 21st Century" or PS21 Movement was launched as a concerted effort by permanent secretaries of the Singapore government, to transform the civil service towards service excellence and change, so as to be "in time for the future." It advocated a climate of continuous change in public-sector organisations, for greater efficiency, responsiveness and cost-effectiveness, to meet the ever-increasing expectations and demands of the public. Its original thrust was based on four functional elements, namely, organisational review, which focused on strategic improvements; WITs & suggestions, which dealt with attitudinal change and situational improvements; quality service, which focused on customers; and staff well-being, which considered the needs of the individual.

In 1995, we were still in the early phase of transformation. ITE had just officially launched its first five-year strategic development plan, "ITE 2000", to restructure and reposition ITE as a post-secondary technical education institution. A development plan was formulated after a comprehensive process of consultation with stakeholders and partners. It was a roadmap of strategies, goals and programmes towards achieving the next vision. I saw the complementary roles of the PS21 and ITE 2000 plan in organisational excellence. As a statutory board under the purview of the Ministry of Education, this PS21 initiative was an impetus giving us access to a higher and wider platform in driving our journey towards organisational excellence.

With this development, the ITE Productivity Steering Committee was restructured and renamed "ITE PS21 Steering Committee". With renewed commitment and intensified efforts, the terms of reference for this steering committee were revised as: "To offer broad direction and review efforts of the PS21 functional committees in cultivating positive attitudes at the individual and establishment levels for continual improvement and in providing quality service to the public." The annual WITs Presentation Day was accordingly renamed "ITE ExCEL Day," in view of the new focus on quality and excellence under the PS21 platform.

A journey towards achieving organisational excellence is a long and never-ending journey. As such, a framework was necessary to plan, track and sustain its momentum and continuity. At the ITE, it was a gradual systematic learning process where new milestones were reached through building consensus, instituting best practices and achieving results. So, as we intensified our efforts, the three key elements, namely, the PS21, Development Plan and Singapore Quality Award were integrated into a holistic organisational excellence framework in 1999 as shown in Figure 5.2.

Under this framework, the "PS21" was the *impetus* for change in preparing and equipping our staff for the impending challenges ahead, and the "ITE Breakthrough" was the *development plan* to achieve a vision supported by goals, strategies and programmes. The Singapore Quality Award served as a *benchmark* against approaches, systems and processes to achieve world-class excellence in our journey of transformation.

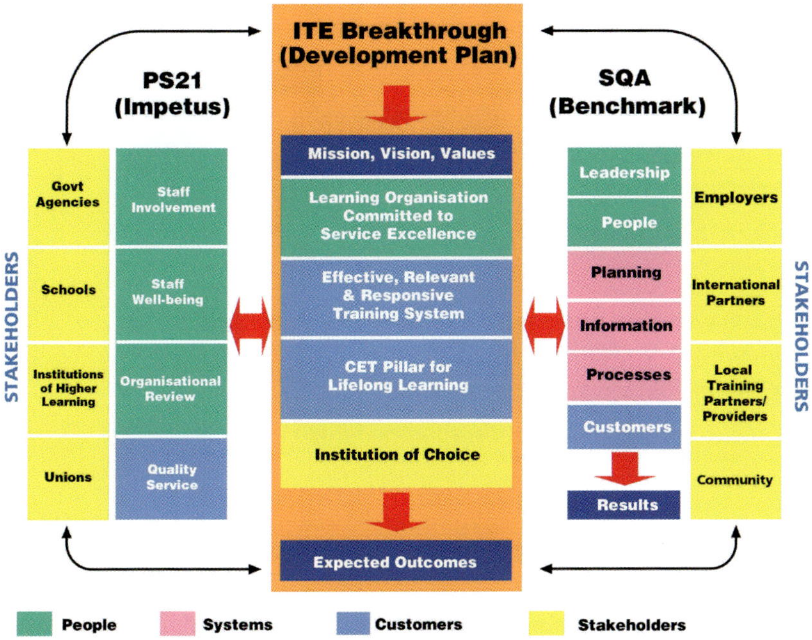

Figure 5.2 ITE's organisational excellence framework

Notes:

PS21 — Public Service for the 21st Century

SQA — Singapore Quality Award

CET — Continuing Education and Training

Supporting these three key inter-locking elements were the common areas of focus on people, systems, customers and stakeholders. It is this holistic organisational excellence framework, when consistently and persistently applied, that eventually led to a breakthrough in the transformation of ITE in Singapore.

MILESTONES IN ACHIEVING ORGANISATIONAL EXCELLENCE

The move towards organisational excellence had its beginnings in the former VITB embracing WITs and people-centred management in the 1980s. However, the systematic process of transformation in ITE began with the implementation of its first five-year strategic development plan, "ITE 2000". Our journey of transformation was driven by the

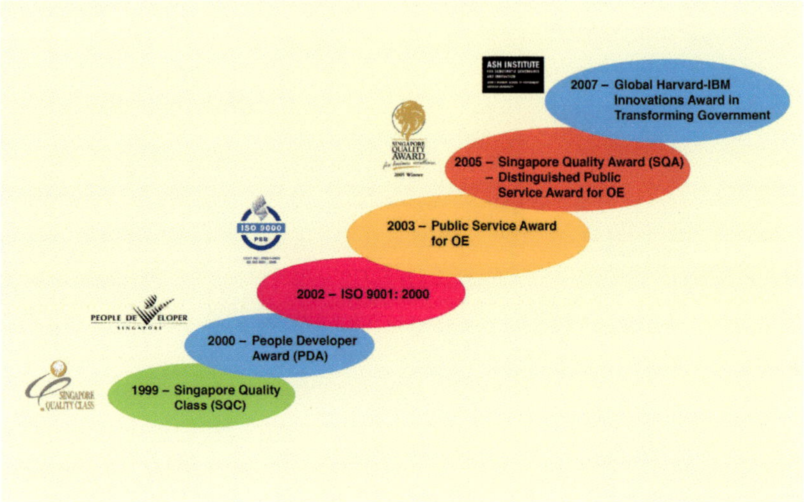

Figure 5.3 Key milestones in organisational excellence

unique challenges facing vocational and technical education and the rising expectations of society and industry. As an integral part of this journey, steps were taken to benchmark against a range of national and international standards within the framework for organisational excellence. The key milestones of achievements over a period of eight years (1999–2007), as shown in Figure 5.3, are a reflection of the intensity in this pursuit of excellence.

Under the Singapore Quality Class system, organisations that are assessed as having achieved a minimum level of excellence under the Singapore Quality Award Model are eligible as members of this system. ITE was, in fact, the first educational institution to qualify for the Singapore Quality Class when the system was launched in 1997. However, we did not join until 1999 as we were then pre-occupied with the implementation of the "ITE 2000" plan. Meanwhile, at the national level, the drive for world-class excellence had gathered momentum in part due to the pressure to restructure the economy and increasing global competition for investment, trade and human resources. Organisations could no longer continue to offer the same goods and services in the same way. To ensure long-term viability, they must continuously improve their products, services and operations. In driving home this message at the national level, Prime Minister Goh Chok Tong, in his National Day Rally speech in 1999 said, "A first-world economy means adopting world-class standards, whatever we do and wherever we operate... Unless our products and services are comparable to the best, we will be out of the running, and will not be a first-world economy" (Goh, 1999).

At this time, ITE was in the process of formulating its second five-year strategic development plan, called the "ITE Breakthrough" (2000–2004). The new vision was to be "a world-class technical education institution for a knowledge-based economy." Unlike the first "ITE 2000" (which was simply "to build ITE into an established post-secondary technical education institution"), the "ITE Breakthrough" was much more ambitious and challenging. However, with a strong and clear support from the ITE Board of Governors, management was ready to benchmark the next phase of ITE's transformation against the Singapore Quality Award model of business excellence. In this respect, a specific goal focusing on "a learning organisation committed to service excellence" was incorporated as part of "ITE Breakthrough". A sign of our growing confidence, this goal was supported by the two strategies of "promoting an environment for continual learning, improvement and innovation" and "nurturing an attitude of service excellence towards customer satisfaction."

To further improve ITE's quality standards, a task force, supported by a number of project teams, was formed to strengthen the key systems, processes and practices. All headquarter divisions and institutes were encouraged to take bold and active steps to build their internal core capabilities and standards. Heads of departments were to benchmark their systems and processes against the various national and international certification schemes. In this context, Lee Ek Tieng, former Head of Civil Service, at the PS21 4th Anniversary Celebration in May 1999, highlighted that:

> The ISO 9000 certification must become a norm. The People Developer Award must become a natural achievement... Singapore Quality Class will not be just aspiration or inspiration: it will be expectation, an expectation not externally imposed but

> an expectation internally driven... This has to be the way forward for the Public Service... a public service that is among the best in the world, worthy of Singapore. (Lee, 1999)

With the completion of ITE 2000 plan, ITE was already viewed as a "best-in-class" organisation with modern campuses, quality programmes and successful graduates. The next challenge was how to achieve excellence as a world-class educational institution? In a speech at the ITE ExCel Day on 28 October 1999, I offered two practical perspectives:

> Firstly, actively seek quality and excellence in your work. Do not be content with the status quo. We must create and innovate. Be open to ideas and suggestions on how you can be more effective in your work or better serve the needs of your students and customers. Take suggestions seriously and implement the changes, where feasible. As a PS21 organisation, we must not be afraid of change, for it is only through continual improvement that we stay relevant to our students, industry and community. Secondly, be proactive in contributing your ideas on how you or ITE can be more effective. Share your ideas on what and how things can be improved, through the WITs, the Staff Suggestion Scheme or feedback to the relevant parties. Every staff must play an active part and take joint responsibility in the spirit of the PS21 vision. If every staff takes pride in his work and is proactive towards improvement and customer service, we can make ITE an exciting and challenging place to work in. (Law, 1999)

In 2000, ITE received the People Developer Award in recognition for its commitment to staff training and development. The goal was to ensure that every staff was professionally trained and well qualified for the job. This was a significant step in building a culture of continual learning and development. Meanwhile, a report of the PS21 Office on the 5th anniversary of PS21 revealed that the PS21 Movement had been successful in raising awareness and standards on customer service and organisational excellence. The assessment was that the PS21 framework had been and would continue to be a useful approach for further change in the public service. However, there was room for improvement as the culture of change advocated under PS21 had yet to be internalised. More had to be done to ensure that the spirit and processes of change and improvement become a natural way of life. Building on the importance of continual change and service, the report advocated a refocus on three new thrusts: "Total Organisational Excellence", "Innovation and Enterprise" and "A Spirit of Openness, Responsiveness and Involvement".

In 2002, ITE's system of design and delivery of training programmes was certified under the ISO 9001:2000 Academic Quality Management System award. Our quality policy stated that "we are committed to provide quality technical education, through continual improvement, to satisfy the needs of our customers." For its achievements under the PS21, ITE was among the first to receive the Public Service Award for organisational excellence in 2003 and the Distinguished Public Service Award in 2005, respectively. What cumulative impact did our active participation in the national productivity and innovation movement and benchmarking have on ITE as an organisation? The result was reflected in key findings on ITE in a PS21 survey conducted by the Civil Service in 2003 that showed:

- 86% agreed that Innovation & Learning Circles (ILCs) encouraged staff to look for ways to improve their work
- 87% thought likewise for the Staff Suggestion Scheme
- 85% agreed that ILCs contributed to teamwork on their departments
- 97% agreed that ILC projects could produce both improvement and innovative outcomes
- 90% believed that they could be creative and innovative through such employee involvements

"ITE CARE" CULTURE

These were strong and powerful signals. Twenty years of commitment and efforts since adopting the people-centred management philosophy in 1983, a "culture of excellence" had taken roots. A new organisational culture had evolved. This was an area close to my heart and crucial in our quest for organisational excellence. We wanted an organisation that was progressive, open to learning, supportive of each other and working cohesively as a team. But, what was that desired culture? What were the underlying beliefs and attributes? What role could staff play in building this culture? We recognised that our key asset was the staff. Each and every one had played an important role in ITE's journey of transformation towards organisational excellence. We would not have progressed this far if not for the excellence in terms of our people and the team spirit fostered under the PS21 and Singapore Quality Award. We would not have a strong foundation to sustain our journey if not for the commitment, dedication and passion of every staff.

It was therefore crucial that we encapsulated an organisational culture that truly reflected our beliefs and aspirations. Towards this end, views of staff were sought as to what were the important specific values they believed in and would like to be included. The consensus of management and staff was the following:

- Integrity — we must be honest and sincere in our words and actions towards others
- Teamwork — we must work and help each other as a team so that we can achieve more
- Excellence — we try to give our best in everything we do to add value to our customers and stakeholders
- Care — we care for our staff, customers and other stakeholders, the community and the environment

In short, this was how ITE's desired culture, the "ITE Care", was born. It means "working with integrity to achieve excellence as a team, caring for all whom we serve." The "ITE Care" constituted the core values that we wanted to promote and inculcate at every level of the organisation. Collectively, these core values represented the fundamental beliefs and principles upon which ITE staff embraced in performing their roles and functions. This culture of "ITE Care", especially the care and concern of staff for our students, is a hallmark of ITE's brand of vocational and technical education.

WINNING THE SINGAPORE QUALITY AWARD

The real breakthrough came in 2005 when ITE won the prestigious Singapore Quality Award for business excellence (SPRING Singapore, 2005). This is a competitive annual award for organisations that have achieved at least 700 points (out of 1,000) through a rigorous and intensive evaluation process. By then, ITE had created a unique brand of a holistic "Hands-on, Minds-on and Hearts-on" post-secondary education under its "One ITE, Three Colleges" model of education and governance. With the opening of the first regional campus, the ITE College East, it was clear in the eyes of the public, that ITE had transformed itself into a world-class institution. This was truly a turning point, a pinnacle of achievement that would not have been thought possible not too long ago.

Winning the award is an honour for any organisation and it was a landmark achievement for ITE, the first educational institution to win the award. Moreover, to win it on our first attempt gave us an even greater sense of its transformation. The model had given us a focused, systematic and sustainable approach in striving for the highest standards in the journey towards organisational excellence. It reaffirmed our belief in offering a unique ITE Brand of College Education. It added meaning and purpose to the work we did for our students and society. It drove home the point that it was all about our attitude and proactive approach in always asking ourselves how we could better serve, add value and meet the changing needs and expectations of our customers and stakeholders.

The three-day SQA Site Assessment for ITE in July 2005 was an intensive and exciting experience. We had never before seen such a high level of enthusiasm and synergy as a team. The seven-member SQA team of assessors interviewed both management and staff. They combed through our systems, practices and results for clarification and verification. What was most heartening to me was their unanimous praise for the strong commitment and passion of our staff and unequivocal care for our students. In taking on the Mission, Vision and Values of ITE, our staff was fully engaged and much inspired by the challenges in the process.

Beyond the SQA was the vision to be "a global leader in technical education". Appropriately, winning the SQA was ITE's springboard in building its global leadership. It injected a greater global perspective in our work through active engagement and collaboration with overseas partners and international organisations. Sharing our experience and expertise with the international community will not only increase the global presence of ITE but help to ensure its continuing relevance, responsiveness and resilience in a global economy. Two years later, the dramatic transformation of ITE was recognised internationally when it won the Harvard-IBM Innovations Award in Transforming Government in 2007. Beyond all dreams, the transformation of ITE has become a Singapore success story in vocational and technical education.

This of course did not mean that the journey of organisational excellence has ended. The work in organisational excellence continues. In fact, six years after winning the SQA, ITE won the SQA with Special Commendation Award in 2011. This is the highest-tier Award that honours the rare few who have scaled the pinnacle of business excellence in Singapore. Bruce Poh, the current CEO of ITE was reported as saying, "Since winning the SQA in 2005, we have further enhanced our capabilities, systems and processes; accelerated our innovations in teaching and learning; and built new world-class 'Colleges of the future'... the SQA with Special Commendation award serves an important external assessment and validation of the progress we have made (since 2005), and helps us examine ways we can still do better" (ITE, 2011).

Chapter 6

The Three Waves of Transformation

There was much optimism and excitement when the Institute of Technical Education (ITE) was established as a new post-secondary educational institution on 1 April 1992. It was a new beginning. Replacing the former Vocational and Industrial Training Board (VITB), it was a milestone in the development of vocational and technical education (VTE) in Singapore. In moving the second reading of the ITE Bill in Parliament, then Senior Minister of State and Minister-in-charge Dr Tay Eng Soon, explained that while VITB graduates with a secondary education were well received by employers and had good starting salaries, the same could not be said for those with only a primary education (Tay, 1992). In line with the national aspiration of moving towards a developed country status as articulated in "The Strategic Economic Plan (1991)", the goal was to upgrade the educational and skill profile of the workforce.

Then Prime Minister Goh Chok Tong was the guest-of-honour at the inauguration of ITE on 31 March 1992. Highlighting the challenge that Singapore faced in order to transform its economy, he said:

> Every human being is unique. His ability, interests and motivation are different. Our challenge is to provide an education system that meets his ability and interests, and which motivates him to do his best. To succeed in this, we have to build up a climate which accords equal respect for good, honest work, whether it be simple or complicated… Those who don't make it to university or polytechnic also play an important role in our economy.
>
> Many kinds of work are necessary to make a society function properly. Each work is useful and of value and must be done well. Our job is to train Singaporeans to do these different kinds of work to the best of their ability. The more highly competent, productive and disciplined we are, the more likely we can be world-class. And indeed, we have to be world-class if we want a world-class standard of living. If our workforce is third-class, we will have a third-world economy and a low per capita income. (Goh, 1992)

A MILESTONE SHIFT IN EDUCATION POLICY

The move to restructure VITB as a post-secondary institution was a consequence of a policy change in the school system. The primary function of VITB had hitherto been to provide pre-employment vocational training for both primary and secondary school leavers under the 1980 New Education System (NES). But, as Singapore moved onto the capital-intensive phase of economic development in the early 1990s, there was growing concern among educators and policymakers that a primary-level education was no longer a sufficient foundation for skills development. With the increasing use of higher technology and skills, a more educated and skilled workforce would be required to sustain continuing economic growth.

Concomitant with social and economic progress, parents whose children opted for VTE held expectations for higher skills qualifications, wider options in occupational choices and opportunities for progression to further education and training. The majority of secondary school leavers who enrolled in VITB were doing well. The outcome for primary school leavers was less promising. While VITB was able to "capture" 85 per cent of students who had completed eight years of primary education under the NES, only 55 per cent managed to go beyond the pre-vocational stage to acquire the semi-skilled National Trade Certificate or NTC-3. The main limitation was the lack of competency in English and Mathematics. This success rate was not satisfactory. The system was not at pace with Singapore's economic development.

These were some of the national concerns, which in July 1990 led to the formation of a Ministry of Education Review Committee on "Improving Primary Education" by former Minister for Education Dr Tony Tan Keng Yam who is now President of Singapore. The Director of Education, John Yip Soon Kwong, was appointed Chairman of the Committee. As Director of VITB, I was the Deputy Chairman. On vocational training, the Report of the Review Committee (Ministry of Education 1991) concluded:

> The present provision of vocational training for primary school leavers is ineffective. This arises from and is compounded by

pupils' low attainment in English and Mathematics, the poor image of vocational training and the limited opportunities for advancement as perceived by both pupils and their parents.

The two recommendations that had direct and significant implications on VITB were that:

- All pupils will receive at least 10 years of general education, including secondary education, before they proceed to further education and training;
- A new secondary level Normal (Technical) course will be introduced for pupils who are not academically inclined to better orientate and prepare them for vocational training.

The decision to provide at least 10 years of basic general education for all pupils was a significant policy change in education. Hitherto, under a system of streaming in primary and secondary schools, the academically weakest students would have had only eight years of primary education before proceeding to vocational training (Goh, 1979). With the change in policy, these pupils would now complete a six-year primary education before progressing to the new four-year secondary Normal (Technical) course. It was, once again, an example of forces driving change and the need to realign the educational system with the dynamics of social and economic development. As a consequence, the government decided to reposition VITB as a post-secondary educational institution. VITB would no longer admit primary school leavers. It would instead focus on providing vocational and technical education for the less academic students who had completed a secondary education.

With this change in policy, I was tasked to chair an internal VITB Review Committee on "Upgrading Vocational Training". The goal was to study the implications and formulate plans to restructure and upgrade the vocational training system. The committee was guided by the need to make the vocational training system more attractive to school leavers and employers. The new system should help to develop a better-educated and skilled workforce to meet the manpower needs of Singapore for the

1990s and beyond. A comprehensive range of proposals, including course restructuring, apprenticeship training, progression opportunities for further education, upgrading of training environment and the renaming of VITB and vocational institutes, were made for the upgrading of VITB.

The Report of the Review Committee concluded that:

> The proposed changes will help further upgrade the status and quality of vocational and technical training in Singapore. The wider choice of training options through a more flexible system of full-time institutional training and apprenticeship schemes will better meet the needs of school leavers and skilled manpower needs of the economy in the 1990s. There will also be better opportunities for VITB trainees to achieve higher-level skills and progress to further education and training. (VITB 1990/1991)

Noticeably, among the proposals, was a name change for VITB. This was a strategic step to move away from the word "vocational" because of the deeply rooted perception that "vocational training" and hence, VITB, was a place of last resort for those who had failed in schools. In view of the poor image, it was proposed that VITB be renamed. Similarly, "vocational institutes" should be renamed as "technical institutes" to reflect the higher-level skills courses to be provided as a post-secondary institution. The total developmental plan to upgrade VITB into a post-secondary institution was estimated at S$250 million.

NEW CHALLENGES AND OPPORTUNITIES

Thus, the new Institute of Technical Education (ITE) was established on 1 April 1992. Repositioned as a post-secondary education institution, this policy shift opened up new challenges and opportunities for the transformation of ITE. As a mission-driven institution, the goal was to provide the best vocational and technical education and ensure the success of graduates in the economy and society. With the emergence of the knowledge economy and its impact in society, in particular, the pervasive use of Information Technology (IT) in the early 1990s, the new challenge was in staying relevant and responsive to the changing needs of students, industry and society. With the increasing pace of economic restructuring and skills upgrading, graduates not only need to have the technical knowledge and skills for the jobs but also so-called "values" for lifelong learning. From the national and institutional perspectives, graduates must not only be well trained, entrepreneurial and confident, but also ready to contribute to society and serve the community.

At a National Day Celebration at ITE East (Bishan) on 8 August 2002, I shared my thoughts on this mission:

> We have broadened ITE's mission as an educational institution to not only create opportunities for our students to acquire knowledge and skills, but also the "values" for lifelong learning. What are some of these important values? They include the ability to think and learn independently. To develop these qualities, you must have the opportunities to set your objectives, do your own planning, make choices and take initiatives in getting things done. While you seek information, you will need to differentiate what may be relevant and what may not be. And in accomplishing all these tasks, you will find that you may need to consult others and collaborate as a team. In the process, you will learn to resolve differences, make decisions and exercise judgment. Our goal is to provide a total development of our students. To achieve this, learning opportunities are created through the introduction of compulsory "life skills" modules, a process-based pedagogic model and a wide range of co-curricular activities. ITE's teaching and learning environment today is designed to prepare you for the more dynamic but potentially disruptive world. (Law, 2002)

The social stigma against students doing vocational training remained the greatest challenge. As an educational institution, how could ITE respond innovatively in the teaching and learning of new skills competencies, lifelong learning and e-technologies? How should ITE restructure and transform itself? With increasing focus on quality and performance outcomes, how could ITE remain focused in its mission? How could attractive educational pathways be created for school leavers? Beyond these educational goals, how could ITE respond to the increasing expectations of stakeholders, partners and customers in terms of organisational excellence, operating systems, processes and best practices?

It was against these educational, economic and social challenges that led the ITE in Singapore to embark on its "journey of transformation" in the early 1990s. So, how did ITE transform itself into a world-class post-secondary institution? How did we manage to change the public image of ITE? How did we transform an institution of "last resort" to one, which is now viewed as "the jewel" of the Singapore education system?

Staying focused on our mission, vision and values was crucial in the process. We called this the "ITE Heartbeat". It was that inner spirit of commitment in always asking how we could better serve, add value and meet the needs of our students, industry and the community. An integral part of the journey was the relentless pursuit of organisational excellence under the Singapore Quality Award framework (see Chapter 5). Another strategic step was the rebranding of ITE (see Chapter 8). So, over a period of 15 years (1992–2007), ITE gradually and systematically transformed what was previously a traditional system of small "vocational institutes" into a modern system of mega "regional campuses".

THE WAVES OF TRANSFORMATION

ITE's journey of transformation was characterised by its consistent use of five-year strategic plans (see Chapter 7). A strategic plan helps to align decisions and actions with the longer-term goals as to the "what, when, how and why" of getting there. It is a roadmap with a new vision to be achieved over the next five years. Each plan was developed through a rigorous and comprehensive process of review and consultation with customers, partners and stakeholders. Endorsed by the ITE Governing Board, the total plan would include a mission, vision, goals, strategies, specific programmes, expected outcomes and corporate values. ITE's five-year strategic plans from 1995 to 2014 are shown in Figure 6.1.

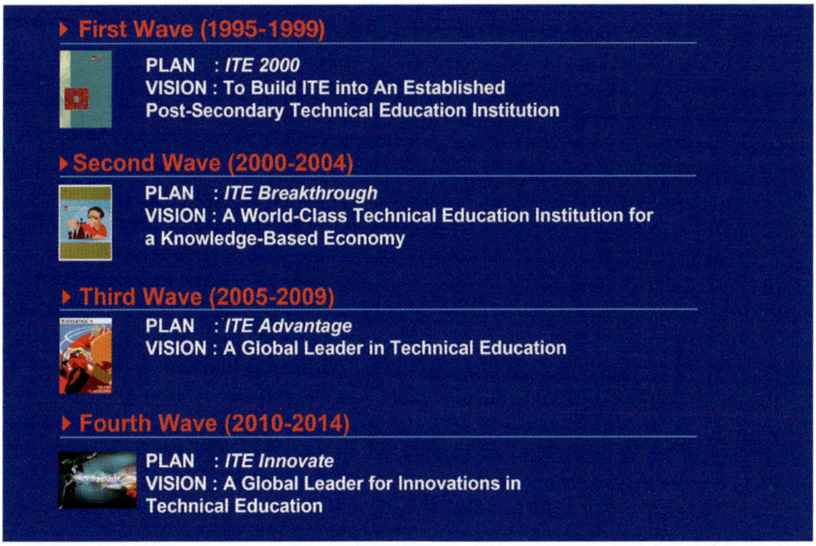

Figure 6.1 Five-year strategic plans

FIRST WAVE OF TRANSFORMATION (1995–1999)

The main thrust in this first wave of transformation was to establish ITE as a post-secondary education institution. With the new educational policy in 1991, all students enrolling in ITE would have completed at least 10 years of basic education comprising six-year primary and four or five-year secondary schooling. This decision opened up new avenues and possibilities for development. It was an opportunity to upgrade and restructure the vocational technical education system to better meet the needs of school leavers, the economy and society. In particular, it was an opportunity to innovate and create a new brand of technical education.

The very first challenge we faced under ITE was the need for a staff restructuring exercise. It was a painful experience. Many of the training programmes under the former VITB had to be restructured and reconfigured to match the new cohort of school leavers. As a result, the qualification and skills of some 400 training staff were rendered irrelevant or inadequate for new and higher-level skills courses. Our first priority was to offer the maximum opportunities and support to upgrade to a diploma level or retrain in the areas of need.

It was especially tough for those in their 50s who did not have the educational prerequisites for upgrading or retraining. It was a major struggle to switch from mechanical-based courses to the electrical or electronics skill areas, which were now in demand. Some chose to leave the system under a Special Resignation Scheme with compensation. Others left to set up their own businesses. We understood their concerns and extended assistance in all ways possible. We consulted our training staff union and talked to every affected staff. If the restructuring process had gone wrong, it would have been a major human resource problem for all concerned. Eventually, 250 staff were retrained and made the transition over a five-year period. Fortunately, it was an issue well managed and satisfactorily resolved.

An early initiative in the transformation of ITE was infrastructural campus development. This was also the most visible part of a changing campus landscape. Initially, seven new campuses were built and three existing campuses under the former VITB system were upgraded from the mid-1990s to 2000. The new campus environment was well equipped with up-to-date training and recreational facilities as shown in Figure 6.2.

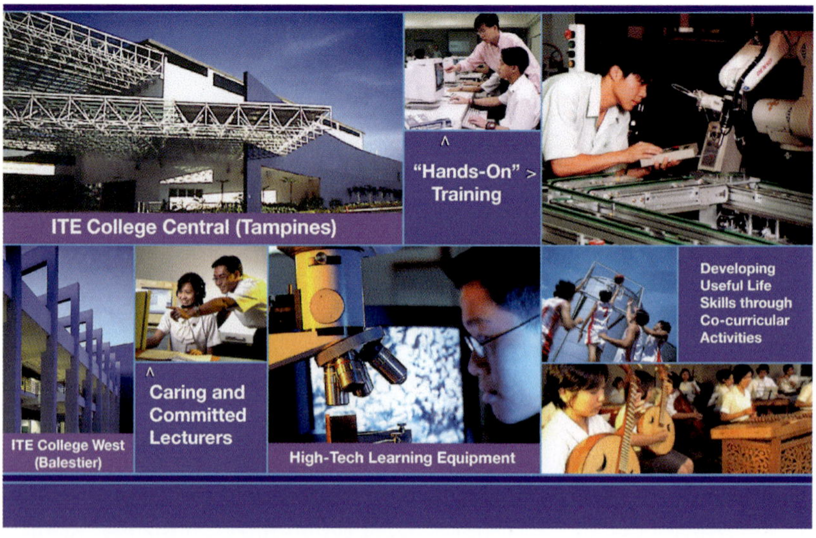

Figure 6.2 Infrastructural campus development

However, conceptually, it was still a traditional system of small vocational institutes. The basic model of governance, management and operation had not changed. The culture was one of dependency for instruction from senior management rather than self-motivation and innovation. This posed both physical and educational constraints as to how many changes could be made in positioning ITE as a post-secondary institution.

The idea of a mega regional campus was first mooted by the Minister for Education Teo Chee Hean in 2001. Reflecting on the rationale for the new model at ITE's 20th Anniversary Dinner on 3 April 2012, he said:

> Instead of using hand-me down premises, ITE students now had access to up-to-date teaching and learning infrastructure, to better prepare them for the needs of modern developing economy. However, these 10 new campuses still carried over some aspects of the previous model of technical education. Each centre was modest in size, with around 1,800 students each, with limited course offerings at each centre. But with students now at the post-secondary level, it was no longer necessary to have many centres spread out across the island for easier access by young teenage students. The opportunity to review this model to derive new synergies arose when more capacity was needed to meet the demand for more training places.
>
> The government decided to consolidate the 10 ITE campuses into three regional campuses, with each campus catering to between 7,000 to 10,000 students. With more students at each campus, ITE could justify specialised equipment and simulators, provide better facilities for inter-disciplinary learning, and better sports, recreation and student interaction spaces for a vibrant campus life to provide the students with self-development activities beyond their courses of study. The first mega campus — ITE College East at Simei — was completed in 2005; and the second ITE College West at Choa Chu Kang in 2010. The third mega campus, ITE College Central at Ang Mo Kio, will open its doors in January 2013… (Teo, 2012)

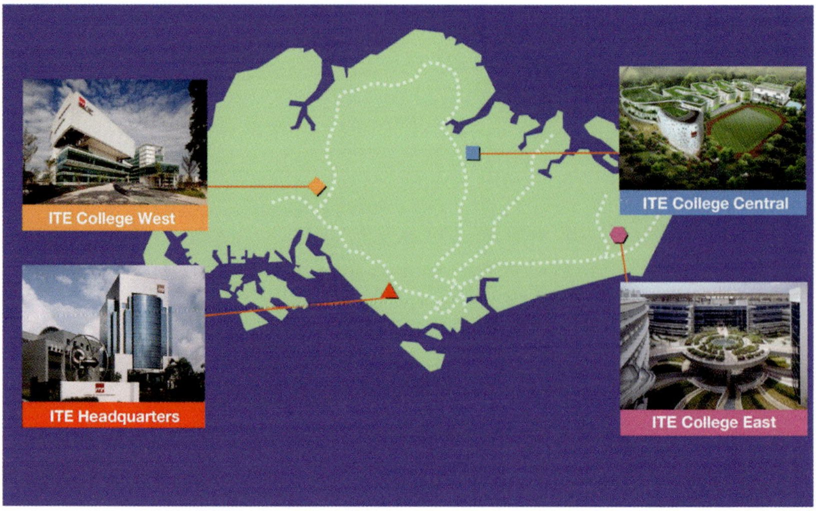

Figure 6.3 System of "One ITE, Three Colleges"

Today, ITE is effectively run and governed as a "One ITE, Three Colleges" system of education as shown in Figure 6.3. Under this model of governance, the ITE headquarters (relocated at ITE College Central since 2013) continues to oversee corporate matters such as policy issues, strategic planning, organisational excellence, certification standards and quality assurance. At the same time, the colleges are empowered with greater autonomy and flexibility to better focus on professionalism in teaching and learning and management of student development and services. With significantly bigger campuses, there was greater synergy in the use of resources. From an educational perspective, the economies of scale was an important factor in promoting a more innovative and vibrant campus environment. Well-equipped with a wide range "real-life" training laboratories, a centre of music and the arts and first-class sports facilities, these mega regional campuses captured the minds and hearts of the students, staff and the public. Purposefully designed, each with its own architectural identity, these mega regional campuses had gone a long way in helping to change the mindset and public perception about ITE.

However, good training infrastructure alone would not be sufficient to build a world-class education institution. Central to education is the professionalism, quality and commitment of the staff. As such, another area

Figure 6.4 Enhancing staff capabilities

of priority was in enhancing staff capabilities as illustrated in Figure 6.4. Focusing on people development, schemes were put in place to help staff upgrade their professional capabilities and pedagogic skills so as to stay relevant and up-to-date with technology and industry practices. Besides technical job skills, other platforms under the Singapore Quality Award framework were introduced to foster teamwork and inculcate a culture of commitment and "ITE Care" values. Regular activities that promoted staff participation such as the Annual Corporate Work Plan Seminar, ITE Teacher Award Ceremony, Innovation and Learning Circles (ILCs) and Staff Suggestion Scheme were introduced.

Our mission was clear and we were focused in what we did. In addition, to be a world-class technical education institution, a key factor must be the quality of teaching staff. Ensuring that teaching staff are well qualified and motivated to provide relevant and high quality training with utmost care for students is fundamental. In October 2001, I was asked by the ITE Board to chair a task force to restructure the existing teaching service into one that was competitive, attractive and responsive to the needs of ITE and its staff.

The review was completed in April 2002. Recommendations were made in five key areas: raising the profile and status of ITE teaching profession; strengthening the compensation, reward and recognition system; expanding career progression opportunities; enhancing the capability and talent development programmes; and creating a supportive work environment. The desired qualification, work experience, job skills and personality traits of ITE teaching staff were redefined. The desired profile was an equal mix of degree and diploma holders in the long term. More importantly, the staff must be pedagogically trained and possess at least three years of relevant industrial work experience.

A crucial outcome was in adopting a more holistic approach to people management. We put in place a human resource framework based on the earlier described people-centred management philosophy and strengthened by the values underlying the Singapore Quality Award and "ITE Care" culture. In line with a competency-based performance system, four career tracks were created: leadership, specialist, technologist and teaching. All staff were encouraged to take advantage of the various schemes and incentives to upgrade themselves so as to stay relevant and responsive to changing needs. ITE's mission is strongly people-focused, be it staff or students; one reinforces the other. Lecturers who find meaning in work are better able to bring out the best in their students and stay true to their profession. Keeping staff committed, dedicated and passionate in doing their work will continue to be an important role of leadership.

SECOND WAVE OF TRANSFORMATION (2000–2004)

The aspiration in the second wave of transformation was to build a "world-class" ITE. Two key elements define the relevance and quality of educational programmes and, hence, the quality of its graduates. The first is the curriculum model representing the content, i.e., what needs to be delivered, as shown in Figure 6.5. In 2000, the curriculum model was reviewed and realigned with the changing needs of the global economy.

ITE's courses are built on skills competencies derived according to industry standards. To ensure a strong foundation in technical skills and high

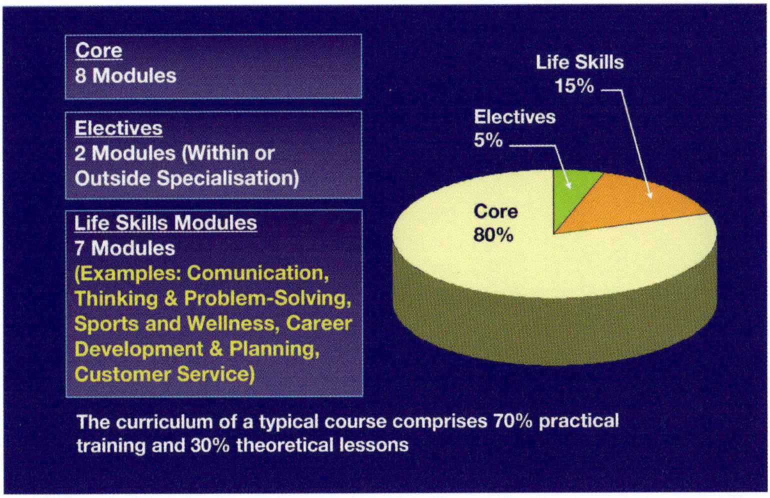

Figure 6.5 A practice-oriented curriculum model

employability, 80 per cent of the total curriculum time is devoted to the "core" modules, which define the occupational areas where the graduates will seek employment. As "hands-on" courses, typically, 70 per cent of curriculum time for these core modules is practical training and 30 per cent theoretical lessons. An "elective" module was also made available for those who wished to pursue a subject of interest within or outside their main course of study. A fundamental change was the introduction of compulsory "life skills" modules for all students. Taking up 15 per cent of the total curriculum time, it ensures that students also acquire the skills of communications, teamwork, thinking and problem-solving, sports and wellness, career development and planning and customer service. In this way, students will be better prepared as lifelong learners and remain adaptable in the global job market.

The second key element of relevance and quality is pedagogy, i.e., how teaching is delivered. The pedagogic model was re-articulated as shown in Figure 6.6. The underlying objective is to develop "thinking doers", graduates who can apply what they have learned into practice. Called the "Plan, Explore, Practise and Perform" or PEPP Model, the approach is interactive and process-oriented. Under the guidance of a teacher, the student plans the work to be done, explores the information required

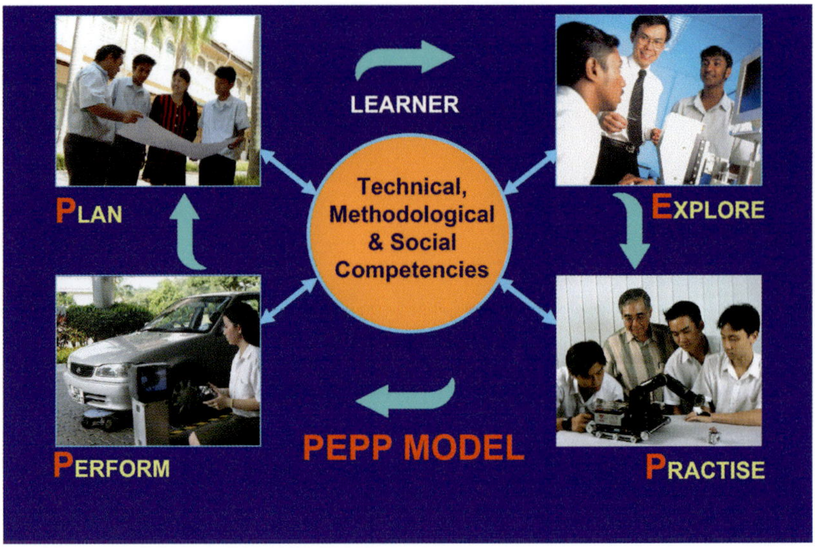

Figure 6.6 A process-oriented pedagogic model

and practises what he or she has learned. Finally, the student performs with competence, the knowledge, skills and values that were mastered. Through this approach, the student acquires key competencies that are technical, methodological as well as social.

Also significant in the second wave of transformation was the creation of an innovative teaching and learning environment. In particular, with the pervasive use of Information Technology (IT) in society and the knowledge economy, it is important that students learn in a rich IT-based environment that better prepares them for the real working world. Guided by the ITE IT Master Plan 2000, two pioneering systems, the eTutor and eStudent, were launched in 2002, as shown in Figure 6.7.

The eTutor is a web-based online learning system that leverages on the advances in IT and e-learning technologies. The eTutor has transformed ITE into a community of connected online learning campuses. It provides flexibility, convenience and easy access to e-learning for students and staff in a personalised, interactive, multimedia and collaborative learning environment. Students would log onto the internet and access web-based

Figure 6.7 An IT-based learning environment

lessons in various forms, including computer-aided presentations, tutorials, drills and practice and assignments. It also served as a campus-wide platform for students to exchange views and collaborate on project work across different fields. Using the same platform, teaching staff were able to assess the students' work online as well as track their progress and communicate with students via discussion board, emails and live chats. As ITE's programmes are highly practice-oriented, e-learning is largely focused on the knowledge and theoretical component of the curriculum. This e-learning system has enabled ITE to deliver 20 per cent of its total curriculum on a web-based platform.

The eStudent, on the other hand, is a web-based fully integrated student services administration system. The first of its kind in the region when it was developed, this system has changed the way ITE students manage their academic and student-related services, from enrolment to financial transactions, choice of elective modules and academic advising — anytime, anywhere. In the process, they learn to take responsibility for planning their studies and taking the initiative to do things independently. This seamless one-stop centre on the web replaces the many otherwise manual and unproductive systems of student enrolment and administration. eStudent has helped ITE redefine its academic structure, streamline processes and improve its student services. Significantly, the eTutor and eStudent systems have created a new way of teaching, learning and living in ITE campuses. They provide an important bridge in preparing our graduates to better face the challenges of the 21st century.

ITE inherited the legacy of a poor image (of the former VITB) when it was first established in 1992. This was the greatest underlying challenge at the time. As the training system was being transformed, parallel efforts were made towards changing its image and public perception. There were deep-rooted negative perceptions about vocational training that needed to be addressed. Parents continued to cherish the hope and aspiration of a university or polytechnic education for their children. There were two aspects to this transformation. The first was strengthening our communications and marketing efforts in reaching out to potential students, teachers, parents and the community. The second was image-building and a rebranding of ITE as an educational institution. The strategies and efforts that eventually led to a turnaround in the image of ITE are described in Chapter 8.

THIRD WAVE OF TRANSFORMATION (2005–2009)

As mentioned earlier, the year 2005 will long be remembered as the historical milestone for ITE. This was the year ITE won the prestigious Singapore Quality Award for organisational excellence. Attracting much recognition and attention nationally and internationally, ITE had achieved its vision of a world-class technical education institution. Appropriately, the SQA was the springboard in launching ITE Advantage, the third strategic five-year plan outlined in Figure 6.8. The main thrust was in re-positioning ITE in an increasingly global world.

The plan was to take ITE to even greater heights — as a global leader in technical education. It was a bold and strategic vision. A global leader is one recognised among peers for leadership, professionalism, innovation,

Figure 6.8 ITE Advantage Plan (2005–2009)

quality programmes, "best-in-class" practices and organisational excellence. Global leadership means staying actively engaged with the wider regional and international community. It means greater collaboration and sharing of knowledge, expertise and experience with partner institutions. While injecting a greater global perspective in our system of operation, we would continue to improve and innovate. Ultimately, it was about building the next generation of a globally competitive and highly skilled workforce.

Supporting the new vision of this plan were four goals, nine strategies and 19 programmes. The first goal was aimed at preparing and orientating students to the realities of an increasingly competitive global environment. Some of the key programmes included a greater flexibility in the curriculum development framework, enhancing the intake selection system and a global education programme for students. The second goal aimed at helping graduates to remain "career relevant" in the fast-changing workplace through special programmes offering a wide range of both formal and short "on-demand" courses for ITE graduates. Offered as a part-time programme, these courses enabled working adults to update their technical knowledge and skills on a continuing basis. Building on the ITE brand name, the third goal was to develop an extended network of strategic alliances and collaboration with the international community. Finally, helping to sustain the first three goals was the final goal, which focused on "an enhanced capability for organisational excellence." The continual focus on enhancing core capabilities is fundamental in building a sustainable world-class institution.

In 2007, the transformation of ITE attracted global recognition when it won the Harvard-IBM Innovations in Transforming Government Award (Garekar, 2007). The following is an extract from a Straits Times report entitled "ITE: From 'school of last resort' to 'jewel in S'pore's crown'":

> As the Harvard citation noted, ITE has gone from being "an institution of last resort for low-achieving students" to being internationally recognised. Its results speak for themselves. In 2005, the ITE also became the first educational institution to win the Singapore Quality Award, a leading business award, for its overall excellence. The same year, it won praise from the World Bank... ITE has come a long way since it rose from the ashes of the former Vocational and Industrial Training Board (VITB) 15 years ago....
>
> There were high hopes the ITE could shed the negative image of vocational institute students as dropouts and low achievers. Speaking in 1992, then ITE director and chief executive officer, Dr Law Song Seng declared: "We want parents and school leavers to realise we have a new image and direction"... Dr Law, an engineer by training who retired as ITE director and CEO in February this year, mapped out ITE's transformation in five-year plans... In its latest plan, it aims to become the global leader in technical education. It has already formed alliances with institutions in Canada, Germany, the United States, Hong Kong and South Korea... The ITE is offering consultancy services to countries in the Middle East and Africa and aims to send 20 per cent of its students overseas. At home, it has helped thousands demoralised by poor results in their earlier school career to further their studies, and hope more will do so... (Ho, 2007)

WHAT'S IN THE FUTURE?

ITE has developed a unique and successful system of vocational and technical education for the less academically inclined in schools. However, in view of the natural aspiration for a university education and ever-increasing drive towards becoming a knowledge economy, what are the prospects of ITE maintaining its unique position and attractiveness as a post-secondary institution? How might the intake of school leavers into ITE be affected in the future?

I believe the intake will be shaped by the future dynamics and challenges in vocational training. It is true that the types and levels of knowledge, skills and values will vary according to the changing needs of the economy. Parents and school leavers will continue to aspire for the prestige of a university degree. As the economy further develops, there will be the growing expectations for higher education in society. Nonetheless, education systems are shaped not only by social expectations but the need to maintain economic relevance and standards in education. At stake are the creditability of the institutions and value of their qualifications.

My belief is that the ITE pathway towards a post-secondary education will remain an important part of the education and training system. It will no doubt have to evolve so as to stay relevant and responsive to changing needs. This was how the former VITB was restructured to the present-day ITE. Beyond the ITE are the multiple pathways for those with the potential to progress to the polytechnic and university. Presently, about one in five ITE graduates progresses to the polytechnic immediately after graduation. The plan is to increase this progression rate to one in four by 2015. While the social aspiration for a polytechnic or university education will continue, progression must be based on good performance and the potential to do well. All economies, including the developed and developing, will always need people with practical technical skills. The issue today is no longer about the importance and value of vocational and technical education. Irrespective of the different pathways in education, the focus will be on building quality and sustainability.

ITE is a social enabler. There will always be a place for an ITE form of college education. What matters most is not so much the intake numbers but that all school leavers have opportunities to develop their potential to the fullest. In this respect, ITE will continue to play a significant role in the social and economic development of Singapore.

Chapter 7

Strategic Planning Makes a Difference

Significant and purposeful outcomes must start with strategic planning, but this is only possible when coupled with strategic execution. As a strategic tool, it helps to align the short-term decisions and actions with the longer-term goals as to the "what, when, how and why" of getting there. It is a systematic way of shaping a future. Having a clear direction and a well-developed blueprint or road map to follow is a good starting point to ensure a common focus and the sustainability of a journey. The approach and process in developing such a plan is of equal if not greater importance. A plan is only as good as its effective implementation. Thus, an inclusive approach involving key stakeholders and partners would help to create greater "buy-in" and commitment towards successful outcomes. The processes involved in the consultation, development, formulation and sharing are an important part of a learning organisation. Collectively, they offer opportunities in reinforcing the spirit and culture of teamwork, collaboration and care.

There would not have been a journey of transformation for ITE if there were no strategic plans to start with. Without a road map, where would ITE be heading? What initiatives would it focus on? How would we know if we were on the right track? How would ITE monitor its progress and outcomes? The consistent use of five-year strategic plans was fundamental to transforming ITE into a world-class education institution. It meant achieving a new vision every five years.

While there are common steps and features that characterise a strategic planning framework, there are also variants that are unique to an organisation. It is with this awareness that I now share the history and evolution of ITE's strategic planning as a "best planning practice" under the Singapore Quality Award framework for business excellence.

HOW DID IT ALL START?

Organisations in general have some forms of "planning exercises and reviews" as part of the governing, managing and operating system. The strategic extent and comprehensiveness vary. At the minimum, it could be a brief report from a senior manager to the CEO or CEO to the Chairman of the Board of Governors on an update of the present position, the key issues and challenges and the plans with goals and outcomes to be achieved over the short term. At times, there could well be special reviews and proposals in response to changes in organisational or market environment. At the high end would be the practice of a rigorous strategic planning process involving analysis and consultation with stakeholders and customers for the long-term on a periodic basis.

Indeed, the first Annual Report (1979/1980) of the former Vocational and Industrial Training Board (VITB), the predecessor to ITE, alluded to a "high" level of planning and development activity. However, it was not a strategic planning exercise as there was no extensive analysis or consultation with staff and stakeholders. The report said that the Board took into account "the revised 'rolling' 10-year manpower budget of the Ministry of Trade & Industry, the re-projected supply of school leavers, the 'catch-up' and forward requirements of the new sectors, the higher levels of training to be provided and restructured curriculum" (VITB, 1979/1980).

The overall proposal was for a substantial expansion of the Board's physical facilities from 1980 to 1986. A high enrolment of 30,900 students was projected for VITB by 1986. There was growing concern about the need to reconfirm the availability of school leavers and the ability of the Board to attract the projected number under a voluntary system of education and training. In terms of process, it was an exercise carried out as part of capacity and resource planning. The outcome was plans to create new training programmes and places to meet operational needs. It was not a formal strategic planning exercise. It was a typical case of a top-down approach in planning and implementation.

The early beginning of a strategic planning exercise was to be found in the development of the "VITB Strategic Plan (1988–1992) — Towards Excellence in Vocational Training" released in May 1988. It was an exercise initiated by the chairman Dr Tay Eng Soon, who suggested that it was timely for VITB to focus its attention on the qualitative aspects of training since it had successfully achieved its quantitative targets. Dr Tay was referring to the completion of the first phase of development (1979–1986), whereby VITB had restructured training programmes and built up an annual intake capacity of 15,000 places in readiness for the 1980 New Education System.

Highlighting the importance on excellence, Dr Tay said:

The Management has formed a Strategic Planning Committee aimed at achieving the following four goals:

- Excellence in Teaching and Training
- Relevance of VITB's Courses and Curricula
- Excellence in the Environment of Training Institutes
- Excellence in Management and Administration

> The review is being undertaken with the realisation that the mission of VITB is not only to provide a place for every school leaver who wishes to take up vocational training, but also to provide the trainee with realistic, relevant and quality training in an environment which is conducive to learning. The aim is to develop the trainee into a skilled and knowledgeable worker, imbued with the correct work attitudes and the necessary flexibility to respond to changing technology and demand. The exercise involves staff at all levels and is expected, when completed in FY 1987, to yield practical strategies for the 1990s. (VITB, 1986/1987)

As part of the formal planning process, a Strategic Planning Committee was formed to develop this plan, where I chaired the committee with senior management staff. Using a framework of four sub-committees and 17 working groups, some 154 officers from various levels of the organisation were directly involved. In addition, many more staff responded through questionnaire surveys and interviews and participated in forums in the exercise. The views and inputs of the Board and VITB Training Staff Union were taken into account in formulating the corporate goals for VITB in striving for excellence in vocational training over the next five years. This planning process was the "most formal" then as it had a consultative process with stakeholders. Nonetheless, it was not as yet a rigorous and comprehensive strategic planning exercise.

MY "TWO-PAGE" NOTE

How did the practice of using five-year strategic planning in the transformation of ITE come about? The origin may be traced to a "two-page" note that I had prepared for the in-coming chairman Eric Gwee Teck Hai in January 1994. Mr Gwee was newly appointed with the untimely passing of Dr Tay in August 1993. In 1994, our main challenge was to establish ITE as a post-secondary education institution. With a private-sector perspective, the new chairman who was the Director of Marine & Supply, Esso Singapore Pte Ltd, had said, "We needed a strategic plan with a clear vision to move forward." The next thing he did was to invite me to lunch. As the saying goes, lunches do not come free. Before the meeting, he had already given me my first assignment. He had asked me to reflect upon and give him my personal assessment of ITE.

We met at his office. I was quite ready to share my thoughts with the chairman. In my hand was my "two-page" note (Box 7.1).

The first three aspects provided a realistic view of how I felt about ITE at the time. I shared that the administration and management systems were in place. ITE was a dynamic and adaptable organisation. However, there were "transitional issues" on building up an identity, upgrading "lower-level" staff, physical development of institutes and creating a "total learning environment". I also pointed out the existing constraints and resistance factors such as the image and status of ITE training, staff quality and the critical need to groom Training Managers and Heads of Departments. There was also the impact of external environment arising from changes in education policies and manpower needs of the economy. These were the key issues facing ITE at that time.

The fourth aspect, in my view, turned out to be the most significant in building a close, supportive and fruitful working relationship between

BOX 7.1 NOTE TO ITE CHAIRMAN ERIC GWEE TECK HAI, JANUARY 1994

Reflection on ITE
(by Director & CEO/ITE)

1. Existing system/direction

   Administration & management in place. A dynamic and adaptable organisation.

2. Vision in establishing ITE as a post-secondary institution

   Transitional phase — building up an identity (among post-secondary institutions), putting programmes (NTC-2) in place, upgrading "lower-level" staff and physical development to create "total" learning environment.

3. Some constraints/resistance factors

   - Image/status of ITE training (not something a school leaver or parent is proud to associate with). The "last" choice for those who fail in schools.
   - Quality/matching of staff arising from restructuring VITB to ITE. Critical to groom TM (Training Manger)/HOD (Head of Department).
   - Impact of external environment such as changes in education policies (Polytechnics, Normal [Technical] stream) and its effect on "quality" of intakes. Fluctuating "pools" of school leavers. Changing manpower needs in industry.

4. How Chairman/ITE can help?

   4.1 Lend moral support /encouragement

   Support and encourage staff on the "difficult" tasks that need to be done. Technical training critical to economic development but not glamorous and may not be fully appreciated by parents, public and government officials (as compared to say, university/polytechnic).

(*Continued*)

BOX 7.1 (CONTINUED)

4.2 Seek support/consensus at Board level

Help articulate ITE goals/projects/initiatives so as to seek support of Board members. "Clearing" the way and give mandate/room for management to move without unnecessary civil service bureaucracy.

4.3 Help promote image/work of ITE

Although restructuring ITE as a post-secondary institution is a significant first step, much needs to be done. Personal involvement at major ITE public functions can help. Can also use influence to involve high-level VIPs as guests-of-honour for ITE functions as appropriate (e.g., ministers)

4.4 Mentor/Advisor to Director/ITE

Keeping watch on general direction or Board but lending support where possible. Useful if Directorate feels Chairman takes a personal interest in their work.

Dr Law Song Seng
14 Jan 1994

a CEO and a Chairman. "How can I help?" the Chairman asked. This was something we would not normally expect a boss to ask (of his subordinates) in the public sector. But to me, it was an opportunity to follow up. It would be foolish of me not to accept the offer of assistance. Obviously, I reflected much on this question to see how best I could maximise its value for ITE.

ITE is a statutory board governed by an ITE Board of Governors. The chairman and members are appointed by the Minister of Education with the approval of the Cabinet. These are non-executive appointments. The Board provides stewardship in governance and guidance in steering ITE towards meeting its mission and goals. By virtue of his position, the Chairman can play a crucial role in influencing the development, accessing political support and shaping the cultural climate in the inner workings of the organisation. The Director and CEO of ITE reports to the Chairman of the Board. Representing the management and staff, he is responsible for the administration, operation and performance of ITE. The ITE, as a statutory board, is ultimately accountable to Parliament through the Ministry of Education.

Underpinning my list of four "wishes" was the view that technical and vocational education was crucial to economic development but not glamorous. Its role in society might not be fully appreciated by parents, the public and government officials, unlike that of the university or polytechnic. I said to the Chairman, "We need a strong sense of mission for ITE staff. You are in a good position to garner the support of Board members. You can help in clearing the way for management to respond expeditiously without excessive civil service bureaucracy. Your personal presence and influence to involve high-level VIPs at major ITE functions such as Ministers will reinforce the importance and image of ITE. As a mentor and advisor to me, you can keep watch on the direction of the Board but lend support where possible. Our Directorate members will feel a greater sense of mission if they feel that [the] Chairman takes a personal interest in their work." In his characteristic way, he responded with a smile, saying, "We face many challenges, but the key is to change the image… I trust that we will find our way forward."

All these thoughts and conversation were exchanged 20 years ago. It was the kind of support a CEO would hope to have. As Chairman of ITE, Eric Gwee had consistently demonstrated a strong passion for the kind of work ITE was doing. By words and actions, he had always given support and encouragement to management, staff and students. He liked to walk about and engage staff at their places of work. His personal visits to the campuses and close engagement with staff and students had helped to foster a stronger sense of mission, culture and commitment among ITE staff. This sense of mission, I believe, had further translated into the kind of care and concern our staff had for students: a special quality that made ITE College Education a unique experience.

His effective chairmanship was instrumental in steering ITE's journey of transformation. Known for his people-centred values, he was a great champion and supporter in vocational education. Personally, he had been an outstanding mentor and advisor. Reflecting on the key challenge at the time, Eric Gwee said:

> To improve ITE's image, there were many steps we needed to do. Therefore, we needed a road map: a road map to find and then create the path to where we wanted to go. The staff's morale was also not high at the time. Many were not clear where they were heading. Vision and forward planning was therefore another key priority for ITE. That was how the Board and management started to envision and create five-yearly strategic plans to guide and bring the staff along a new journey of reinventing ITE. (ITE, 2012)

STRATEGIC PLANNING IN ITE — AN EVOLUTION

With much encouragement and support, ITE started the formal practice of five-year strategic planning in 1995, as described in Chapter 6.

The process in this first strategic planning exercise was "top down" in nature. The ITE 2000 Plan was developed by senior management, endorsed by the ITE Board of Governors and then discussed at a Training Managers' Conference. Following further discussions of the plan with management, supervisory staff and union officials at an ITE 2000 Seminar, the plan was subsequently disseminated to all ITE staff. It was a comprehensive plan supported by five goals, eight strategies and 27 programmes.

The experience in formulating and implementing the first five-year plan led to considerable refinements in the strategic planning process for the second five-year plan. The mission statement was updated as: "To create opportunities for school leavers and adult learners to acquire skills, knowledge and values for lifelong learning." The words "values for lifelong learning" were added in view of the changing global economy. Built upon the successful completion of the first plan, the vision was now more ambitious. In taking a bolder step, the ITE Board decided on the vision: "A world-class technical education institution for a knowledge-based economy." This time around, the process was more rigorous, consultative and comprehensive.

A distinguishing feature of ITE's strategic plans is the set of specific programmes and action plans that arise for implementation. A strategic plan is only as good as its successful execution. As an evolving process, new features such as "corporate values" and "expected outcomes" were subsequently added. Ambitious but realistic, the "ITE Breakthrough (2000–2004)" was instrumental in demonstrating what was achievable and what VTE could be in a modern economy and society.

ITE STRATEGIC PLANNING — A HOLISTIC FRAMEWORK

Improved over time, the ITE strategic planning framework was assessed as a best practice under the Singapore Quality Award Model in 2005. Aligned and integrated, it defines a holistic framework for charting the directions, setting the goals, assessing the outcomes and monitoring the performance of an organisation through the development of various plans on a cyclical review and formulation basis. As depicted in Figure 7.1, there are the long-term "Five-year Strategic Plan", short-term "Annual Corporate Work Plan (CWP)" and "Annual Functional Plans". Supported by an annual corporate budget plan, these plans are deployed to the establishment and individual levels and subjected to mid-term and year-end performance reviews. Similarly, the balanced scorecard approach in aligning key performance indicators to strategic objectives is cascaded in a holistic manner to the various establishments. Here, we use ITE's third strategic plan, the "ITE Advantage (2005–2009)," to illustrate how this plan was formulated.

AN ILLUSTRATION — THE "ITE ADVANTAGE" PLAN (2005–2009)

The underlying strategic challenges in charting the future direction for ITE as a technical education institution are its relevance, responsiveness

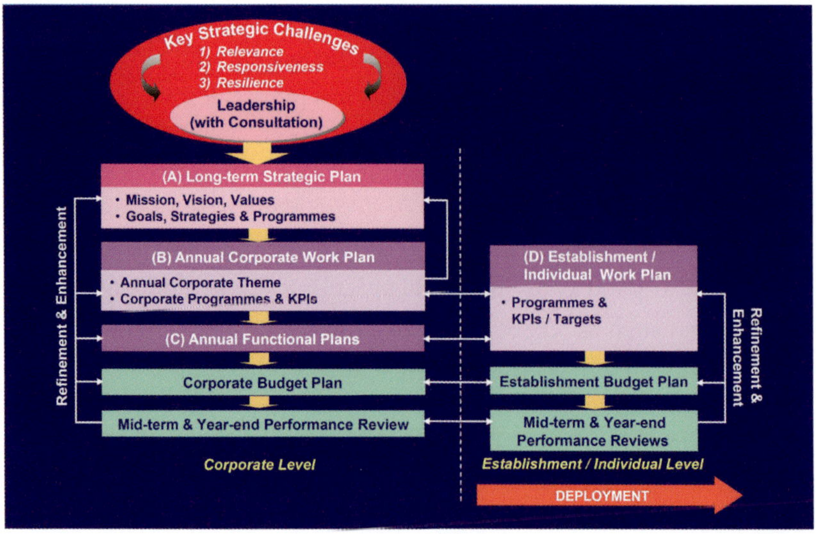

Figure 7.1 Aligned and integrated planning framework

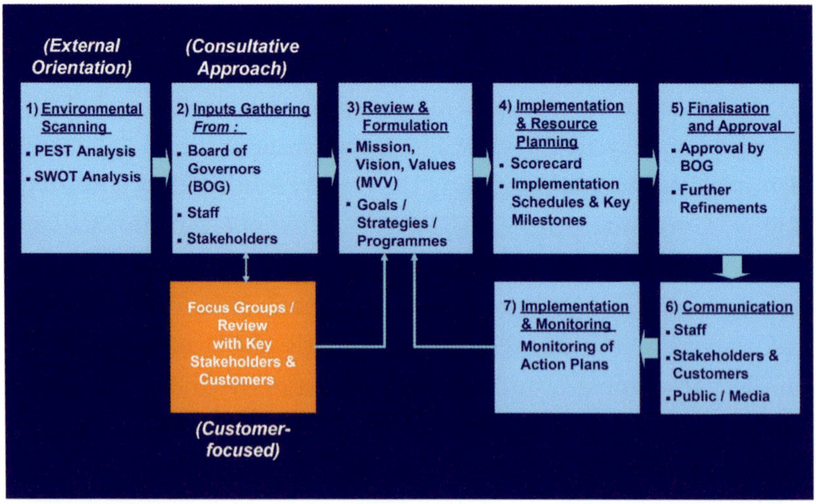

Figure 7.2 Long-term strategic planning cycle

and resilience. The holistic seven-step long-term (five-year) strategic planning cycle is shown in Figure 7.2. It has a unique focus on three important features: external orientation, consultative approach and customer-focused. The key planning methodologies would include "Political, Economic, Social and Technological" or PEST, "Strengths, Weaknesses,

Opportunities and Threats", also known as SWOT, "Balanced Scorecards", surveys and comparative and benchmarking studies. The development of a five-year strategic plan would normally take from six to nine months.

The formulation of the strategic plan was driven by the senior management team and led by me. Members included Dr Benjamin Tan Lin Boon, Heng Guan Teck, Aw York Bin, Dr Ricky Tam Yin Jun, Tan Seng Hua and Dr Yek Tiew Ming. Secretariat support was provided by the Corporate Affairs Division led by Sabrina Loi. The first step in the planning process for the "ITE Advantage" plan was a scanning of the external environment by the corporate planning unit. At the national level, the strategic responses formulated by the government in the reports of the Economic Review Committee and the Remaking Singapore Committee were especially relevant at the time. The political, economic, social–cultural and technological developments and their potential impact on ITE were reviewed and analysed. For example, from the political perspective, the national goal of "remaking Singapore" in the areas of Research & Development, building a "first-class" Polytechnic and ITE education, promoting a culture of service excellence and remaking the whole city was highlighted.

On the economic front, it was reported that the Economic Development Board was targeting to double the manufacturing output to S$300 billion, double the value-add to S$80 billion, raise the percentage of skilled workers from 31 to 50 per cent and create 21,500 new jobs by 2018. The new growth engines would be nanotechnology, biotechnology, alternative energy and biomaterials. Among the issues arising from an increasingly global environment were those relating to new investment opportunities in education, innovation and enterprise, high-end Business Process Outsourcing (BPO), service standards, lifelong learning and "job re-creation". From the educational perspective were possible directions and ideas to build a more flexible and diversified educational system.

Complementing this external environmental scanning was an internal SWOT analysis that would identify the organisational strengths and weaknesses based on inputs from the various heads of departments in ITE and feedback from key stakeholders. By 2004, ITE had already achieved significant strengths in many areas of organisational excellence and best practices under its journey of transformation. On the other hand, there were concerns such as coping with the speed of change in ITE, operational constraints imposed by the physical location of campuses, training specifications arising from a unified academic system that were too prescriptive, the need to enhance and formalise the pedagogic model and global opportunities for staff capability development. The results of these PEST and SWOT analyses mentioned earlier provided the primary bases for the senior management team to begin its deliberation and formulation of the strategic direction for the new five-year strategic plan.

The second step was a rigorous and extensive consultative process of gathering inputs from the ITE Board of Governors, staff and key stakeholders. In this "customer-focused" approach, specific focus group dialogues were held with governmental agencies, unions, employers, teachers, parents and students. In step three, the proposed tentative strategic plan would be subjected to further deliberations and an intensive review process by the senior management team. As the plan began to take a more definite shape, the scorecard, implementation schedule and key milestones were worked out and proposed under step four, i.e., implementation and resource planning. The proposed "ITE Advantage (2005–2009)" plan was eventually finalised and approved by the Board in step five. Under step six, the plan was disseminated to staff, stakeholders and public media. Equally important in having a strategic plan is its implementation. In closing the loop in the planning process, step seven provided the platform for the implementation and monitoring of the action plans.

The "ITE Advantage" articulated ITE's mission, vision and values; set out four goals, nine strategies and 19 programmes; and identified key performance indicators and expected outcomes (Box 7.2). The mission statement differed from that in the previous five-year plan only in four words: "in a global economy". The addition of these four words recognised that changes in the global environment was going to affect the workplace in Singapore and that ITE graduates need to be equipped

BOX 7.2 FACTSHEET ON THE ITE ADVANTAGE PLAN

The ITE Advantage (2005–2009) was the third five-year strategic plan. Built on the strengths of the two previous plans, the intent was to create "competitive advantages" for ITE students and stakeholders in facing the challenges of a global economy. Moving from being "a world-class institution" to "a global leader in technical education", it would extend the brand name of ITE and its global presence.

Mission

To create opportunities for school leavers and adult learners to acquire skills, knowledge and values for lifelong learning in a global economy

Vision

A Global Leader in Technical Education

ITE Values

We work with integrity to achieve excellence as a team, caring for all whom we serve

ITE Care: Integrity, Teamwork, Excellence and Care

Goals

1. An ITE Education for a Global Economy
2. Lifelong Employability for ITE Graduates
3. An Increased Global Presence for ITE
4. An Enhanced Capability for Organisational Excellence

Strategies

1. Provide Flexibility to Customise Learning
2. Nurture Enterprising ITE Students
3. Build Global Mindset
4. Deliver "On Demand" Continuing Education and Training (CET)
5. Widen Collaborative Partnerships with Industry
6. Build Strategic Alliances in Global Community
7. Strengthen ITE's Brand Name
8. Enhance Staff Capability for Global Challenge
9. Pioneer Core Capabilities in Vocational & Technical Education (VTE)

(Continued)

BOX 7.2 (CONTINUED)

<u>Programmes</u>

1. Flexible Selection System
2. Differentiated Learning Programmes
3. New Flexible Curriculum Framework
4. Student Leadership Development
5. Student Enterprise Development
6. Student Community Outreach
7. Global Education Programme
8. ReNEW Plus Programme
9. Joint Certifications with Industry Players
10. International Certification
11. International Collaboration
12. Corporate Branding
13. Alumni Network
14. ITE Staff Academy
15. Competency-Based Performance Management System
16. Centres of Technology
17. SME Consultancy Programme
18. College Development Plan
19. Centre of Excellence for VTE

<u>Key Performance Indicators (KPIs)</u>

1. Cohort Capture Rate
2. Success Rate
3. Employers' Satisfaction with ITE Graduates
4. Graduates' Employment Rate within six months and after 5 and 10 years in labour market
5. Proportion of ITE Graduates in ITE CET Programmes
6. ITE Brand Equity Index
7. No. of Active Overseas Partners

(*Continued*)

BOX 7.2 (CONTINUED)

8. SQA Band Score for Organisational Excellence
9. Number of New VTE Initiatives

Expected Outcomes

1. Graduates will be market-relevant, enterprising and adaptable in a global economy
2. Graduates will remain lifelong learners for lifelong employability
3. ITE brand name will be recognised locally and globally
4. Staff have capabilities to pioneer and set new benchmarks in VTE

with the skills required in the new environment. Built upon the success of two previous strategic plans, the new vision was to be "a global leader in technical education". In nurturing a culture of values and care, "ITE Care" was adopted in upholding "integrity, teamwork, excellence and care" — the care for staff, students, customers and the community. Being a "global leader" means a commitment to world-class excellence, taking on responsibility in sharing the ITE experience and staying actively engaged with the international community. It was this newfound confidence and spirit of global engagement that led to the recognition of ITE as a global leader in technical education.

SHORT-TERM (ANNUAL) PLANNING PROCESS

A long-term (five-year) strategic plan such as the "ITE Advantage" is not a "static" or "fixed" plan only to be reviewed once in five years. On the contrary, it was revisited and reviewed annually to ensure its continuing relevance and responsiveness to changing needs. To achieve this, the long-term strategic planning process was supported by an annual planning process as shown in Figure 7.3. While the long-term strategic plan set the broad direction for ITE, the annual corporate work plan ensured that the functional plans at the establishment, college and individual levels were

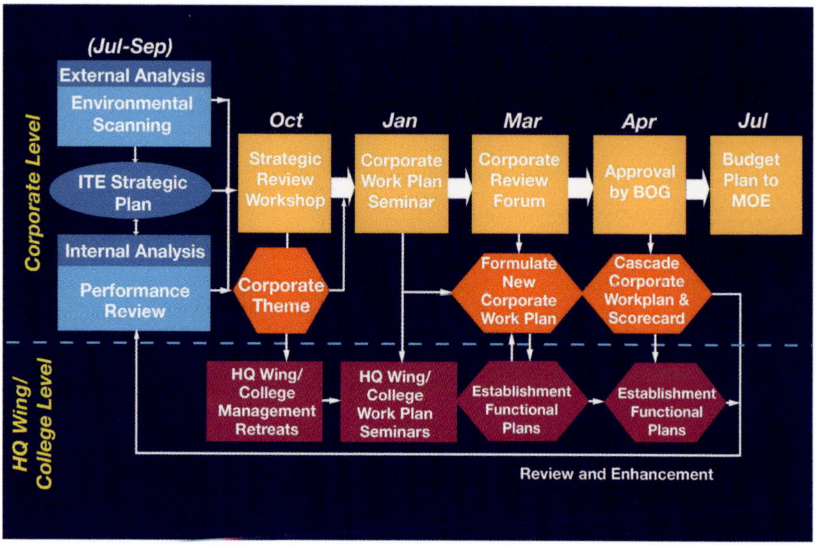

Figure 7.3 Annual planning cycle

aligned with the corporate direction and objectives. An ITE corporate work plan also included a performance review of the corporate score card and key programmes.

For example, in developing the FY2006 ITE corporate work plan, the first step was the conduct of external and internal analyses with reference to the long-term strategic plan from July to September 2005. A strategic review workshop involving all senior management staff was then held in October 2005 to identify the corporate theme and key programmes to be added or carried forward for implementation in FY2006. This was followed by an ITE corporate work plan seminar in January 2006, involving some 400 staff and representatives from the staff unions. These annual activities were not only useful for the formulation of an annual corporate work plan but also acted as effective platforms for fostering teamwork, staff commitment and alignment of individual and organisational interests. The proposed ITE corporate work plan was further deliberated and reviewed by senior management team at a special corporate review forum followed by approval of the Board in April 2006. It was then cascaded to the various establishments in the headquarters (HQ) wings comprising various divisions and colleges as illustrated in Figure 7.4.

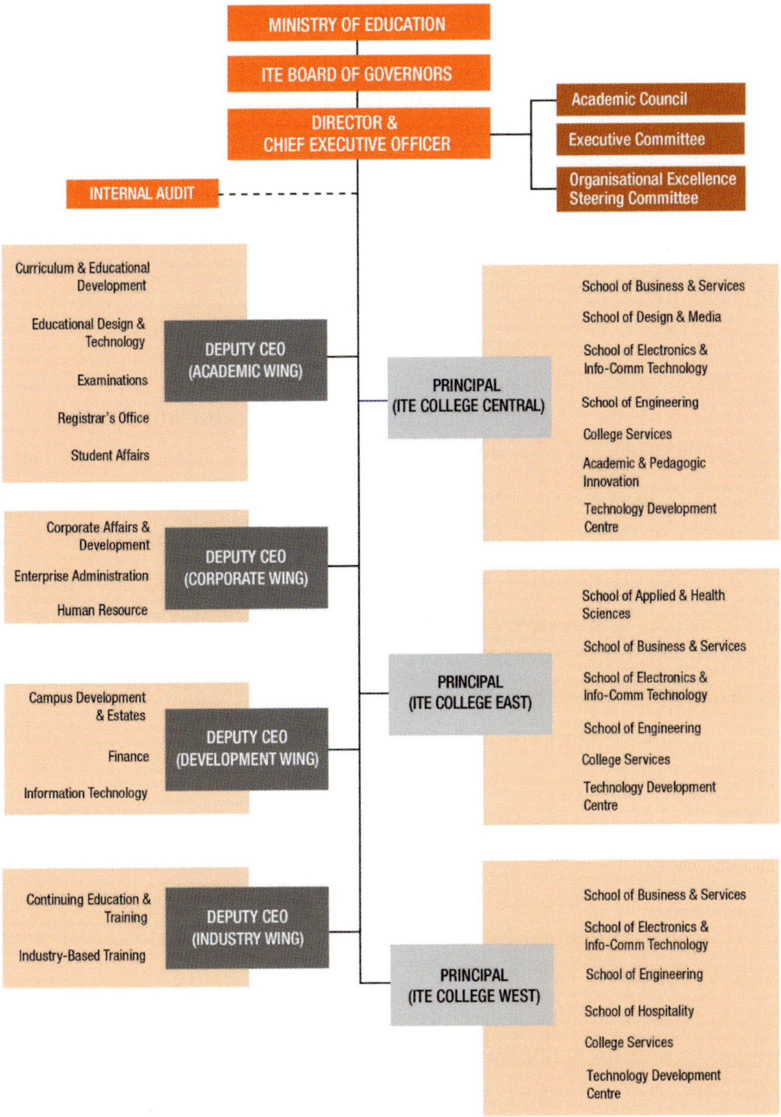

Figure 7.4 Organisational structure

STRATEGIC REVIEW WORKSHOPS AND CORPORATE WORK PLAN SEMINARS

The strategic review workshops and corporate work plan seminars are signature ITE annual events. As an integral part of the annual planning and review exercise, they have become important platforms for the ITE leadership team and staff to take stock of the progress, revisit the strategic five-year plan and gather fresh inputs for formulating the annual ITE corporate work plan. It is a time to reflect, examine the present, address new challenges and identify opportunities emerging in the horizon. The corporate planning unit responsible for these events would have prepared a well-researched document of rich information for discussion and planned activities. It was a rigorous process requiring much hard work but also a meaningful learning exercise.

Personally, I have always enjoyed and looked forward to these annual events. It became a tradition for me, as the Director and CEO of ITE, to share my assessment of ITE's performance for the past year. These were important occasions for management and staff to review and assess the forces driving change, the plans, strategies, programmes and performances. It was an opportunity to model the role of a leader through speeches and open engagement with management and staff. I would in my addresses, remember to encourage participants to "be ready to speak up, challenge the assumptions, seek new ideas, create new solutions, think 'out of the box', be open and constructive." Facilitated by an external consultant, these events served a wider purpose in building leadership, teamwork and commitment.

While the main focus was in developing the annual corporate work plan, I would strongly advocate, for example, that "this seminar is as much about formulating plans as it is about cultivating leadership and inculcating cultural values. It is a never-ending journey of learning about our own leadership and the values we uphold. So, take this opportunity to get to know your peers, understand each other better, encourage the values of 'ITE Care' and strengthen your networking across the ITE system and Colleges." As a matter of tradition, I would introduce and ask the participants to join me in extending a warm welcome to all new members of the management team who were attending the corporate work plan seminar for the first time.

In line with the corporate vision, a management book on leadership was selected to encourage continuous learning as part of leadership development. For the FY2006 corporate work plan seminar, for instance, the book was *Why Great Leaders Don't Take Yes for an Answer* by Michael A. Roberto. I shared what I had learned from some key ideas taken from the book, for instance, sharing that I liked the last chapter of the book "Leading with Restraint" best, as it showed insights on leadership which each of us had a responsibility for in ITE.

THE FY2006 ITE CORPORATE WORK PLAN

The FY2006 ITE corporate work plan, the final plan before I retired as CEO and Director, was a document laying out the strategic direction and focus for ITE in FY2006. Comprising two key elements: (1) ITE Corporate Scorecard and (2) FY2006 Strategic Programmes, it is a plan approved by the Board. In adopting a new five-year strategic plan, the "ITE Advantage", ITE had ended FY2005 on a high note. With the achievement of several major breakthroughs and milestones, the year 2005 was not just another successful year. The changes were fast, visible and dynamic.

We met or exceeded our key performance indicators. There was positive feedback from our students, stakeholders and the public. The image and public perception had improved significantly. ITE's first regional campus, the ITE College East, opened its doors in January 2005. It represented in reality, what a modern and quality vocational and technical education could be. This dramatic transformation of ITE was publicly endorsed by Prime Minister Lee Hsien Loong in his National Day Rally speech highlighting the uniqueness of an ITE College Education in the world (Lee, 2005). We received six national-level awards and accolades in 2005, including the Singapore Quality Award.

Inspired by the new vision to be "a global leader in technical education", ITE was beginning to orientate and prepare itself for a more active engagement with the region and international community. The desire was to increase the global presence of ITE. Efforts were stepped up in forging new partnerships and collaboration with industry leaders and overseas institutions. Having set a new benchmark in technical education, ITE was gearing itself to meet the higher expectations and demands of its customers and stakeholders.

In keeping with the spirit to seek new peaks of excellence beyond the Singapore Quality Award, management and staff decided on the corporate theme "Beyond the SQA — Selectivity, Scalability and Sustainability". It reflected the need to stay focused on projects of significance, leverage on strengths to scale outcomes and sustain the journey of organisational excellence. Driving the FY2006 corporate work plan were key developments and challenges arising from economic and educational perspectives. In the light of globalisation, there was increasing importance in innovation, enterprise, and research and development. There was interest in creating more pathways to success in the educational system by increasing flexibility, choices and diversity for students with different needs, interests and aspiration.

Under the ITE corporate scorecard, the Board decided on five strategic performance indicators for ease of monitoring and reporting. The five were student enrolment, graduate employability, student satisfaction with ITE education, student success rate and brand equity index. The actual performance, existing targets and projected targets for these indicators were reviewed and reset taking into consideration the achievements, prevailing conditions and challenges ahead. A key interest was setting a "stretch target" of 60 per cent for the brand equity index, reflecting the relentless efforts to enhance the image of ITE. Based on the inputs from management and staff at the various platforms, 11 strategic programmes were proposed for the FY2006 corporate work plan. As part of the annual planning process, programmes under the "ITE Advantage" were also reviewed, as a result of which some realignment and changes were made. This was how the FY2006 ITE corporate work plan was formulated. As a matter of practice, this is the way ITE sets out to align all staff and establishments towards a common mission, vision and goals, even today, as part of its culture in corporate and strategic planning.

Chapter 8

Changing the Image

Vocational and technical education has long suffered from a "poor image." Unlike the university that offers academic and professional degree courses, such institutions were and are still viewed as places for those who have failed in the school system. The poor image remains an obstacle in the ability to attract students in many countries. The rebranding of ITE took us many years of concerted efforts in changing the mindset and societal attitudes towards vocational training. Viewed in a wider context, it was a sustained effort and strategy in building a quality product (an ITE education) and a new brand. The strategic approach and continuing efforts to mitigate the poor image are elaborated in this chapter.

POOR IMAGE — AN OLD LEGACY

In a review on "Vocational Education's Image for the 21st Century", based on three journal issues over a 10-year period from the American Vocational Association (AVA) and reflecting the context of the problem in the United States, an ERIC Digest in 1998 reported:

- A good image begins with good programmes that meet the needs of students, employers and the community
- Vocational education continues to compete against others in the arena of education for a shrinking student population and resources
- Vocational education is mostly for high school students who do not plan to go to college
- Groups that benefit most from vocational education include students not going to college, adults who need job skills, and students with disabilities
- Generally, adults and youth have heard of vocational education, but they have no clear idea of what it is

In the same review, it was said that "for many, the word 'vocational' doesn't work" (Digest, 1998). In fact, quite a few states in the US had resorted to changing the name of their vocational education system and in many more instances school districts had changed the names of vocational centres or programmes.

The challenge of poor image in vocational training is universal and pervasive in both developed and developing countries. In an article dated 1 June 2010 in the *Modern Ghana News*, it was reported that the Council for Technical and Vocational Education and Training in collaboration with the City and Guilds Centre for Skills Development, UK, had embarked on a project aimed at changing the perception held by Ghanaians about technical and vocational education and training (COTVET, 2010). The expected outcome of the research was to help the council develop its publicity and promotional strategies aimed at tackling the image of technical and vocational education and training. At a stakeholders meeting in conjunction with the launch of the project, concerns were also expressed about the lack of interest on the part of parents letting their children pursue vocational and technical education and that only seven per cent of those who completed basic education had the interest in enrolling in a private or public institution for technical and vocational education and training.

Concern for the poor image was also echoed in efforts to restructure the vocational education system in Malaysia. In a 2011 article "Making vocational education a popular choice", *The New Straits Times* reported,

> Technical and vocational education is in need of a new shift... It is seen as timely in raising the 'nobility' of vocational education and making it a preferred choice of students... The restructuring of the vocational education is eagerly awaited by various parties who would like to see this discipline progress into a core thrust of the national educational system. It is therefore important that public perception of vocational education be changed. Over the years, many people assumed vocational students were weak or 'second-class'. A large-scale transformation is aimed at removing this stigma... ("Making vocational education," 2011)

The poor image in vocational and technical education was a subject of much interest in an International Research Project on "Vocational Training and Education" (Metzger et al., 2001). As discussed in Chapter 2, the study, conducted over four years from 1996 to 2000, focused on the role of vocational training and education in the changing social and economic context in Switzerland, Japan, Singapore and the United States. Among the key findings that cut across the four countries was a clear consensus on the "poor image" of vocational training. We attributed this to the phenomenon of "college mania" or "paper chase". The ultimate aspiration of parents and society is a university degree.

Testifying to the importance of a degree, a parent of an ITE student in Singapore, when interviewed, said, "Our society is like that. It is so obvious. In recruitment advertisements, the good jobs specify a university degree as a requirement." According to Singapore's teachers, the competitive education environment and the importance attached to good grades in the paper chase had produced examination-smart students. The research team member from the United States reported that "though just a phrase, I was struck by the number of times the students we interviewed said that they had 'disappointed' someone — themselves, parents and, their school — by not scoring higher on one entrance exam or another. The consequence, they knew, was a slot lower down the pecking order."

Culturally, scholars have been held in high esteem in societies for many centuries, perhaps more so in the Asian culture. To obtain good grades in school was extremely important. Parents today continue to cherish the hope and aspiration that their children will make it to university. However, unrealistic expectations from parents and sometimes, teachers, generate intense competition and pressure in the schools. The fallout of these pressures is a prejudice against and less-than-positive image of vocational training and education.

Vocational education in Japan faced a similar challenge. The research team member from Japan had reported that "VTE at the secondary level is faced with a lack of motivation and low self-esteem among their students as well as a pronounced stigmatisation. Alleviating the stigma — and as a result, helping to improve the students' motivation and self-esteem — has proven to be a hard task. In part, the challenge exists because the stigmatisation is rooted in the education system, and in part because the incentives for making efforts to pursue a better life are eroding as affluence arises. The stigma problem seems more serious in the United States and Japan due to their highly expanded education systems and their associated school cultures, which value general education and higher academic credentials."

OUR EARLY EXPERIENCE

All these negative perceptions and the struggle to build a more positive image had been very much a part of our earlier experience in vocational education in Singapore. As a former British colony largely dependent on entrepôt trade, Singapore began industrialising without the benefit of tradition or experience in production and manufacturing. The society had little understanding and much less appreciation of the value of vocational and technical skills. Education only meant one thing — having good GCE "O" and GCE "A" educational qualifications. There was a deep-rooted preference for an academic education. Parents and teachers honoured those who excelled in academic studies. The respect for the "scholar" and disdain for the "mechanic" and all the negative associations with those who do not do well in school and lower-level manual work perpetuated the poor image.

When vocational education was first introduced in the secondary school system under the Technical Education Department (TED) in 1968, special efforts were undertaken to change people's mindset. Public campaigns on "using the hands" were organised and basic workshop subjects such as metalwork, woodwork, technical drawing and basic electricity were made compulsory for lower secondary students. Top-of-the-trade television competitions and Apprenticeship of the Year awards were introduced to create awareness and promote the importance of technical skills among the young. However, this early phase of vocational education within the secondary school system remained unattractive. Within five years, the basic system of skills development under the Technical Education Department was no longer adequate in responding to the fast changing skilled manpower needs in an evolving industrial economy. Vocational students were looked down upon and branded as failures in schools. There was a strong societal prejudice against vocational students.

The question then was how best to respond to the increasing need for more skilled manpower created by newly emerging industries. The policy response was the establishment of the Industrial Training Board (ITB), the first statutory board with a special mission on vocational training in 1973. Replacing TED, it marked the formalisation of a system of vocational training outside the school. Constituted as a statutory board, it was empowered with greater autonomy and flexibility to respond to changing skilled manpower needs. Subject to the challenges and dynamics, the ITB was subsequently restructured as the Vocational and Industrial Training Board (VITB) in 1979. However, despite the greater efforts to expand and upgrade the quality of training, the poor image of vocational training remained a challenge for many more years.

The report on *Improving Primary School Education* identified the "poor image of vocational training" as one of the underlying concerns in the system of vocational training for primary school leavers (MOE, 1991). In a parallel *Report on Upgrading Vocational Training* (VITB, 1991), the report strongly advocated a renaming of VITB and vocational institutes. The rationale was that "pupils and parents have a poor image of vocational training. The term 'vocational' as in 'vocational training' is often associated with a low image... This is mainly due to the perception that vocational institutes are for school failures... Similarly, in view of the negative perception that VITB is a place for school failures, it is proposed that VITB be renamed... Removing the term 'vocational' would help to break the negative associations, long entrenched in the local context."

The acceptance of vocational training in Singapore was the result of a gradual process in building image and public perception. By early 1990s, it was clear that the key challenge to resolve the many interrelated issues surrounding vocational training was to change its image. This was also the most difficult challenge. The opportunity for a breakthrough came when the government decided that vocational training should be repositioned at the post-secondary level (MOE, 1991). It was a crucial education policy decision.

When the Institute of Technical Education (ITE) replaced the former VITB in 1992, an editorial entitled "A welcome fillip" in *The Straits Times* on 3 April 1992 commented thus:

> Few Singapore parents, it would be safe to say, would declare with pride that their son or daughter is studying in a vocational and technical institute. For too many years, many people have been prejudiced against such trainees. One reason could be Singapore's preoccupation with high-flying achievers and the focus, over the last few years, on concepts such as gifted education programmes and independent schools[1]... It is no exaggeration to say that for some Singaporeans, technical training is regarded as a dead-end route only for school dropouts, and delinquent ones at that... There is a sense of excitement about the road ahead for the ITE. The name itself has a nice ring to it... But, while the ITE is doing much that is laudable, it would be idle to pretend that social value systems can be changed overnight; prejudices about technical education are not likely to be discarded quickly. ("Editorial," 1992)

With policy change and a new name, ITE earnestly embarked on a journey of transformation in pursuing organisational excellence and building a world-class technical educational institution. Over a period of 15 years (1992–2007), the former traditional system of small vocational institutes under the VITB was transformed into a modern system of mega regional colleges. Described by the Education Minister as "the

[1] Independent schools are government-funded schools. Enjoying a greater autonomy in curricular innovations, implementation of programmes, administration, student admissions and setting of fee structures, they are also acknowledged as schools for elite students.

shining jewel" of the education system, this transformation helped to change the image of ITE.

CHALLENGE IN BUILDING A NEW IMAGE

Sharing his thoughts on building a new image, former ITE Chairman Eric Gwee Teck Hai said:

> Image was a very serious concern then… What is ITE's image and how do we change the perceptions of ITE? Image is about how you project yourself, your product, ITE graduates and how they project themselves in society. So, obviously, the priority must be on ITE students and graduates and, hence, the staff, too. We had to first build the image among the students and graduates, and then build the image of the staff. These will reflect on the organisation… Image was the key to transform ITE, but it was a very difficult thing to do at the time. I visited every campus then just to have a feel of what they were at that point. After the visits, it was very clear that we needed the support of the ITE Board of Governors and the Ministry of Education, and everyone had to work together to achieve the image we desired for ITE. (ITE, 2012)

We knew that the road towards changing the image was not going to be easy. Simply changing the name from "VITB" to "ITE" was not going to change the image. It was only a beginning and an opportunity to rebrand "ITE". In fact, the detractors would cynically say that the acronym "ITE" stood for "It's The End". The challenge was enormous. The stakes were high. Yet, a successful rebranding was a necessary condition in building a credible and attractive pathway for school leavers. While we needed to define our brand and communicate with the public we also had to be realistic.

We were not competing with the academic or tertiary educational institutions. ITE was entrusted with the mission to address the needs of the less academic in schools. Without the prestige of a university or polytechnic, we needed to create a unique product that would truly reflect the relevance, quality and experience of an ITE education. The name "ITE" should be synonymous with high graduate employability, excellence in organisation and a world-class institution with strong public endorsement. As a brand, it must be able to reach the minds and hearts of the people. Organisationally, it must capture the mission, vision and values, the "heartbeat" of ITE, as an educational institution.

A lot depended on the ability to change the image. How do you change the image of vocational training that had been so negatively rooted in society? The strategy to rebrand ITE had to be viewed in the wider context of repositioning ITE as a post-secondary educational institution in Singapore. It was very much an integral part of the journey of transformation. Changing the image of ITE would not have been possible without the many other concurrent initiatives in creating a unique ITE college education (as described in Chapter 6). It was a sustained strategy in building a unique product and simultaneously seeking the support of political leaders, public media and stakeholders.

Starting with ITE's first five-year strategic plan, the "ITE 2000" in 1995, one of the goals was to focus on achieving "an improved public image and recognition of technical training". Reflecting the strategic importance of promotional efforts and increased public visibility on ITE, four initial programmes were identified: (1) Introduce Experience ITE Programme for GCE Normal (Technical) Students, (2) Establish Networking System between Training Institutes and Schools, (3) Promote Status of Technical Training through Skills Competitions, and (4) Implement a Public Education Programme. In the second strategic plan, the "ITE Breakthrough", one of the strategies was aimed to further raise the profile of ITE as a post-secondary technical education institution. The goal was to make ITE an institution of choice for technical education.

The turnaround in the public perception of ITE came when ITE won the Singapore Quality Award (SQA) (see Chapter 5) in 2005. It was a clear public endorsement for organisational excellence and the new brand of "Hands-on, Mind-on and Hearts-on" education. Reflecting the positive mood at the time, there was a strong sense that ITE had transformed itself. In the eyes of the public, a new ITE image had emerged, an image visibly associated with the opening of the first regional campus, the ITE College East. The physically impressive facilities of the college were a clear statement of the government's continuing commitment in ITE as a post-secondary institution.

This change in image gave us the confidence in formulating an even more ambitious third strategic plan, "ITE Advantage". It advocated "an increased global presence for ITE". The rebranding of ITE took on a global perspective with two specific strategies. One was in building strategic alliances in the global community with two programmes — (1) International Certification and (2) International Collaboration. Another was on strengthening ITE's brand name. It had two supporting programmes — (1) Corporate Branding and (2) Alumni Network. Helping to extend the brand name overseas was the ITE Educational Services. A consultancy arm of ITE, this leverages on the experience and expertise of ITE in sharing the Singapore experience by undertaking consultancy projects and services internationally. Today, ITE's unique brand of vocational and technical education has attracted much worldwide attention and recognition.

BENCHMARK PUBLIC PERCEPTION STUDY

The first step towards building a marketing and branding strategy was an understanding of how ITE was perceived by stakeholders, opinion leaders and the public. For this purpose, AC Nielsen (Singapore), an independent research agency, was commissioned to undertake a benchmark public perception study in 1997. As part of this study, a Brand Equity Index (BEI) was developed based on a comprehensive analysis of perceptions gathered from focus group interviews with and questionnaires completed by eight targeted respondent groups, including prospective students, opinion leaders (i.e., teachers, parents, employers and general public) and ITE (i.e., students, graduates and lecturers).

The 16-image attributes that were most commonly associated with and that captured the perception of ITE and other post-secondary educational institutions were identified during this developmental phase of the same study. The image attributes included statements such as those relating to the relevance of courses in equipping students for the economy, a creative teaching and innovative environment, employment prospects and progression to further education and training. The index, once validated, was then used as benchmark in monitoring and tracking the image in the rebranding of ITE.

The results of this benchmark public perception study showed that ITE was seen as a "place of last resort" associated with "losers, low achievers and school dropouts". The study also showed that the poor perception was caused mainly by a lack of information about ITE amongst the public and key opinion leaders. There were misconceptions about vocational training, prejudice against the former VITB heritage and non-favourable impressions of ITE students. The second step was using these findings as the basis in developing a marketing and branding strategy. The first branding campaign commissioned in 1998 was mainly targeted at the general public and opinion leaders like teachers, parents and employers. The aim was to address the information gaps and position ITE as a relevant, credible and quality post-secondary institution.

Since then, an image-tracking study has been conducted on a triennial basis, at the end of each three-year branding campaign cycle, starting in 2000. The same survey protocol, based on face-to-face interviews with targeted respondents at secondary schools, ITE institutions, companies, parents and general households in all parts of Singapore, was adopted. These image tracking studies have been useful in providing ITE with an independent assessment of the effectiveness of the branding campaigns, public perception towards ITE and basis in formulating its next marketing and branding strategy.

IMAGE BUILDING — COMMUNICATIONS AND REBRANDING

A brand can only be as good as its product. As the product — an ITE Education — was being developed (1992–2005), parallel steps were taken to cultivate public support and build a new image. There are two aspects to

Figure 8.1 Communications and marketing

this. The first was the communications and marketing approach illustrated in Figure 8.1. The key issue was how to effectively communicate and reach out to the community at large and targeted groups of stakeholders, in particular, prospective students, parents and teachers. The thrust was to address the lack of awareness in ITE, its value and information gaps identified in the benchmark public perception study.

In reaching out to the community at large, ITE adopted a three-pronged approach in enlisting the support of political leaders, public media and stakeholders. Firstly, the support of political leaders was crucial. For example, in championing the cause of an ITE education during the Parliamentary Budget Debate in May 2002, Education Minister Teo Chee Hean, said, "The real success of ITE has been the fact that it has raised the prospects and maximised the potential of young Singaporeans who, in other education systems all over the world, would have been left behind. The fact that youth unemployment in Singapore is not a problem, even in the middle of a recession, is evidence of the success of ITE" (Teo, 2002).

Minister Teo, presently Deputy Prime Minister, then proceeded to extend an open invitation to his parliamentary colleagues and the public "to come and see" for themselves how well ITE students were doing. The result was that he personally hosted the biggest group of 43 members of parliament over three visits to ITE campuses in 2002. All came away very much impressed and surprised by what they saw in the students, courses and facilities. The media publicity generated not only helped to move the hearts of the public but also changed the perception of policymakers. It was the icing on the cake in image building. On other occasions, the presence of the Prime Minister and Ministers at official functions, such as the launching of new ITE campuses and graduation ceremonies, had helped to showcase our progress and reinforce the important role of ITE in society. Indirectly, winning the endorsements and support of political leaders was also an effective way in reaching out to the various constituencies and community at large.

Secondly, ITE took active steps to cultivate good relations with the public media including the newspaper, radio and television. Besides the English newspapers, the vernacular media (Chinese, Malay and Tamil) were effective channels in reaching out to the public at large in a multi-racial society like Singapore. Recognising the time value of news and information, we adopted an open policy of sharing newsworthy stories with the media. I was personally not averse to media interviews and must have given some 200 interviews and speeches, many of which were reported between the period of 1981 to 2007. Among the news reports were 15 front-page features and a live telecast. By 2005, ITE was receiving about 300 to 400 positive media mentions a year. I have no doubt that the value of the media in highlighting our work has helped in our efforts in rebranding ITE.

Thirdly, in reaching out to the stakeholders, ITE has over time developed a comprehensive marketing approach in engaging four specific groups of stakeholders, i.e., prospective students, educators, parents and the public. Annually, promotional talks and open houses are organised for potential students in secondary schools. Prospective students in Secondary Two and Three continue to participate in a two-day "Experience ITE Programme" on ITE campuses. The objective is to enable these students, when they are still in secondary schools, to experience the relevance of an ITE college education to themselves, the economy and society. The highlight of this experience is an exposure to a range of hands-on learning projects reflecting the real world through an integrated simulated learning system. This innovative approach in strengthening the linkage between school education and vocational training at an early age has been hailed as a best practice. It is a crucial step to orientate these students in following through with their further education in ITE when they complete their secondary education.

As for educators, they represent the teachers and education leaders who have a direct contact with and influence on students in schools and their parents. In partnership with the National Institute of Education, the teacher training college in Singapore, all trainee teachers undertake an "ITE Discovery Programme" as part of their course of training. Since its inception in 1998, more than 18,000 trainee teachers have visited ITE campuses and experienced first-hand the relevance of ITE training in the real world. As teachers, they are positioned to better appreciate and provide advice and guidance to students interested in a career-oriented technical education. Periodically, seminars are held for school leaders on the strategic changes and development in technical education. Similarly, presentations and road shows are organised at appropriate times of the school year for parents and the public. This comprehensive marketing approach reaches out to some 50,000 individuals a year.

Another strategic initiative in raising the profile and image of vocational and technical education was skills competitions. Encouraged by then Prime Minister Goh Chok Tong, ITE took the lead in spearheading Singapore's participation in the WorldSkills Competitions in 1995. Held biennially, the mission of WorldSkills International is "to promote through the cooperative actions of members, a worldwide awareness of the essential contributions that skills and high standards of competence make to the achievement of economic success and individual fulfilment." ITE is the official delegate representing Singapore in the WorldSkills. As Chairman of the WorldSkills Singapore Council, ITE organises the national-level competitions in Singapore in conjunction with the polytechnics. Keenly contested among polytechnic and ITE students, the winners of the national competitions are selected and groomed to represent Singapore at the WorldSkills International Competition. The competition is the equivalent of the Olympics for vocational and technical skills. The Singapore team has continued to maintain high standards and do Singapore proud at each competition. Winning a medal in an international competition is never a certainty and it takes great effort in organisation, teamwork and support from all experts, coaches and other team officials to ensure continuing success. Singapore was ranked 16th among 28 countries when it participated for the first time in France in 1995. It was placed 7th in overall medal ranking in Switzerland in 2003, winning two gold medals in IT (PC & Network Support) and Mechatronics, a silver in IT (Software Application) and a bronze in Graphic Design.

Despite the increasing competition over the years, Singapore had its best showing when it was ranked in 6th position among 51 countries in the WorldSkills Competition in the United Kingdom in 2011. The team of 22 polytechnic and ITE students won a total of seven medals, including four gold medals in IT Network Systems Administration, IT Software Solutions for Business, Beauty Therapy and Caring, a silver in Mechanical Engineering Design — CAD and two bronzes in Information Network Cabling and Visual Merchandising. Singapore continues to do well and was ranked 7th in 2013. These sterling performances have raised the image of Singapore in the international arena and reflect well the quality and standards of the polytechnic and ITE systems in Singapore.

The second important aspect of image building is the rebranding of ITE. To create a new brand of education, the community and public need to be able to identify with ITE, its role in skills development, industry, society and values. By conducting triennial branding campaigns, the approach was to create public empathy and credibility in line with the transformation of ITE. The key focus was to engage stakeholders, opinion leaders and the general public in building belief and acceptance in the value of an ITE education. The messages were kept simple and direct. Since 1998, ITE has launched five branding campaigns with creative themes such as "ITE makes things happen" (1998–2000), "ITE — a force behind the knowledge-based economy" (2001–2003), "Thinking hands create success" (2004–2006), "We make you shine" (2007–2009) and "I believe" (2010–2012). Each message was created to reinforce the ITE brand.

Figure 8.2 Creative rebranding of ITE

As illustrated in Figure 8.2, the message underlying the creative theme "Thinking hands create success" (2004–2006) was that ITE students are uniquely talented. With "thinking hands", they were portrayed as "thinking doers" who excel in skills through experiential learning and building a successful future for themselves and Singapore. Professionally commissioned and executed through a mix of advertising media such as newspapers, posters, buses and mass rapid transit (MRT) systems, the underlying messages were focused on the success of ITE graduates and its dynamic transformation as a world-class education institution. Ultimately, it is the students, graduates and staff who will shape the image and represent the ITE brand.

In endorsing the success of ITE's brand of education in his 2005 National Day Rally Speech, Prime Minister Lee Hsien Loong said, "This is a brand of education which is unique in the world. Their tagline is 'Thinking Hands'. You think about it. It's a very good slogan because with hands, you are doing something, but the brain behind it, it knows what to do. Smart. So, when they train, they are training people to be hands-on, minds-on and hearts-on. So, you develop a complete rounded person" (Lee, 2005).

Indeed, as an outcome of its transformation, ITE has created a unique brand of training called "Hands-on, Minds-on and Hearts-on" as shown

Figure 8.3 "Hands-on, Minds-on and Hearts-on"

in Figure 8.3. It is a holistic brand of education that provides the motivation, assists student learning and develops graduates all round. It is an innovative brand grounded on sound curriculum, pedagogic and educational principles. The "hands-on" training ensures that students acquire a strong foundation in technical skills. "Minds-on" learning develops independent-thinking and flexible practitioners who are equipped to cope with changing technology and diversity in the work environment. And "hearts-on" develops the "complete" person with the passion for what they do with confidence and care for the community and society. It underpins an educational environment where students are able to integrate theory with practice through coursework, projects, community service and global education. The outcomes are relevant to the market, enterprising and adaptable graduates with lifelong learning skills.

TURNAROUND IN IMAGE

The brand equity index (BEI) model that tracked the image and public perception of ITE every three years had given ITE a BEI of 34 per cent in 1997 as shown in Figure 8.4. It was 37 per cent in year 2000, a small but statistically significant improvement of 3 percentage points

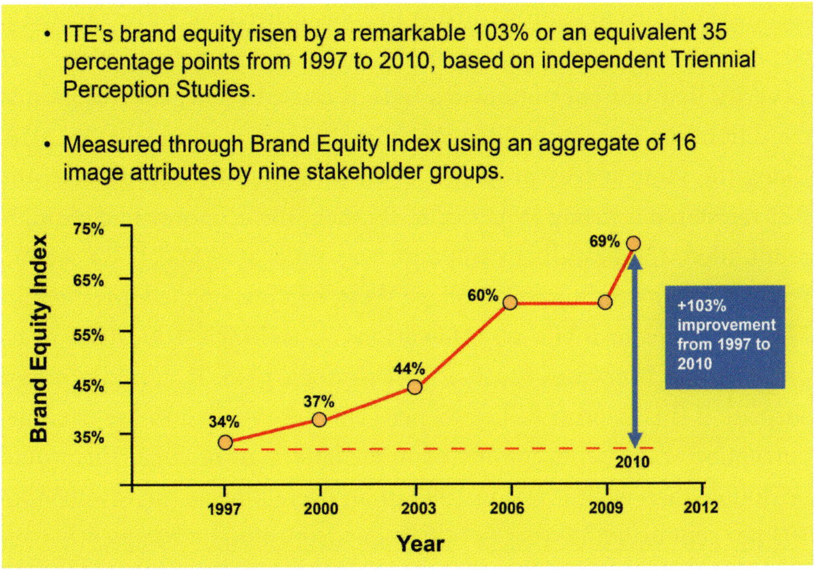

Figure 8.4 Turnaround in ITE's image

based on a 95 per cent level of confidence. In 2003, the public image of ITE improved by another 7 percentage points with a BEI of 44 per cent. The improvement was evident across many target respondent groups, especially the opinion leaders (i.e., teachers, employers and the general public). By 2006, the BEI for ITE had increased significantly by another 16 percentage points to 60 per cent. This steep turnaround in the image of ITE was attributed to the convergence of three milestone events, through the opening of the first regional mega campus at ITE College East, public endorsement of ITE's "Hands-on, Minds-on and Hearts-on" education by Prime Minister Lee Hsien Loong at the National Day Rally and ITE winning the Singapore Quality Award in 2005. The change in perception was visible. There was great excitement, enthusiasm and exuberance all round within ITE and in the public that ITE had transformed itself. Against all odds, the image of ITE had improved by an impressive 76 per cent over a nine-year period from 1997 to 2006.

The new image was a summative reflection of ITE's transformation as a post-secondary education institution. Based on a projected trend, the

BEI was expected to improve further in 2009. Instead, the BEI stagnated at 60 per cent amid a severe economic downturn and uncertainties. In order to verify that this aberration was indeed caused by negative economic conditions, an interim public perception study was conducted in 2010. Using the same survey protocol, albeit using half the sample size, the BEI registered a strong 69 per cent. By then, the economy had strongly rebounded, the branding campaign was reinstated and ITE's second regional mega campus, ITE College West, had just opened. Meanwhile, ITE continues to focus on innovations in technical education in its present "ITE Innovate" (2010–2014) strategic plan. It should not be a surprise if this interim BEI of 69 per cent was rectified in the triennial perception study being conducted in the latter part of 2012. This would be double than what it was in 1997 or an overall image improvement of 103 per cent over a 15-year period. Indeed, the study subsequently confirmed that the BEI for ITE in 2012 was 70 per cent or an improvement of 106 per cent. This is the strongest endorsement yet of how ITE has made a difference in vocational and technical education.

Chapter 9

ITE: A World-Class Educational Institution

The present system of vocational training under the ITE was established in 1992. Repositioned as a post-secondary technical education institution, ITE is an integral part of Singapore's national education system (see Appendix A). Its birth was both a result of policy change in education and response to Singapore's 1991 Strategic Economic Plan. The changes as captured in Chapter 6 were fundamental, innovative and visible.

In the process, the concept of vocational training was challenged and redefined. With new visions, pioneering initiatives and ingenuity, a unique ITE brand of college education, "Hands-on, Minds-on and Hearts-on," was created. The traditional system of small "vocational institutes" was transformed into a system of modern mega "regional campuses." ITE's brand of education is synonymous with world-class standards and global leadership in technical education. Capturing the hearts, minds and aspirations of society, ITE has effectively rebuilt itself.

THE ITE MODEL

The ITE today is vastly different from the system inherited from the former VITB as described in Chapter 4 when the journey of transformation started in 1992. Built on strong foundation and fundamental principles, the strengths of the ITE Model are as follows:

(A) CLARITY OF MISSION AND GOVERNANCE:

- **Mission-focused:** Constituted as a statutory board under the education ministry, ITE follows its own mission, vision and values. The institution's journey of transformation has been sustained by the "ITE Heartbeat" — that inner spirit of leadership, commitment and teamwork in always asking how to better serve, add value and meet the needs and expectations of students, partners and stakeholders. It is an educational institution built on organisational excellence, standards and best practices. It is a continuing journey characterised by the consistent use of five-year strategic plans.

- **Effective model of governance:** The traditional system of ten small "vocational institutes" has been transformed into a modern system of three mega "regional campuses". Called the "One ITE, Three Colleges" system of education and governance, the colleges, each headed by a principal, are empowered with greater autonomy and flexibility. With greater synergy in the use of resources and the economy of scale, there are greater possibilities in innovations and creativity in teaching and learning. The college model has enhanced the capability to stay relevant and responsive to changing needs.

- **Modern campus infrastructure:** Purposefully designed and built to meet the needs of ITE students who do well in an experiential rather than academic learning environment, ITE's world-class campus facilities never fail to impress visitors. The campuses are well equipped with extensive workshops, "real-life" laboratories, an IT-rich web-based environment, student support services and facilities for sports, music and arts. Representing the best practices in vocational training, these modern campuses have been an important factor in changing public perceptions and image.

(B) EFFECTIVE AND RESPONSIVE MANAGEMENT IN SERVICE PROVISION:

- **Holistic "hands-on" education:** ITE's brand of vocational education is unique in the world. The "Hands-on, Minds-on and Hearts-on" education is a holistic one that aims to provide the motivation, assist student learning and develop all-rounded graduates. Supporting students who learn better in a "hands-on" training environment, ITE is an education of choice for 25 per cent of a school cohort in Singapore. Known for its quality, relevance and values, ITE's graduates are highly employable (at 90 per cent in 2014) and ready to take on the challenges in a modern global economy.

- **Experiential pedagogic model:** ITE uses the "Plan, Explore, Practise and Perform" or "PEPP" pedagogic model. An interactive and process-oriented approach facilitated by well-qualified staff with practical experience, the aim is to develop "thinking doers," i.e., graduates who can apply the knowledge, skills and values they have mastered and apply them in practice. Addressing the needs of kinaesthetic learners, the focus is on acquiring the three key competencies, i.e., technical, methodological and social, which are essential skills in the real world of work.

- **"ITE Care" culture:** Founded on a people-centred management philosophy that believes in people and their potential, the "ITE Care" (Integrity, Teamwork, Excellence and Care) culture is deeply entrenched throughout the organisation. It means "working with integrity to achieve excellence as a team, caring for all whom we serve". Beyond professional expertise and skills, the dedication and passion of ITE staff is what makes an ITE education so unique in transforming the lives of young Singaporeans. In particular, the "ITE Care" culture is pervasive, especially the care and concern of staff for the students.

- **Quality brand:** The ITE brand of education is founded on quality training and successful graduates. ITE is recognised as a world-class educational institution and global leader in technical education. The strategic rebranding of ITE has changed public perceptions and image. With comprehensive communications, marketing and creative publicity campaigns, the ITE brand equity index has improved by a remarkable 103 per cent from 1997 to 2012.

(C) INDUSTRY RELEVANCE AND PARTNERSHIP:

- **Industry-relevant curriculum:** ITE's courses are competency-based and developed using the rigorous curriculum process. Facilitated by curriculum specialists, it ensures that the competencies and occupational standards are aligned with the needs of employers in major sectors of business and industry. In building a strong foundation in technical skills, 80 per cent of total curriculum time is allocated to the occupational core modules. Typically, 70 per cent of curriculum time for these core modules is practical training and 30 per cent are theoretical lessons.

- **Close industry partnership:** Built on mutual needs and benefits since the early days of Singapore's efforts in industrialisation, this close partnership has further strengthened in terms of level and quality of engagement. Leveraging the knowledge, expertise and skills of industry technology leaders, linkages with industry take various forms, including partnership in curriculum development, apprenticeship training, college advisory committees and joint centres of excellence across sectors of industry, business and services. These supportive partnership and practices help to ensure the relevance and quality of training.

WHAT MAKES ITE WORLD-CLASS?

Why is ITE a world-class education institution, one may ask? A rhetorical but nevertheless relevant question given that there is no league table in the ranking of vocational and technical institutions. Model institutions do exist and are occasionally featured in special studies commissioned by international organisations such as the World Bank, UNESCO or OECD. The aspiration to be a world-class institution was first articulated in ITE's second strategic plan, the ITE Breakthrough (2000–2004). The vision was to be "a world-class technical education institution for a knowledge-based economy." Since then, ITE has received many accolades in its pursuit of organisational excellence, best practices and innovations. As an organisation, ITE has achieved world-class results based on strategic performance indicators. There is national and international recognition based on external endorsements and competitive awards. Taken together, this wide recognition by peers and the wider impact on its graduates in industry and society is proof that the ITE today is a world-class institution and global leader in technical education.

WORLD-CLASS RESULTS

As a matter of good governance, ITE started the formal process of five-year strategic planning in 1995 (see Chapter 7). The process soon evolved into a holistic framework for charting future direction, aligning goals and mission, setting targets, monitoring outcomes and the formulation of annual corporate plans. Strategic objectives and performance indicators are aligned using the Balance Scorecard approach. ITE would not have been able to win the Singapore Quality Award in 2005 without the ability to demonstrate "world-class" results based on its strategic performance indicators: student enrolment, graduate employability, students' satisfaction with ITE education, employers' satisfaction with ITE graduates, completion rate and brand equity index.

The total student enrolment more than doubled to 23,000 from 1995 to 2005. This was the result of the successful repositioning of ITE as a post-secondary institution and ability to attract 25 per cent of a school cohort. Graduate employability has remained consistently high and was 90 per cent in 2005. Students' satisfaction with ITE education was at a high of 94 per cent from 80 per cent in 2001. Employers' satisfaction with ITE graduates was at a high of 95 per cent. The student completion rate significantly improved from a low of 61 per cent in 1995 to a high of 78 per cent in 2005. This was an outstanding achievement in the context of vocational training where low completion rates are the norm. Underscoring the transformation of ITE was the turnaround in the public perceptions and image of ITE. The brand equity index of ITE improved by a remarkable 76 per cent over the nine-year period from 34 per cent in 1997 to 60 per cent in 2006.

Five years after winning the Singapore Quality Award in 2005, the updated strategic performance indicators for 2010 are as shown in Figure 9.1. The results showed that ITE was able to maintain or further improve on its performance indicators. In fact, the quality and sustainability of the ITE system was reaffirmed in 2011 when it won the SQA with Special Commendation Award.

Beyond the statistics, I also wanted to see for myself and feel the pulse of the real ITE today, now that I have retired more than five years ago. I was warmly received when I met some staff and students on "A-day-in-campus" in ITE College West on 19 July 2012. ITE College West is the second mega regional campus to be built in 2011, the first being ITE

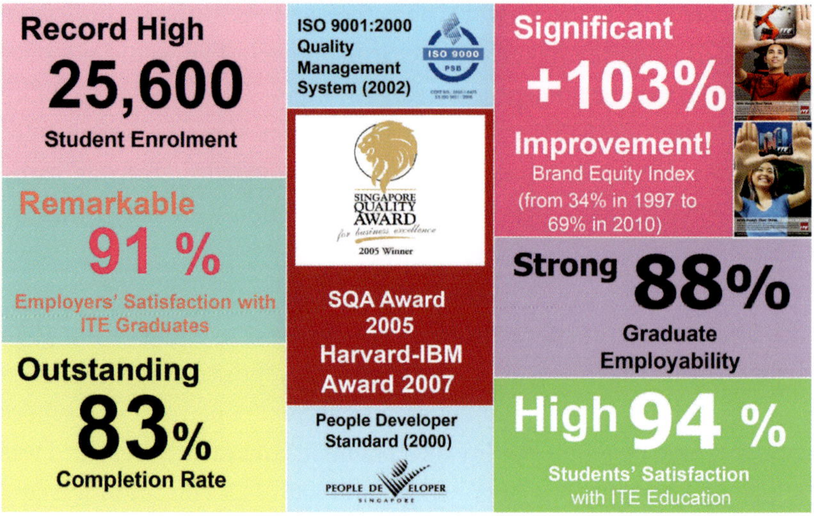

Figure 9.1 World-class results (2010)

College East in 2005. It was like a homecoming for me. The following are the impressions I shared with Dr Yek Tiew Ming, Principal of ITE College West, after the visit:

> The dedication and passion remain strong among leaders and staff. The staff are passionate in what they do and continue to stay relevant and up-to-date through continual learning and development. Confident and articulate, the student leaders carry themselves well. It is clear that they are personally appreciative of how ITE has touched their lives. Inevitably, they attribute their success to ITE staff for the care, inspiration and motivation. The ITE Care values live on. Although the students are mainly from the lower socio-economic strata of society, they do not show any sign of being disadvantaged. This augurs well not only for themselves, but also for Singapore as a society. There is diversity and vibrancy all round.

I obviously enjoyed the visit and I came away reassured that the ITE Model is not only unique, but truly world-class. It has achieved quality and sustainability.

GLOBAL IBM INNOVATIONS AWARD

On 25 September 2007, ITE won the inaugural Global IBM Innovations Award in Transforming Government given by the Ash Institute for Democratic Governance and Innovation at Harvard University's John F. Kennedy's School of Government, now known as the Harvard Kennedy School. This is the highest order of recognition ITE has ever received at the international level. Open to international competition, this award was created to recognise exemplary government programmes for their innovation, measurable results, collaborative practices, scope and potential global replication. The award attracted over a hundred nominations from 30 different countries. Selection was made by an international panel of distinguished experts and practitioners in good governance.

On ITE winning this Harvard-IBM Innovations Award, Professor Stephen Goldsmith, Director, Innovations in American Government Program, Harvard University, said:

> Singapore's Institute of Technical Education has not only improved the lives of its students, it has created a highly sustainable model of transforming poorly performing educational institutions worldwide... We are pleased to honour the Institute's achievements and commend the outstanding dedication of multiple administrations of ITE leadership in collaboration with an international portfolio of technology and business partners. ITE's contributions extend far past the schoolroom and have a direct impact on youth employment rates, community safety and the Singapore economy. (ITE, 2009)

In a special video, *Experiential Learners Change a Nation*, commissioned by the Ash Institute and aired over PBS in the United States from July to August 2008, the opening lines introduced ITE thus:

> Novel concepts, new solutions and inventive approaches to old problems don't spring out of thin air. They happen when you look at a situation from a different angle. That was what happened

> on the island nation of Singapore and it led to one of the most successful approaches in technical education in the world. The Institute of Technical Education or ITE was once seen as a place of last resort for low academic achievers. It is now an institution of choice in Singapore for 25 per cent of students... Instead of being seen as academic failures, these young people were viewed as experiential learners who blossomed in a technical environment. This single shift in perspective combined with a massive restructuring of ITE had made Singapore the envy of the world. (Mosher, 2008)

Tharman Shanmugaratnam, then Minister of Education, who was interviewed in the video, explained it this way:

> If I am a young kid going there [ITE], I feel as if I am going to university like any other. I am being developed all round, but I am also developing some pretty deep specialised skills... It is not so much in the numbers or the statistics of success. But when we meet an individual who succeeded because he took an alternative path and did well, it proves to everyone that it is not just one talent that counts, but different talents that make up a society, and make up a country that keeps looking to the future.

Singapore Prime Minister Lee Hsien Loong, in his congratulatory statement, said:

> We are very proud of ITE. ITE has developed a unique brand of education, to train students with "thinking hands" who excel in technical vocations. A first-class ITE system is critical to enabling every Singaporean to maximise his potential, and participate fully in Singapore's growth and progress. The ITE staff and students have worked long and hard to make this vision a reality. The award shows that they are succeeding, and winning international recognition. (ITE, 2009)

EXTERNAL ENDORSEMENTS

In addition, the recognition of ITE as a world-class institution in vocational and technical education has been widely endorsed by observers external to ITE:

> We have witnessed ITE's many great transformations and innovations in one short decade. We note that ITE has already established a very comprehensive and robust Organisational Excellence and Quality System for Vocational Training that is global in class and mature. ITE's VTE system is comparable with or even better than the world's best in advanced countries like Germany, Switzerland, Japan and the United States of America. (Rau, 2002)
>
> **— H.E. Helmut Rau, Deputy Minister for Education, Youth and Sports, Baden-Württemberg, Germany, 2002**

> Singapore has developed one of the most sophisticated and strategically placed programmes for vocational and technical education anywhere in the world. Its [ITE's] new facilities are world-class, its teaching staff are eager and qualified. ... It was evident that efforts in promoting the importance of technical training had visibly elevated the image of ITE in Singapore. (Metzger et al., 2001)
>
> **— Professor Robert Zemsky, Institute for Research on Higher Education, University of Pennsylvania, 2001**

> It [ITE] has achieved significant breakthrough by establishing itself as a post-secondary institution... It has effectively rebuilt and transformed its former "vocational" institutes into top-line educational colleges... and achieved a world class standing in its own right... ITE has given skilled occupations a new social and economic importance, creating viable careers for its graduates. (Pillay, 2005)
>
> **— Gerald F. Pillay, Consultant, South Asia Region, The World Bank Report, 2005**

I think it [ITE] is one of the success stories of Singapore that we are able to uplift the academically less-advantaged 25 per cent and use their other skills, hands-on skills and ability to improvise, to give them that added value so that they can make a contribution to life, to society and to make a good living. (Goh, 2008)

— Singapore Minister Mentor Lee Kuan Yew, 2008

Until recently ITE — dubbed "It's The End" by ambitious middle-class parents — was the dark side of the Singaporean education. The city-state streams pupils rigorously… But such a system also produces losers — many of the bottom third who do not make it to university come to ITE… Since the 1990s the government has worked hard to change ITE's image… And it has encouraged students who are used to failure to take pride in their work… ITE has sports teams and concerts just like any university. The attention to detail has paid off. … Singapore, already near the top of most educational league tables, has created yet another centre of excellence that is beginning to attract foreign visitors. ("Go East," 2011)

— "Go East, young bureaucrat", Special Report,
***The Economist*, 17 March 2011**

If I had to rank ITE and compare this organisation to the more than 30 countries we have been engaged with over several decades, they would be my first choice in the top of my ranking scale… Having worked in Alberta's publicly funded system for over thirty years, I can honestly state that few can measure up to the ever high standards set by ITE… which serve as a benchmark for others to attain. (ITE, 2012)

— Dr Irene Lewis,
President and Chief Executive Officer,
SAIT Polytechnic, Canada, 2012

ITE's development since its foundation in 1992 is a success story which, as far as I can see, is unparalleled in the world… Through my career as Professor of Higher Education Management

> and University President… I have seen more than 200 higher education institutions worldwide. Among them, ITE stands out among the top league institutions for organisational excellence and quality education globally. (ITE, 2012)
>
> **— Professor Dr Rainer Kuenzel,**
> **Faculty of Economics, University of Osnabrück,**
> **Germany, 2012**

IMPACT ON GRADUATES AND SOCIETY

The greatest value of ITE is the wider impact on its graduates and society. ITE takes in students mainly from the lower socio-economic strata of society and equips them with market-relevant skills and values for the modern economy. An ITE survey on the 1998 intake cohort had shown that 74 per cent of ITE students came from families with a monthly household income of S$2,000 or less. Students who were once viewed as failures in schools can now blossom in a world-class learning environment. ITE is where many students who have experienced disappointment in life rebuild their self-esteem and confidence. With renewed motivation, it is a place where individual students can take pride in their abilities to do well as Singaporeans. With the support of dedicated and caring teachers, students are made to feel that they are understood and encouraged to pursue their interest and develop their full potential.

Employers value ITE graduates highly for their technical knowledge, skills and values. Parents are grateful to ITE teachers for reaching out to their children and transforming their lives. Far from being the end, graduating from ITE is the beginning of many opportunities and possibilities. The majority will enter employment and build their professional careers. Others continue to further their education in the polytechnic and university. Some will pursue their dreams in entrepreneurship in industry, business and services. In keeping with the new image and reassured of their value and role in society, ITE graduates wore mortarboards and graduation gowns for the first time during the ITE Annual Graduation Ceremony in 2012.

ITE MODEL GRADUATES

Ultimately, the success of ITE is measured by the success of its graduates. Giving hope and opportunities to 25 per cent of a school cohort to learn and develop into confident and productive members of society is the greatest value not only for the individual but society. ITE has contributed significantly towards meeting the expectation of a post-secondary education among school leavers, enhancing competitiveness of the Singapore workforce and building a more inclusive society. Not to succeed would have serious social implications.

There are many success stories of ITE graduates. Each one is an inspiring story. Here is a sample representing many others in different fields:

- Elson Koh, ITE Lecturer (Box 9.1)
- Mohamed Akbar Khan Akhtar, Research & Development Engineer (Box 9.2)
- Fanddy Bin Halil, Structural Designer (Box 9.3)
- Sivachandran Murugasu, Entrepreneur in ambulance services (Box 9.4)
- Lim Lili, Entrepreneur in retail fashion (Box 9.5)

WIDER IMPACT ON SOCIETY

There are different opportunities and possibilities in achieving success in society. Upgrading the level of education, building professional careers or pursuing entrepreneurship are the main pathways for ITE graduates in moving up the socio-economic ladder. Many have done so. While the extent of mobility will vary, they have all benefited from an ITE education. In addition, what is the wider impact of ITE on its graduates and society? A study was conducted by ITE, albeit in a limited way, in tracking the 1998 intake cohort of graduates who first entered the employment market in 2002. They were tracked again after working for 5 and 10 years. Given the data available, the social profile of the graduates was tracked by two parameters: educational qualification and occupation.

The results are grouped into four bands as shown in Box 9.6. The "moving" profile of graduates as defined by the percentages in these four bands is

BOX 9.1 ITE GRADUATE: ELSON KOH

ITC in Mechanical Engineering, 1996

Elson left school prematurely at Primary 5. His mother worked as a cleaner and his father was an odd job labourer, and both were unable to provide an ideal environment for him to study. However, the turning point came when he joined the former Vocational & Industrial Training Board (VITB) in 1988 for Basic Vocational Training. He also took night classes to improve his English and Mathematics.

It was tough going as he had to work part-time at a fast food restaurant to contribute to the family income. Through perseverance, he managed and progressed to National Trade Certificate Grade 2 (NTC-2) in Precision Engineering. He went on to graduate with a Certificate of Merit for the Industrial Technician Certificate (ITC) in Mechanical Engineering in ITE in 1996 where he topped his course and won the prestigious National Trades Union Congress (NTUC) medal.

He worked for a year in industry before enrolling in the Singapore Polytechnic and was offered the Tay Eng Soon Scholarship. With hard work and consistent efforts, he graduated within the top five per cent two years later. When interviewed by the polytechnic's magazine, he credited ITE for his success. An extract from the article reads, "Elson is grateful to ITE for what they had done for him. 'The staff are more understanding and given their knowledge of our background, they are more patient.'"

In 2000, he pursued a degree in Queensland University of Technology, Brisbane, Australia. He had decided to be an ITE Lecturer and was offered a scholarship by ITE to complete his degree programme. He graduated at the top of his cohort. Elson completed his part-time master's degree in Industrial System Engineering at National University of Singapore in 2008.

Now an ITE Lecturer, Elson (on the right) wants students to know that a degree dream is not beyond reach.

BOX 9.2 ITE GRADUATE: MOHAMED AKBAR KHAN AKHTAR

NTC-2 Electronics (Computer Technology), 2002

Mohamed Akbar Khan Akhtar rose from humble beginnings as a pupil in the weakest primary stream to become a first-class honours graduate in Electrical Engineering at the National University of Singapore (NUS).

Mohamed Akbar received a Gold Medal for his active involvement in Co-curricular Activities. He was among the top students from the National Technical Certificate Grade 2 (NTC-2) course to progress to the Singapore Polytechnic. There he received the Lee Kuan Yew-STEP (Scholarship to Encourage Upgrading) Award and the Tay Eng Soon Scholarship. He graduated with a Merit Diploma in Electronics, Computer and Communication Engineering. He qualified for direct entry to the second year degree programme at NUS.

Mohamed Akbar said that ITE staff had touched his life. "I considered myself to be very fortunate to have two great lecturers at ITE who groomed me to be a better person in life. One of them is Miss Chan Lay Lee, who was then Section Head at ITE. She was consistently checking the performance and maintaining the discipline of every single student. She was always encouraging us to do well. Besides her were other wonderful teachers such as Mr Samuel Sim, Mr Lim and Mr Tay — all very friendly and approachable."

"Another great teacher of mine is Mr Sugumar, Section Head of Physical Education. He was my sports teacher and my fencing coach. He used fencing as a way to motivate students in studies and help us apply sporting skills to our personal life in order to be a better person. There was so much to learn from him in sports, academic and life."

Mohamed Akbar is currently working as an R&D Engineer at A*STAR.

BOX 9.3 ITE GRADUATE: FANDDY BIN HALIL

Higher Nitec in Mechanical & Electrical Engineering Design, 2004

"My ITE education has given me a strong skills foundation to build on. At ITE, I discovered my interest in the oil and gas field," Fanddy Bin Halil shared when asked about how he felt about his ITE education.

Fanddy came from the Normal (Technical) stream in secondary school and first took up the Nitec in Mechanical Servicing course. He then moved on to graduate from ITE with a Higher Nitec in Mechanical & Electrical Engineering Design in 2004.

He started as a Draughtsman in B. T. Engineering Pte Ltd for four years, before progressing to J. Ray McDermott Asia Pacific Pte Ltd as a Structural Designer in 2008. In this position, he holds his own and works alongside other diploma and degree holders. He has also demonstrated a high level of commitment to ensure he could catch up with the industry. "For the first few months of my working life, I would bring home reference materials at the end of each day to prepare for the next day," said Fanddy.

B. T. Engineering was so impressed with Fanddy's commitment that its Engineering Manager, Mr C. S. Foo, described him as one who is well equipped for the job. "He has the potential to progress to any discipline that an Offshore Oil & Gas field could offer, be it in strength design, inspection, contract administration or procurement. He is well placed for the future," assured Mr Foo.

Fanddy (on the right) currently works as a Structural Designer at J. Ray McDermott.

BOX 9.4 ITE GRADUATE: SIVACHANDRAN MURUGASU

Nitec in Nursing, 2008

Sivachandran's helping hands made him realise his passion. He had a vision and the perseverance to defy the odds to do well for himself and his family. He believed in himself, and turned his life around.

Today, he is a successful nursing entrepreneur enjoying a more than comfortable life. His is a Nurse Director managing his own ambulance services business.

After his national service in the army, Siva, who did not do well in the GCE "O" Level examination, was adamant about *not* going to ITE. After being an ambulance driver and realising the value of an ITE education, Siva became interested in joining the Nitec in Nursing course. However, he was rejected twice. He persisted, and was third time lucky. Despite his interest in his studies, he had the financial burden of supporting his pregnant wife, and often did not turn up for classes. His lecturers remained a source of strength, and continued to support and motivate him.

Upon graduation, with just S$800 and an ITE certificate on hand, the gung-ho nursing graduate started his own ambulance service company. His hands-on skills and entrepreneurial mind have enabled him to grow his business and live the dream he always imagined.

Siva said, "Unlike what I believed earlier, the ITE certificate is very well recognised, and has enabled me to pursue my dream. I am thankful for the opportunities. The care of ITE lecturers has been a great source of encouragement and motivation for me in becoming what I am today."

BOX 9.5 ITE GRADUATE: LIM LILI

Nitec in Service Skills (Retail), 2007

She fondly remembered her time in ITE. Lili confessed that she was never her teacher's favourite during her secondary and ITE school days. Back then, she was a dreamer in class and was often late for lessons. However, till this day, she remains very grateful to her Class Advisor, Anna Chin, for her patience and mentorship.

After graduation, Lili embarked on several short desk-bound job stints before realising her dream in fashion. She subsequently responded to an advertisement for sales assistant and was hired by The Blog Shop Pte Ltd. In the first three years of learning the trade of wholesale and retailing of ladies' fashion, Lili was promoted several times. By 2010, she was already the General Manager of The Blog Shop overseeing the operations of two retail and three wholesale shops.

Finally in July 2011, Lili realised her dream — setting up her own retail store in Far East Plaza called Online Shoppers. Lili said, "I'm very thankful to the ITE teachers who taught me during my retail course. It was very useful and relevant to my previous jobs and current business. It still feels like a dream having my very own shop." As a shop owner and manager, Lili is personally involved in all aspects of the business functions, from inventory, sales, advertising and promotions to procurement and visual merchandising to trend forecasting, accounting, budget and human resource. On days when the shop is shorthanded, she will attend to the shop personally and becomes both fashion consultant and cashier.

She was very much encouraged by the response of her customers and subsequently, she opened another outlet in City Plaza in December 2011. Most recently in January 2012, she opened her third outlet in Haji Lane. An entrepreneur within four years of graduation, this feisty young lady has bigger dreams.

captured for the years 2002, 2006 and 2011 in Table (a) and Table (b). Within the first five years, 28 per cent of ITE graduates have upgraded to a polytechnic diploma. Another 2 per cent have already earned a university degree. While the data show that the majority of 65 per cent continued to hold on to an ITE qualification within 10 years, it is notable that 9 per cent have now earned a degree.

The occupational clusters are grouped with reference to the skills associated with the occupational groups and the Singapore Standard Occupational Classification (SSOC). ITE fresh graduates will enter the job market as skilled personnel (72 per cent) or associate professionals and technicians (28 per cent) respectively. Within five years, the percentage of graduates working at the associate professionals and technician band has about doubled at 54 per cent, and 7 per cent have reached the higher end of the occupational ladder. More encouragingly, within 10 years, a total of 18 per cent of graduates work as managers, working proprietors and professionals.

What the results of this study have shown is that an education at ITE has a wider impact on the social progress of its graduates than is previously known.

BOX 9.6 TRACKING THE SOCIAL PROFILE OF ITE GRADUATES

Table (a) — Educational Qualification

Qualification	2002	2006	2011
Degree & above	0%	2%	9%
Polytechnic Diploma	0%	28%	26%
ITE/Post-secondary	100%	70%	65%
Secondary & lower	0%	0%	0%

Table (b) — Occupation

Occupation	2002	2006	2011
Managers, Working Proprietors & Professionals	0%	7%	18%
Associate Professionals & Technicians	28%	54%	44%
Skilled (e.g., Service & Shop Sales Workers, Production Craftsmen & related Workers)	72%	39%	38%
Unskilled (e.g., Cleaners, Labourers & Related Workers)	0%	0%	0%

EARLIER DAYS (1961–1981)

As a scout on board M. S. Ruys with the Singapore Contingent (front row, first from right), en route to the Hong Kong Scout Jamboree, December 1961.

Pre-university 2 (Science 1) Class (sitting, fourth from right), Victoria School, 1964.

First Professional Year (second row, seven from left) at Ardmore School of Engineering, University of Auckland, New Zealand, July 1965.

Dr Law (sixth from right) with his second-year students in Singapore Polytechnic, Prince Edward Road, 1968.

Conducting an experiment in a Three-Dimensional Photo-elasticity research laboratory, University of Wisconsin - Madison, Wisconsin, USA, 1970.

Giving a lecture in Industrial & Systems Engineering, National University of Singapore (1973–1983).

VITB (1981–1992)

The Vocational and Industrial Training Board (VITB) Headquarters (1979–1992). (Courtesy of ITE)

A vocational institute in the early 1980s: Singapore Vocational Institute. (Courtesy of ITE)

My first official function as Guest-of-Honour at Master Printers' Association, 44th Anniversary Dinner, Shangri-La Hotel, Singapore, 29 August 1981.

Chairman, Dr Tay Eng Soon (sitting, fourth from right) with VITB Board of Governors, 1983.

Dr Law (with Mrs Law) meeting President C. V. Devan Nair during reception after receiving the Public Administration (Gold) Medal (PPA(E)) on 23 November 1984.

Mr Goh Chok Tong, then First Deputy Prime Minister (sitting, fourth from left) sharing views with students at Ang Mo Kio Vocational Institute, 30 May 1986.

Dr Law speaking at his alma mater, Bukit Panjang Government High School, on Annual Speech Day, 1986.

VITB management team in a seminar conducted by consultant, the late Mr Wong Chai Kee (sitting, third from left), Cameron Highlands, Malaysia, June 1988.

Dr Tony Tan Keng Yam (in dark suit), Minister for Education (1985–1991), observing students in a training session in Bedok Vocational Institute, 1991.

A study visit, led by then Senior Minister of State (Education) Dr Tay Eng Soon (third from left) to the Ministry of Education, Youth and Sports, Baden-Württemberg, Stuttgart, Germany, 4 June 1991.

ITE (1992–2012)

Inauguration Ceremony of Institute of Technical Education (ITE) by Guest-of-Honour, Prime Minister Goh Chok Tong, 31 March 1992.

Mr Lee Yock Suan (third from right), Minister for Education (1992–1997), visiting ITE Bedok, 1992.

Chairman Dr Tay Eng Soon (third from left), at Ground Breaking Ceremony for ITE's new Headquarters and Technical Institute at Dover Drive, 18 May 1993.

Mr Eric Gwee Teck Hai (second from left), ITE Chairman (1994–2007), visiting ITE Bukit Merah, 1995.

Dr Law (fifth from left) with the first Singapore contingent to the International Youth Skills Olympics (now WorldSkills), Lyon, France, October 1995.

A Vocational Institute, ITE Bedok, built in 1986, that was upgraded in 1996. (Courtesy of ITE)

Mr Teo Chee Hean (second from right), Minister for Education (1997–2003), sharing his thoughts during a visit to Tampines Technical Institute, 1997.

Dr Law (sitting, first from right) with members of the International Research Team on Vocational Technical Education visiting Japan, 16 October 1998.

Minister Mentor Lee Kuan Yew donating S$552,500.00 to ITE in a presentation ceremony on 21 November 1998.

Dr Law (second from left) holding a sharing session with students at ITE Macpherson, 2001.

Third MOU between ITE and Ministry of Education, Youth & Sports, Baden-Württemberg, signed by Minister of State (Education and Manpower) Dr Ng Eng Hen and Minister for Education Mr Helmut Rau, Baden-Württemberg, Germany, 29 October 2002. (Courtesy of ITE)

The first ITE mega regional campus, ITE College East, opened its doors in January 2005. (Courtesy of ITE)

ITE winning the Singapore Quality Award, 2005. (Courtesy of ITE)

The musical "Joseph and the Amazing Technicolor Dreamcoat" was presented by ITE's Centre for Music and The Arts (CeMTA), 2006. (Courtesy of ITE)

Minister of State (Education and Manpower), Mr Gan Kim Yong (centre), officiating at the Opening of WorldSkills Singapore Competition at ITE College West (Balestier Campus), 13 July 2006. (Courtesy of ITE)

Dr Law speaking at Seminar on "Vision of Education and Training," Jubail Industrial City, Saudi Arabia, 29–30 October 2007.

Mr Tharman Shanmugaratnam (sitting, fourth from left), Minister for Education (2003–2008), congratulating ITE on winning of the Global Harvard-IBM Innovations Award, 2007. (Courtesy of ITE)

Dr Law (third from left) chairing the Singapore-World Bank Workshop on Leadership in Education and Training, Singapore, January 2008. (Courtesy of ITEES)

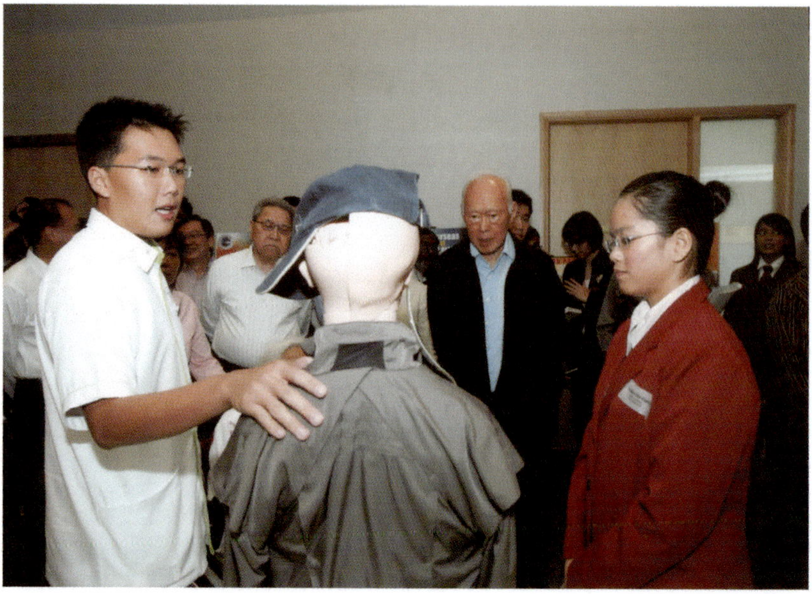

Minister Mentor Lee Kuan Yew visiting ITE College East, 21 February 2008. (Courtesy of ITE)

Dr Law speaking at the 2nd High Skills Development Forum, ILO-Chinese Ministry of Human Resources and Social Security, Shenyang, China, October 2008.

Dr Law (front, third from right) leading a Feasibility Study Team to Maputo, Mozambique, July 2009. (Courtesy of ITEES)

Dr Law (sitting, fourth from right) with participants from Industrial Training Fund (ITF), Abuja, Nigeria, in a "Train-The-Trainer" Programme in ITE, Singapore, January 2011. (Courtesy of ITEES)

The young faces behind ITE's success, ITE Headquarters at Dover Drive (1995–2012). (Courtesy of ITE)

Part III

Implications for Developing Countries

Chapter 10

Some Lessons on Building Quality and Sustainability

Building quality and sustainability in technical and vocational education and training — this is a goal that many countries aspire to achieve. This is a necessary foundation to sustain social and economic development. What would such a system be? A quality system is one focused on meeting its targeted outcomes based on strategic performance indicators such as graduate employability, student completion rate and student satisfaction rate. Sustainability means the ability of the system to adapt and transform in an increasingly competitive and global environment. Built on a sound foundation and fundamental principles, it should be able to withstand the dynamics and challenges of its operating environment. However, what will it take to build such a system — one that will continue to stay relevant, responsive and resilient? In reality, this goal remains a difficult challenge for many. Drawing on the Singapore ITE experience and international perspective in undertaking overseas projects, this chapter will share some lessons and fundamental principles on building quality and sustainability.

INTERNATIONAL CONTEXT

International organisations such as the World Bank, OECD, UNESCO and ILO, in partnership with development agencies including the United States Agency for International Development (USAID), German Society for International Cooperation (GIZ), Japan International Cooperation Agency (JICA), and Human Resources Development of Korea (Korea HRD), have extensive technical cooperation experience in education in many developing countries. While emerging countries that gained independence in the 1950s to 1960s have made successful inroads in expanding primary and secondary education, efforts at creating educational pathways in technical and vocational education and training at the post-secondary level have not been as successful. Many still face difficulties in building relevant and responsive systems. Despite the demand in the economy for graduates with technical skills, technical and vocational education and training remain an unattractive option for school leavers.

Without quality and sustainability, the image, standards, outcomes and values will remain elusive. More importantly, without a major transformation, it would be difficult, if not impossible, to achieve and sustain social and economic development. In fact, skills gaps between countries that have access to skills development and those that do not are likely to widen. The disparity in the supply and demand of well-trained technicians and skilled manpower is already apparent in both developed and developing countries. Building quality and sustainability in technical and vocational education and training are a matter of urgency for governments.

CONNECTING WITH AFRICA

I have dedicated my entire career in education for some 40 years. While I first started my work in the polytechnic and university, the later and most significant part of my career was the development of VITB (1981–1992) and transformation of ITE (1992–2007) in Singapore. Switching from the familiar in academia to vocational training which I knew little meant learning from others, working from basic principles and redefining practices. We undertook study missions to learn from the more advanced economies in Europe, America and Asia. We went in search of experience and professional expertise to build up our core capabilities. Indeed, we learned much and adapted some of the key concepts and practices that were relevant to our needs. The ITE model today is, in essence, a unique system based on a composite of international practices and our own innovations.

Looking back, I could not have anticipated that one day, I would have the privilege to reciprocate and share the Singapore ITE experience with the international community. The story of ITE's transformation began to attract international attention with the opening of ITE's first mega regional campus, ITE College East, in 2005. Following my retirement in 2007, I continued to stay engaged with overseas governments, international organisations and education institutions. It was in this advisory and consultancy capacity that I was invited, together with four other colleagues from educational institutions in Singapore, on a needs assessment mission organised by the International Enterprise Singapore (IE Singapore) in collaboration with the World Bank, to three African countries — Madagascar, Ghana and Mozambique — in March 2007. Fortuitously, it was my introductory step to Africa.

In the foreword to a World Bank publication, *An African Exploration of the East Asian Education Experience*, Dr Yaw Ansu, then Director of Human Resource Development for African Region at the World Bank, wrote:

> In their quest for educational development, African leaders are keen to examine the experience of other countries for possible adaptations to their own contexts. The story of East Asian countries holds special appeal in this regard. Four or five decades ago many of these countries started from conditions quite similar from African countries, and since have managed to turn their colonial-era systems into highly effective instruments for national development... Responding to this interest, the World Bank sponsored an education study tour to Singapore and Vietnam in June 2006. Among the participants were senior education policy makers from six African countries... Perhaps the most striking is the indispensable role assigned to the education and training system as a driver of sustained economic growth and social development. (Fredriksen & Tan, 2008)

Commenting specifically on the importance of technical and vocational education and training, Fredriksen and Tan wrote:

> For most participants, the discussions and the visits to TVET [technical and vocational education and training] institutions in Singapore and Vietnam were perhaps the single-most interesting aspect of the study tour... Successful cultivation of TVET capacities is perhaps the most complex of all the education and training challenges facing industrial and developing countries alike... The site visits revealed other attractive aspects of the Singapore system. For example, the teaching equipment at all the TVET institutions typically was current by industry standards;

> students routinely worked on projects commissioned by private industry as part of their final year studies; and graduates enjoy high rates of employment. By creating strong demand from employers, the "poor image" problem traditionally associated with TVET institutions, has been kept at bay. (2008, p. 15)

The interest in the Singapore ITE experience by African countries further deepened when I was invited by the World Bank to share the Singapore experience on three platforms in Maputo, Mozambique, in May 2008.

The first was at the "Third Meeting of the External Advisory Panel for a Regional Flagship on Tertiary Education and Economic Growth & Competitiveness in Africa". In reference to the urgency for a technological catch-up, the conference report *Accelerating Catch-up — Tertiary Education for Growth in Sub-Saharan Africa* said, "East Asian economies are all committed to knowledge-based development because they now see the advances in technological capabilities as inseparable from growing economies" (World Bank, 2009).

Secondly, I had the privilege to share "A Peer Review Process" research methodology as a resource person for the Caucus of Ministers of Education Meeting held in conjunction with the Biennial Conference of the Association for the Development of Education in Africa (ADEA). The interest was to see how this qualitative ethnographic approach (Metzger et al., 2001) could add new perspectives to an existing pilot project on "Peer Review in Education in Africa".

Thirdly, I was invited to speak on "Pathways for Post-Secondary Education — The Singapore Experience" in a parallel session at the ADEA Biennial Conference. The conference is the most important meeting of the educational cooperation community in Africa. A sub-theme of this 2008 Conference was "Skills Development and the World of Work". Birger Fredricksen, who chaired the session, shared with me that:

> Many people told me after the session how much they appreciated learning about the Singapore experience… Indeed, I think that

> how to go about addressing these challenges [in TVET] was perhaps the single-most frequently raised concern in the many sessions during the conference. This illustrated both the urgency and complexity of how to move ahead... Among other things, I think your presentation made them appreciate the key role TVET must play in supporting a dynamic economy... ITE is already having a positive influence on the way policymakers in many African countries think about how to reform their TVET system.

MY PERSONAL PERSPECTIVE

Africa is the second largest continent with a land mass of 30.2 million square kilometres, home to 57 countries and a population of over one billion people. The needs assessment mission to Madagascar, Ghana and Mozambique in 2007 and the ADEA Biennial Conference 2008 in Maputo, Mozambique, had given me a wider perspective of the realities and enormous challenges faced by political leaders and policymakers in Africa. I saw the challenging conditions in schools and vocational institutions. However, in the political, social and economic diversity, there is potential and opportunity for change. Africa has a young population and is open to foreign investment. There is a sense of hope and achievement driven by the keen desire to learn from the success and experience of other countries.

Africa has vast natural resources (e.g., minerals, agriculture and marine) but face problems in long-term economic growth. The investments in the 1960s have not been easy to sustain. While many countries have greatly expanded primary education, they face tremendous difficulties in introducing market-relevant secondary and post-secondary education. Some countries spend 4 to 6 per cent of GDP in education but failed to achieve results comparable to the East Asian countries. Reform policies and strategies have not met expectations. Existing systems continue to reflect a strong preference for an academic education. The attempt to provide TVET in the school curriculum as a transition from school to work has not been successful. The common issues concerning a poor image, lack of qualified teachers with practical experience, inaccessibility and limited resources for TVET persist.

International conferences on TVET have shown that there already exists a rich resource of information, experience and analyses. Leaders and policymakers recognise the importance and urgency in skills development. There is no shortage of ideas and suggestions from the many research studies and analyses, e.g., World Bank (1991, 2007), Johanson and Adams (2004) and OECD (2010). There are no secrets to success. What then could be the missing elements? For some, it may be the lack of focus on the "what, when, how and why" of strategies and realistic action plans. While no two TVET systems are the same, valuable lessons and fundamental principles can be adapted to local needs. It is not feasible to simply transplant a training model, which may have worked successfully in another country. Building a quality and sustainable TVET system is a long-term commitment. It takes perseverance, efforts and resources.

The opportunity to dialogue with political and educational leaders has enabled me to reflect more deeply and distil the Singapore ITE experience in having addressed the dynamics and challenges of our transformation. The underlying question is how the Singapore experience may help to make a difference in developing countries? What are some key lessons and fundamental principles we can draw on and share with others? It is in this spirit that I was moved to write this book. In this way, I hope that Singapore's experience can be shared with a wider audience.

LESSONS FROM SINGAPORE'S EXPERIENCE

Singapore ITE's system of vocational and technical education may be a world-class model today, but it had its share of obstacles and challenges in the earlier years of development. The political, social and economic conditions following independence in 1965 were difficult and made the country vulnerable. The birth of Singapore as an independent nation through separation from Malaysia was sudden. For a tiny island left on its own, without natural resources or a hinterland, the problems of survival as a young nation seemed insurmountable. The earlier than planned pullout of the British naval bases soon after compounded an already volatile environment with political instability, high unemployment and social unease in a growing population. Many believed at the time that Singapore would not make it. Indeed, the nation's survival was at stake.

However, through the sheer political will of the people, hard work and a strong and effective government, Singapore eventually succeeded in transforming itself from a "Third World" nation to the "First World" (Lee, 2000). It was under these conditions that saw the evolution of a TVET system focused on responding to the skilled manpower needs of an emerging economy. In this respect, it took a government that not only believed in but also invested heavily in education at all levels to make a difference. In particular, attention was not only paid to the university and polytechnic but also vocational and technical education. This political foresight, prioritisation of resources and continuous commitment eventually led to the development of the system of vocational training in Singapore.

The following are some key lessons.

Policy Shift Towards TVET and Economic Development

There was very little TVET prior to Singapore's independence. The limited primary and educational places available in general education were geared towards preparing white-collar workers for the clerical and administrative jobs in the colonial civil service. This posed a major obstacle when priority shifted towards economic development through the process of industrialisation. There was limited education and training infrastructure, a dearth of trained manpower and a workforce without the relevant skills. It was therefore a farsighted government that began to pursue a policy of relentless and systematic development of education and training in keeping with each phase of economic development. The role of the Singapore Polytechnic and vocational schools in the educational system was realigned with the manpower needs for industrialisation.

It was a painful and slow process in the beginning. With limited resources, the expansion of the technical education system had to make do with basic school buildings, shared centralised workshop facilities and even crash programmes for training of technical teachers. With each phase of economic restructuring and development, the educational and training institutions were called upon to respond to the needs of emerging industries. Then there was the urgency in establishing the first Industrial Training Board (ITB) in 1973. It was a clear policy shift to expand TVET and to do it through the formalisation of a system of pre-employment training for young school leavers outside the school system. As a statutory board, ITB was empowered with greater autonomy in governance. The objective was to have the flexibility to respond to changing social and economic needs. This then became the present day model of TVET in Singapore, a system that is subject to periodic reviews and restructuring. Another milestone policy decision change was the repositioning of vocational training from a post-primary to a post-secondary system under the present ITE in 1992 (see Chapter 6).

Changing Public Perception and Image

Singapore started industrialisation without the benefit of tradition or experience in production and manufacturing. Culturally, there was a steep preference for an academic education. Parents want their children to attend university. The desire for a university degree is pervasive in society. The respect for the "scholar" and disdain for the "mechanic" and all associations with those who do poorly in school and perform manual labour only helped to perpetuate the poor image of vocational training. To overcome this barrier and change people's mindset, public campaigns on "using the hand" were necessary and basic workshop subjects such as metalwork, woodwork, technical drawing and basic electricity were made compulsory for all secondary students. Top-of-the-trade television competitions and Apprenticeship of the Year awards were used to create interest and promote the importance of technical skills among the young. Eventually, as the economy grew and vocational graduates were recognised with high employability and successful careers, the acceptance of TVET and its image gradually improved.

Extensive efforts in communications, marketing and branding continue even today towards building a positive image of TVET in Singapore.

Modern and conducive teaching and learning campuses, strong support of political leaders and success of graduates have all helped to achieve a significant turnaround in the public perception and image of ITE. Today, ITE's unique brand of college education, "Hands-on, Minds-on and Hearts-on", is synonymous with world-class standards and global leadership in technical education.

Leveraging on Industry Partnership

The main approach in TVET in Singapore is a full-time pre-employment system of institutional training for school leavers with ten years of general education. The availability of technical manpower was an important strategic tool used by the Economic Development Board (EDB) in promoting foreign direct investment in Singapore. However, the formal system at the time was not able to ensure the sufficiency and range of skills required by industry. It was necessary, especially in the early phases of industrialisation, to leverage on the experience, skills and technology that resided in the private sector companies. Many of these were foreign MNCs that needed specialised skills and had in-housing training capabilities that were not available or too costly to develop in the formal TVET system. To meet these skills gaps, incentives were offered as part of total investment packages by the EDB in setting up joint government training centres and technical institutes in cooperation with MNCs and foreign governments. These institutions were eventually absorbed into the Nanyang Polytechnic and ITE. This experience demonstrated an important phase of economic development when it was necessary to leverage on foreign government assistance and private sector industry partners in complementing the formal TVET system.

There are other forms of partnership that are important to ensure that the TVET system stays relevant and responsive to changing manpower needs. ITE, for example, works closely with major sectors of business and industry in the curriculum development process. Industries, as potential employers, have much to contribute in defining the skills competencies, standards and values required of the graduates. It also promotes and facilitates industry-based training (IBT) by employers. In this respect, various IBT schemes, such as the Traineeship Scheme, Approved Training Centre, Certified On-the-Job-Training Centre and Approved Training Provider, have been established over the years. These industry-based training schemes are designed to better meet the needs of individual employers and are partially funded by government. To stay technologically up to date, joint centres of excellence are established in ITE campuses in partnership with industry leaders. This close partnership between ITE and industry complements the formal national TVET system for the continuous development and upgrading of the workforce.

Transformation of TVET: It can be done

ITE is neither a university nor a polytechnic. It is a government-funded post-secondary institution focusing on vocational and technical education. Today, it is widely recognised for its transformation into a world-class education institution. The first to win the Singapore Quality Award in 2005, ITE has created a unique brand of college education for a quarter of every school cohort and many working adults in Singapore. It has achieved a breakthrough in TVET.

So, what are some of the success factors? Strong political commitment, appropriate policy decisions, community partnership, management leadership and staff commitment are necessary ingredients. In ITE, there is constancy of purpose in pursuing its mission, vision and values. The consistent use of five-year strategic plans has provided a clear focus and platform for implementing many of the initiatives and programmes. It has built a strong team of leaders and staff who are professionally qualified and dedicated to the cause of TVET. Their commitment and enthusiasm to achieve the mission and goals are reflected in the "ITE Care" culture, especially the care and concern of the staff for the students. Embedded in this culture is the relentless pursuit of organisational excellence and pro-active approach in always asking how they can better serve, add value and meet the needs of students, stakeholders and partners.

There is an open willingness to learn from and adapt the best practices from other educational systems in building our own — in using the pedagogic concept of key competencies from Germany, the Developing a

Curriculum (DACUM) methodology from the United States and on-the-job-training practices from Japan. The goals and concerns in TVET may be the same, but the systems are unique and shaped by the schools, industry and needs of the local community. And so with a strategic plan and new vision every five years, the journey of ITE's transformation continues.

FUNDAMENTAL PRINCIPLES

The dynamics and challenges of TVET are complex and unique. Underlying the key lessons are the sorts of leadership, policy choices, governance system, expertise, capabilities, investments and ingenuity needed to achieve a major transformation. But, beyond these key lessons, are the fundamental principles. They represent the foundation that adds strength and robustness to a sustainable TVET system. They are the benchmark against which an existing system may be assessed and validated. Consultants and experts may have their own approaches and methodologies in the conduct of strategic reviews and needs assessments. But, a checklist of fundamental principles can serve as a useful guide for professionals and practitioners in building quality and sustainability. This practical guide will also be useful to teachers who want to have a better understanding of the inner workings of a TVET system.

Such a guide on fundamental principles was developed as shown in Box 10.1. Based on a practitioner's experience, it has been refined in the course of presentation in leadership training workshops. Viewed from a total systems perspective, the principles are broadly banded in three levels: strategic, tactical and operational. All principles are of fundamental importance. Each fundamental principle carries a brief description of the kinds of qualitative elements one would expect to find in the system. For example, on the fundamental principle on "leadership" at the strategic level are the important elements of visionary leadership, political support, transparency and consultative engagement. The principle on "organisational excellence" at the tactical level would underline the drive to pursue excellence and better serve students and stakeholders. Likewise, under the operational principle on "culture and care", are the elements of commitment, ownership and a culture of care for students.

BOX 10.1 FUNDAMENTAL PRINCIPLES ON BUILDING QUALITY AND SUSTAINABILITY

No.	A. Strategic	Qualitative Elements
1.	Leadership	Visionary leadership with political and governmental support at the highest level. Valuing and respecting people. A leadership that inspires commitment, teamwork and trust in management and staff. Leadership sets clear direction, the tone and culture in leading the organisation to achieve its mission and goals. Being transparent and consultative in engaging with staff and stakeholders.
2.	Mission and governance	Clarity in statutory provisions on system of governance, responsibilities, autonomy and accountabilities. Staying focused on mission, vision and values. Policies, goals and objectives are well aligned at the governing board, departmental and institutional levels.
3.	Long-term commitment	Long-term commitment in funding and assurance of stable and adequate resources. Up-to-date and well-maintained training facilities and a conducive teaching and learning environment. Financial support for students in need.
4.	Positioning of TVET	Strategic positioning and coordination as an integral part of the education and training system. Addressing the needs of the less academic cohort of school leavers and working adults. Earning the trust and support of parents, principals, teachers and the community.
5.	Economic alignment	System aligned with and responsive to national skilled manpower needs. Market-relevant, enterprising and adaptable graduates with high employability for a global economy.
6.	Brand and image	Changing public perception and building a positive image. Creating a unique brand attractive to school leavers. Efforts in communicating, marketing and branding. Reaching out to schools, parents, industry and community.

(*Continued*)

BOX 10.1 (CONTINUED)

No.	B. Tactical	Qualitative Elements
7.	Strategic plans	Consistent use of strategic plans with clear goals, strategies, programmes and values. Adequate information system in tracking change and transformation. Adopting strategic performance indicators, setting targets and regular reviews of performance and results.
8.	Organisational excellence	Continuous pursuit of organisational excellence at all levels. Pro-active in seeking better ways to serve, add value and meet needs of students and stakeholders. Open to learning and benchmarking against best practices.
9.	Industry partnership	Leveraging on the knowledge, skills, experience and technology in industry to stay current and responsive to change. Partnerships in curriculum design and development, supporting industry-based training and joint establishment of centres of excellence.
10.	Curriculum and pedagogy	Rigorous competency-based curriculum design and development model. Strong foundation in core occupational modules and life skills for lifelong learning. A process-oriented pedagogic model promoting "thinking doers" and focusing on three key competencies: technical, methodological and social.
No.	**C. Operational**	**Qualitative Elements**
11.	College management	Management leadership in TVET colleges that achieves educational outcomes. Professionally qualified teachers who stay relevant and up-to-date through continual learning and development. Providing a conducive teaching and learning environment with supportive student services.
12.	Holistic "hands-on" education	An education that goes beyond the traditional acquisition of "hands-on" vocational skills. The modern economy requires graduates who have lifelong learning skills and

(Continued)

BOX 10.1 (CONTINUED)

		are being developed holistically through extra-curricular activities such as sports, arts, music, community service and a global education.
13.	Culture and care	A sense of commitment and ownership, among leaders and staff. Believing and living a culture of care, especially, the care and concern of the teaching staff for students. Staff with dedication and passion, reaching out to and transforming the lives of students.

A practical guide is useful, but on its own, will not bring about change. On the other hand, it would be difficult and too presumptuous for anyone to prescribe the "solutions" in developing a TVET system without a deep understanding of the dynamics and conditions in individual countries. In this respect, I believe that the approach to and manner of engagement in undertaking TVET projects in developing countries need more care and attention. There must be a clear understanding of the goals, objectives and commitment among cooperating partners. Advisors and consultants can help to shape better policy decisions, define strategic directions and formulate project proposals. This is a necessary and important step. The consultative approach should be holistic and strategic with clear outcomes to make an impact in the people, systems and processes. Ultimately, the political leaders, overseeing government authorities and partner institutions must collectively take charge and responsibility in seeing through the commitment, coordination and implementation.

SHARING ITE'S EXPERIENCE

The first step of engagement in a consultancy project for a government agency or institution is normally a strategic review, feasibility study or needs assessment, depending on the overall scope and objectives. The consultancy approach begins with a systems view of the total environment in which TVET operates and the needs for change. The project goals should be strategic but not too idealistic. Here, one must ensure that the leader and team of consultants are selected with the relevant level of experience and expertise. A project of strategic importance, for example, would need a senior advisor or team leader whose experience and insights will help to shape better policies and decisions. Building a TVET system is not a theoretical or academic exercise. The "solutions" should be practical and customised to local needs. Expectations are better tempered with relevance, quality and sustainability. It is to be expected that political, social and cultural differences will arise in undertaking international projects. These challenges should not be underestimated.

Building credibility, mutual trust and flexibility among partners are crucial aspects in a successful project implementation. To achieve this, leadership, wisdom, experience and judgment can make a difference. In this respect, it would be an advantage if the project were undertaken directly by a consultancy company that can readily leverage the wider in-house experience and resources in an established educational institution. It was with this in mind that ITE Education Services (ITEES) was established in 2003 as a private consultancy company to better engage and share ITE's experience with other countries.

Leveraging on the experience of ITE and its predecessor institutions of more than forty years, ITEES has shared and extended the Singapore experience with other countries (Box 10.2). The needs for each project are assessed taking into consideration, the local conditions, key lessons and fundamental principles. One of the first projects undertaken on behalf of the Singapore government was the Vietnam-Singapore Technical Training Centre in Ho Chi Minh City, Vietnam. The objective was to provide quality technical training to high school leavers in support of the skilled manpower needs of the Vietnam-Singapore Industrial Park as part of Vietnam's industrialisation plan.

Carried out over eight years, this project included the design and development of five courses, setting up the facilities and training 30 Vietnamese

BOX 10.2 FACTSHEET ON ITEES' KEY OVERSEAS PROJECTS

No.	Country	Project
1.	Vietnam (Aug 1997–Dec 2005)	Establishing and operating a Vietnam-Singapore Technical Training Centre in Binh Duong Province. Under an MOU between the Governments of Singapore and Vietnam, the objective was to train high school leavers for the skilled manpower needs of the Vietnam-Singapore Industrial Park (VSIP) in support of Vietnam's industrialisation programme. A project funded by the Singapore government, the consultancy services included needs assessment, curriculum development, equipment purchase, workshop set-ups, training of instructors and administrators and on-site deployment of ITE staff. Five ITE-type courses in Electrical Maintenance, Mechanical Maintenance, Machining, Electronics and Mechatronics were adapted at two appropriate skills levels for an annual intake capacity of 300 students.
2.	Jordan (Jul 2006–Sep 2007)	Setting up a Regional Vocational Training Centre (RVTC) for the Vocational Training Corporation of Jordan in its Technical Training Institute in Amman, Jordan. The aim was to provide short training courses in air-conditioning to upgrade the skills of practitioners from public and private institutions in the Middle East. The consultancy involved curriculum development and teaching materials, equipment purchase, installing and commissioning and conducting short training courses. Funded by the Singapore government, the Centre has a training capacity of 40 places a year.
3.	China (Apr 2007–Jun 2008)	The design, development and implementation of two Overseas Training and Test Centres (OTTC) for Rotary Engineering Limited, a Singapore listed company, in Dalian and Fushun, China. The setting up of these centres is part of Rotary's Global Workforce project to further enhance its position as a leading service provider in EPCM (Engineering,

(Continued)

BOX 10.2 (CONTINUED)

No.	Country	Project
		Procurement, Construction and Maintenance) in the Process Industry. Privately funded by the company, the consultancy included identification of skills competencies and standards, development of courses, workshop set-ups, instructor training and on-site skills training and testing.
4.	Nigeria (Oct 2008–current)	Establishing a Model Skills Training Centre (MSTC) for the Industrial Training Fund (ITF) Board of Nigeria in Abuja, Nigeria. The goal is to upgrade the quality and standards of vocational training by modelling after the Singapore ITE system and its best practices. The Centre will conduct five ITE-certifiable two-year full-time courses in Facility Technology, Information Communications Technology, Mechatronics, Electronics and Culinary Skills (Western). A project funded by ITF, the comprehensive range of consultancy services covers needs assessment, project formulation, curriculum development, instructor training, equipment specifications, workshop set-ups, on-site staff deployment and project execution and management. The Centre is built for an annual intake capacity of 100 students.
5.	Thailand, Philippines, Vietnam, Cambodia, Indonesia, Myanmar, Laos and Sri Lanka (2009–2012)	These are capacity building projects for leaders, administrators, curriculum specialists and training instructors customised to the needs of different countries. Largely funded by the Temasek Foundation, a non-profit philanthropic organisation based in Singapore, these training programmes provide a valuable first-hand learning experience for participants in ITE. The sharing of experience includes the transformation of ITE, leadership, organisational excellence, governance, strategic planning, curriculum development, pedagogy and college management. A total of 2,500 participants have benefited from these projects.

instructors and administrators. A team of one director and seven department heads from ITE was also deployed over different periods in Vietnam to spearhead the management and operation of the centre before its transfer to the Vietnam management staff in 2005. In this case, short but intensive six-month courses were customised to meet the needs of new investors in the Industrial Park. Priority was placed on building capability in curriculum development and the training of instructors. The Vietnam-Singapore Technical Training Centre, with its modern campus environment, up-to-date training facilities, professionally trained staff and close links with industry, was held up as a model for quality training in Vietnam.

Similarly, the same approach and principles were applied in formulating proposals for the projects in Jordan, China and Nigeria. The needs varied from the upgrading of instructors to skills certification of workers and pre-employment training of young school leavers respectively. More recently, working in partnership with the Temasek Foundation, a non-profit philanthropic organisation based in Singapore, ITEES has been focusing on capability development projects for leaders, administrators, curriculum specialists and instructors. Since 2009, the participating countries include Thailand, Philippines, Vietnam, Cambodia, Indonesia, Myanmar, Laos and Sri Lanka. In this model of collaboration, ITEES is the project manager while ITE is the "expert" institution with in-house professional experience and expertise. Temasek Foundation is the major funding partner for these projects. With programmes conducted both in the receiving partner countries and Singapore, participants can see and experience for themselves what it takes to build a world-class educational institution in vocational training.

Chapter 11

Concluding Reflections

The "what, when, how and why" as captured in this book tell the story of ITE's breakthrough in vocational and technical education in Singapore. Does this mean that the ITE model is the only possible way to a successful system in vocational training? The answer is an emphatic "no". There are other very successful models such as the dual system of apprenticeship in Germany or Switzerland. Neither should it be assumed that a model that works well in one country can be easily transplanted without care and due adaptation. Any purposeful transformation or restructuring of a system will take much concerted efforts in time, coordination, commitment and resources. In the case of ITE, the transformation was driven by dynamics and challenges involving many factors — political, educational, social and economic. A successful outcome was never a given. Underlying the policy changes and initiatives are leaders and people. Building a vocational training system is a long-term commitment. With political will, the right policies and support of all stakeholders, change is possible. ITE is one such story. Even then, the work is never done as ITE must continue to adapt and transform itself to remain relevant as social and economic conditions change.

PERSONAL RECOLLECTIONS

At the retirement dinner held in my honour on 2 February 2007, I jokingly said:

> As this is my last official function as CEO of ITE, I hope that you will bear with me if my response this evening seems to take longer than my normal speeches. After all, I will be sharing with you a journey of 39 years of continuous service in education, including the Singapore Polytechnic, National University of Singapore (NUS), VITB and ITE. There are so many things to tell. But, personally, the last 25 years of challenges in the transformation of VITB and ITE has been the most exciting, meaningful and rewarding. And for this, I want to thank all of you this evening for having contributed to, supported and travelled with me in this educational journey.

The call to serve VITB came from the late Dr Tay Eng Soon, then Minister of State for Education in 1981. At 36 years old and not knowing much about vocational training, I accepted the assignment. Switching from the academic world at NUS to take administrative charge of VITB was an act of faith. The task was daunting. I committed myself, followed my heart and persevered. What was supposed to be a two-year secondment lasted 25 years. And I have no regrets. In stepping down, I have the great satisfaction in knowing that ITE has made a real difference in the lives of many Singaporeans. A dream beyond all dreams, ITE has become a Singapore success story.

I take with me many fond memories. But the most memorable moment must be ITE winning the Singapore Quality Award in 2005. This will long be remembered as the hallmark in the history of vocational training in Singapore. Receiving the award on behalf of ITE on 4 October 2005, I said:

> Winning the SQA is a milestone achievement for any organisation. For ITE, it means the national recognition of our transformation as a world-class post-secondary institution focusing on vocational education and skills. It reaffirms our belief and success in offering a unique ITE brand of "Hands-on, Minds-on and Hearts-on" college education... To my staff in ITE, I thank you all for seeing us through in this journey of continuous and dynamic transformation. This award belongs to each and every one of you.

The Singapore Quality Award was our top prize. ITE was hailed as a technical education institution equal to the best in the world. There were imminent signs that ITE was going to be a strong contender for the SQA in 2005. The first indication was the opening of ITE College East, in January 2005. The public was amazed by what they saw in the mega regional campus — a sprawling college with modern teaching facilities. Foreign visitors were impressed and wished that they could have the same. Secondly, people were talking about ITE's creative rebranding campaigns. Portraying the success of ITE graduates and their role in society, the public perception and image of ITE had turned around. The confidence of ITE staff and students was further boosted when ITE's brand of "Hands-on, Minds-on and Hearts-on" education was publicly endorsed by Prime Minister Lee Hsien Loong in his National Day Speech in August 2005.

When news of ITE winning the Singapore Quality Award broke, the feeling was simply euphoric. We received many congratulatory messages. The excerpts below convey the kinds of feelings and extent of internal and public endorsement:

- "I want to say 'thank you' for leading ITE to such honour and glory. Yesterday, as I watched you receiving the coveted SQA, I went through an indescribable mixture of feelings — of gratitude, of being blessed to be part of our beautiful organisation, and mostly of pride that we have come this far. I want to add that I have been and shall always be proud and honoured to be part of ITE, and to have worked under your able leadership..." (ITE staff, e-mail dated 5 October 2005).
- "Your winning shows the commitment to quality and demonstrates that everyone in Singapore can be a winner. Being an institution with humble beginnings ourselves, I am equally excited about your winning and achievement — and I am motivated to follow the lead that you have shown..." (private education institution, letter dated 5 October 2005).
- "The award is a solid testament to your efforts in operating a world-class business environment... ITE has produced well-rounded graduates and elevated its status among the technical education community through its philosophy — 'Hands-on, Minds-on, Hearts-on'..." (international company, e-mail dated 13 October 2005).
- "ITE has managed to overcome all the challenges before it... The indomitable spirit and adaptability of ITE epitomises the essential attributes of excellence that any organisation must possess in order to sustain and remain competitive over time and geographical boundaries..." (member of ITE advisory committee, letter dated 25 October 2005).

Strategic plans, initiatives and innovations are important building blocks of a system or institution. Lest we forget, these are only the means, the "hardware" and "software" in the form of regional campuses, training programmes and institutional capabilities. What a successful and high-performing organisation must also have are the "leaders and people" who share a common mission, vision and values. Approaches to leadership may vary but an organisational transformation would not be possible unless rooted in a culture of commitment, teamwork, trust and engagement that binds together the leaders and people involved. This culture is the "heart ware" behind ITE's success.

Good leadership is fundamental in setting the direction, tone and organisational climate. In ITE, the "ITE Care" culture is the most valuable asset. Nurtured and strengthened over the years, ITE Care is not just for the management and staff. It expresses that extra sense of dedication, passion and care in the way lecturers engage with students. How would I view my own leadership? A quiet servant-leader, I would say. I believe in people-centred management. I take a systems approach in problem-solving. Setting high standards, I encourage management and staff to work collaboratively as a team through open discussion and consultation. This bears itself out in the feedback from others:

- "I credit you, your team and your Board for your strength of vision..." (president of a foreign educational institute, October 2002).
- "Looking back, I must say that I have learned a lot in terms of the way you question underlying assumptions in papers, you constantly challenge us to map our ideas against market realities and you single out details in the most meticulous way without losing sight of the BIG Picture..." (senior college staff after leaving ITE, October 2005).
- "I would like to thank you for your mentoring and guidance over the years. I have learned much from you, in particular, your high standards, objectivity, focused approach to problems and sharp analysis..." (retired ITE management staff, December 2005).
- "Your conviction and belief have infused the Institution with the attitude of continuous improvements and motivated ITE students to reach new heights of excellence..." (Minister for Education, December 2006).
- "Your visionary leadership, steadfastness in implementation and care for your staff and students is an example to all of us..." (ITE Board member, February 2007).

In achieving all that we did, ITE did not work alone. We had many champions and supporters among the stakeholders, including political leaders, the ITE Board, Ministry of Education and other government agencies, unions, industries and community. We had learned from our international partners especially in the earlier days of our development. Moreover, the success of ITE needs to be measured ultimately by the success of our graduates, not by what we did. To me, the graduates' success has always been our commitment. It has been a privilege and honour to have served in a sector that matters most in society. I also thank the late Dr Tay Eng Soon for his trust in me. We may not always be the authors of our life journey but I have no regrets in having said "yes" when I was called to serve. The Bible has a verse that says, "In his heart a man plans his course, but the Lord determines his steps." My wish is that ITE will continue to play a key role in Singapore's education system and expand its global leadership in sharing its experience with the international community.

CLOSING THOUGHTS

The dynamics and challenges in TVET are unique. The Singapore experience is not and cannot be expected to be the same as that of Germany, Switzerland, United States, Japan, South Korea or China. Each system has evolved over time. What we see are the different models reflecting the social and economic needs of the nation and people. The important test is that the system is relevant and responsive to changing needs.

What then are the implications for developing economies? What are the possible steps and choices? What general advice do I have? Taking the next steps towards change will always be challenging. The first step is the most difficult but necessary. Each country must first carefully assess and decide what system or model is best suited to their needs. There are key lessons and fundamental principles one can consider. Making the right policy decisions and choices is of strategic importance. One should never stop learning from the experience of others.

Given its importance, governments should take primary responsibility for TVET. There must be a clear mandate and commitment to invest in its development. A degree of continuity in political support and professional leadership is necessary to achieve longer-term goals. It would help if there were a champion for TVET at the highest level of government. This individual should be someone who can garner support among partners and stakeholders in government, industries and unions. The "traditional" model of vocational education in schools as a transition to work may no longer be sufficient or relevant in meeting the needs of a modern society and economy. Such a system needs to be redefined and empowered with greater autonomy and flexibility if it were to respond to changing social and economic needs.

In closing, the question today is no longer about the importance and value of TVET. Irrespective of the different models, the focus should be on building quality and sustainability for economic growth and transformation. There are strategic policy decisions, priorities and choices to be made. I hope that leaders and practitioners will find in this account an inspiration to shape a vision that will transform TVET systems according to their needs.

> Some men see things as they are and ask, "Why?" I dream things that never were and ask, "Why not?"
>
> — Robert F. Kennedy

List of Abbreviations

ADEA	Association for the Development of Education in Africa
AEB	Adult Education Board
ATC	Approved Training Centre
AVA	American Vocational Association
AVC	Alberta Vocational College
BEI	Brand Equity Index
BEST	Basic Education for Skills Training
BOG	Board of Governors
BPO	Business Process Outsourcing
BSC	Balanced Scorecard
BVT	Basic Vocational Training
CBS	Certificate in Business Studies
CET	Continuing Education and Training
CETE	Center on Education and Training for Employment
CoC	Certificate of Competency
COJTC	Certified OJT Training Centre

COM	Certificate of Merit
COS	Certificate of Office Skills
COTVET	Council for Technical and Vocational Education and Training
CPTE	Council on Professional and Technical Education
CVT	Centre of Vocational Training
CWP	Corporate Work Plan
DACUM	Developing a Curriculum
EDB	Economic Development Board
ERC	Economic Review Committee
ESC	Economic Strategies Committee
GCE "A"	General Certificate of Education "Advanced" Level
GCE "N"	General Certificate of Education "Normal" Level
GCE "O"	General Certificate of Education "Ordinary" Level
GDP	Gross Domestic Product
GIZ	German Society for International Cooperation
IBT	Industry-based Training
IE	Singapore International Enterprise Singapore
ILC	Innovation & Learning Circle
ILO	International Labour Organization
IMechE	Institution of Mechanical Engineers
IPSC	ITE Productivity Steering Committee
IPSSC	ITE PS21 Steering Committee
ISC	ITE Skills Certificate
ISE	Industrial & Systems Engineering
IT	Information Technology
ITB	Industrial Training Board
ITC	Industrial Technician Certificate
ITE	Institute of Technical Education
ITEAASB	ITE Administrative and Ancillary Staff Branch
ITEES	ITE Education Services Pte Ltd
ITF	Industrial Training Fund
JICA	Japan International Cooperation Agency

KM	Ministry of Education, Youth and Sports, Baden-Württemberg, Germany
Korea HRD	Human Resource Development of Korea
KPI	Key Performance Indicator
MNC	Multinational Corporation
MOE	Ministry of Education
MOM	Ministry of Manpower
MOST	Modular Skills Training
MOU	Memorandum of Understanding
MVV	Mission, Vision and Values
NAS	New Apprenticeship System
NCRVE	National Center for Research in Vocational Education
NES	New Education System
Nitec	National ITE Certificate
NMC	National Manpower Council
NPB	National Productivity Board
NPCEC	National Productivity and Continuing Education Council
NQCC	National Quality Control Circle
NTC	National Trade Certificate
NTU	Nanyang Technological University
NTUC	National Trade Union Congress
NUS	National University of Singapore
OECD	Organisation for Economic Cooperation and Development
Off-JT	Off-the-Job Training
OJT	On-the-Job Training
OTTC	Overseas Training and Test Centre
P8E	Primary 8 Extended
P8M	Primary 8 Monolingual
PAP	People's Action Party
PBS	Public Broadcasting Station
PCM	People-Centred Management
PDA	People Developer Award

PEPP	Plan, Explore, Practise and Perform
PEST	Political, Economic, Social and Technological
PS21	Public Service for the 21st Century
PSC	Public Service Commission
PSLE	Primary School Leaving Examination
PTT	Public Trade Test
PUB	Public Utilities Board
PVT	Pre-Vocational Training
QC	Quality Circle
QCC	Quality Control Circle
RVTC	Regional Vocational Training Centre
SBF	Singapore Business Federation
SDF	Skills Development Fund
SIT	Singapore Institute of Technology
SMA	Singapore Manufacturers Association
SME	Small and Medium-Sized Enterprise
SMU	Singapore Management University
SNEF	Singapore National Employers Federation
SP	Singapore Polytechnic
SPI	Strategic Performance Indicator
SPUR	Skills Programme for Upgrading and Resilience
SQA	Singapore Quality Award
SQC	Singapore Quality Class
SSS	Selectivity, Scalability and Sustainability
STI	Singapore Technical Institute
SUTD	Singapore University of Technology and Design
SWOT	Strengths, Weaknesses, Opportunities and Threats
TAC	Trade Advisory Committee
TEC	Training & Enterprise Council
TED	Technical Education Department
TIME	Training Initiative for Mature Employees
TVET	Technical and Vocational Education and Training
UITS	Union of ITE Training Staff

UNESCO	United Nations Educational, Scientific and Cultural Organization
UniSIM	SIM University
USAID	United States Agency for International Development
VITB	Vocational and Industrial Training Board
VPSC	VITB Productivity Steering Committee
VSIP	Vietnam-Singapore Industrial Park
VSTTC	Vietnam-Singapore Technical Training Centre
VTE	Vocational and Technical Education
WDA	Workforce Development Agency
WITs	Work Improvement Teams
WISE	Worker Improvement through Secondary Education
WSQ	Workforce Skills Qualifications

References

Achievements of overseas students praised (1967, December 29). *The New Zealand Herald.*

Chan, C.B. (lead author). (2002). *Heart Work*. Singapore: Singapore Economic Development Board and EDB Society.

Chan, C.K. (1961). *Report of the Commission of Inquiry into Vocational and Technical Education in Singapore*. Singapore: Government Printing Office.

Chan, F. (2010, July 3). ESC panel offering ideas on productivity. *The Straits Times.*

Chiang, M. (1998). *From economic debacle to economic miracle: The history and development of technical education in Singapore*. Singapore: Times Edition.

Chua, C.H. (2003, December 27). Harnessing China's people power. *The Straits Times.*

COTVET. (2010, June 1). COTVET, city and guilds to change image of skills training. *Modern Ghana News.*

Davie, S. (2011, October 28). More new varsity places for poly grads. *The Straits Times.*

Digest. (1998). *Vocational education's image for the 21st Century*. Columbus, Ohio: ERIC Clearing House.

Dobby, E.U.G. (1953). *Report of the Committee on a polytechnic institute for Singapore*. Singapore: Government Printing Office.

Dr Law is new VITB director (1981, June). *The Business Times.*
Editorial: A welcome fillip (1992, April 3). *The Straits Times.*
Federal Ministry of Education and Research. (2003). Brochure. Germany's Vocational Education at a Glance. Bonn: Federal Ministry of Education and Research.
Fredriksen, B. & Tan, J.P. (Eds.). (2008). *An African exploration of the East Asian education experience.* Washington, D.C.: The World Bank.
Garekar, B. (2007, September 25). ITE wins prestigious Harvard award. *The Straits Times.*
Go East, young bureaucrat (2011, March 17). Special Report, *The Economist.*
Goh, C.L. (2008, February 22). ITE route a Singapore success story: MM. *The Straits Times.*
Goh, C.T. (1992). Speech at Inauguration of ITE, Singapore, March 31.
Goh, C.T. (1999). National Day Rally Speech, Singapore, August 27.
Goh, C.T. (2001). National Day Rally Speech, Singapore, August 19.
Goh, K.S. (1979). *Report of the Education Study Team on the Ministry of Education 1978.* Singapore: Singapore National Printers.
Hiatt, F. (2011, October 26). Too many graduates in South Korea. *The Straits Times.*
Ho, A.L. (2007, February 13). Man who made ITE world class calls it a day. *The Straits Times.*
Ho, A.L. (2007, September 30). ITE: From 'school of last resort' to 'jewel' in S'pore's crown. *The Straits Times.*
ITE. (1992). Brochure, Celebrating the Inauguration of ITE. Singapore: ITE
ITE. (2009). Brochure, Transforming Lives through Innovations in Technical Education — The Singapore ITE Story. Singapore: ITE
ITE. (2011). *Infinite, A Bi-monthly Publication of ITE,* Issue 109 (Sep–Oct).
ITE. (2012). *Reliving ITE's Transformation, 20th Anniversary.* Singapore: ITE.
Johanson, R.K. & Adams, A.V. (2004). *Skills development in Sub-Saharan Africa.* World Bank Regional and Sectoral Studies. Washington D.C.: The World Bank.
Law, S.S. (1984). *Trend of vocational training in Singapore.* VITB Paper No. 1. Singapore: VITB.
Law, S.S. (1985a). Speech at Third VITB WITS Presentation Day, Singapore, 21 November.
Law, S.S. (1985b). *The vocational training system — Its development and challenges.* VITB Paper No. 4. Singapore: VITB.
Law, S.S. (1990). *Vocational training in Singapore.* VITB Paper No. 6. Singapore: VITB.
Law, S.S. (1999). Speech at ITE Excel Day, Singapore, 28 October.
Law, S.S. (2002). Speech at National Day Celebration at ITE East (Bishan), Singapore, 2 August.

Law, S.S. (2004, August 13). *Vocational technical education and training — An international perspective*. Presentation made at the International Symposium on Vocational Education — Challenges and Strategies, Suzhou, China.

Law, S.S. (2007). Interview by Patricia Lee, Oral History Centre, National Archives of Singapore. Accession No: 3124/CF 3/CF 1-3, National Heritage Board, 7 March.

Law, S.S. (2009). *Vocational technical education and economic development*. Singapore: ITEES.

Law, S.S. (2010). *Case study on "National policies linking TVET with economic expansion: Lessons from Singapore"*. Paper commissioned for the EFA Global Monitoring Report 2012. Bonn: UNESCO.

Law, S.S. & Low, S.H. (1997). An empirical framework for implementing lifelong learning systems. In M.J. Hatton (Ed.), Lifelong learning — Policies, practices and programmes (112–127). Ontario: Humber College.

Lee, E.T. (1999). Speech at PS21 4th Anniversary Celebration, Singapore, 7 May.

Lee, H.L. (2005). National Day Rally Speech, Singapore, 21 August.

Lee, K.Y. (1979). Speech at Opening of Singapore Polytechnic's New Campus at Dover Road, Singapore, 7 July.

Lee, K.Y. (2000). *From Third World to First World, the Singapore story: 1965–2000*. Singapore: Singapore Press Holdings and Times Editions.

Lee, S.K. Goh, C.B. Fredriksen, B. & Tan, J.P. (Eds.). (2008). *Toward a better future — Education and training for economic development in Singapore since 1965*. Washington D.C.: The World Bank and National Institute of Education, Singapore.

Lin, R. (2010, July 29). "Singapore brand" can be its strength. *The Straits Times*.

Lu, Z.F. (2004, August). Vocational education: The driving force behind social and economic development. *Shanghai Business*.

Making vocational education a popular choice (2011, September 20). *The New Straits Times*.

Mathavan, S.A. (2007, February 12). Thank you, Mr ITE. *The New Paper*.

Metzger, C. Fujita, H. Law, S.S. Zemsky, R. Berset, J.E. & Iannozzi, M. (2001). *Different paths, similar pursuits — The economic and personal potential of Vocational Training and Education in an international context*. Studies and Reports 12. St. Gallen: University of St. Gallen.

Ministry of Education (MOE), Singapore. (1991, March). *Report of the Review Committee on improving primary school education*. Singapore: MOE.

Mosher, B. (2008). *Experiential learners change a nation* [DVD].

Ng, E.H. (2008, June 11). *Higher education: Past, present and future*. Keynote address at the 6th Australian Universities Alumni Convention, MOE, Singapore.

Ng, E.H. (2008, August 14). Speech on "Educating the Next Generation" at the 4th Anniversary Public Lecture, Lee Kuan Yew School of Public Policy, MOE, Singapore.

Ng, W.H. (1983, June 23). Foreign help for Best teachers. *The Straits Times.*

NorthLight School. (2009). *Transformed by the mission — Stories of hope and change.* Singapore: NorthLight School.

Organisation for Economic Co-operation and Development (OECD). (2010). *OECD policy reviews of Vocational Education and Training (VET) — Learning for jobs.* Retrieved from http://www.oecd.org/education/country-studies/learningforjobs.htm.

Pillay, G.F. (2005). Technical & Vocational Education (TVE) systems of selected East Asian countries — Singapore, The South Asia Region, The World Bank, 25 June.

Rau, H. (2002). Speech at renewal of MOU between ITE and KM (Germany), Singapore, 29 October.

Spaeth, A. & Macintyre, D. (2005, November 14). Breaking through. *Time Magazine.*

SPRING Singapore. (2005, Nov–Dec). World-class excellence in technical education. *Enterprise Today.*

Tan, M. (2011, December 14). Push for more "master craftsmen". *The Straits Times.*

Tay, E.S. (1992). Speech at Second Reading for Institute of Technical Edcuation (ITE) Bill, Singapore. 27 February.

Teo, C.H. (2002). Speech at Parliamentary Budget Debate, Singapore, May.

Teo, C.H. (2012). Speech at ITE's 20th Anniversary Dinner, Singapore, 3 April.

VITB. (1991). Report on "Upgrading Vocational Training", March. Singapore: VITB.

VITB. Annual Reports 1979/1980, 1981/1982, 1983/1984, 1986/87, 1990/1991. Singapore: VITB.

Wong, K.H. & Lim, D. (2010, August 6). $165m Temasek move to honour 5 pioneers. *The Straits Times.*

World Bank. (1991). *Vocational and technical education and training: A World Bank policy paper.* Washington, D.C.: The World Bank.

World Bank. (2007). *At the crossroads: Choices for secondary education and training in Sub-Saharan Africa.* Conference edition, Africa Human Development Series. Washington D.C.: The World Bank.

World Bank. (2009). *Accelerating catch-up: Tertiary education for growth in Sub-Saharan Africa.* Washington, D.C.: The World Bank.

Yip, J.S.K. (1993, November 8–10). *Education and training in Singapore.* Paper presented at the Singapore International Foundation African Leadership Forum, Singapore.

Appendix A

An Overview of Singapore's Education System

The ITE today is firmly positioned among the post-secondary institutions as shown in the Figure A.1. An integral part of the national education and training system, there are clear lines of demarcation with respect to the missions of the university, polytechnic and ITE. ITE's mandate is to create an attractive pathway for those who do not progress to the junior college or polytechnic. As a matter of policy, all students receive at least 10 years of general education in schools, comprising six years primary and four or five years secondary education.

The first six years of primary education are compulsory. Students are streamed at Primary Four according to their academic abilities in English Language, a second language and Mathematics in the same school. The objective is to enable students to better cope with their pace of learning using a differentiated curriculum. The underlying principle is to lay a strong foundation in the basic subjects for further education and skills development. This approach has helped to reduce the number of early school leavers (Ng, 2008). Since 2004, schools have been given the flexibility in the use of "subject-based banding" and assessment system. At the secondary level, students are streamed into the Secondary Express, Secondary Normal (Academic) and Secondary Normal (Technical) courses. The Express is a four-year course for those who are most academically inclined. The Normal (Academic) also offers an academic-based curriculum but at a slower pace to enable students to complete the Singapore-Cambridge General Certificate of Education (Ordinary) or GCE "O" level in five years. A fundamental shift in 1991 was the introduction of a Secondary Normal (Technical) track for the less academically inclined. Students in this track take fewer academic subjects. They all take more applied subjects such as computer applications, elements of office administration, art and design and technical studies. These students are orientated towards further vocational training in ITE.

Depending on their academic achievements, aptitudes and interest, over 90 per cent of a primary one cohort would progress to junior college, polytechnic or ITE. The two-year junior college programme provides a rigorous academic high school education for the top 25 per cent of

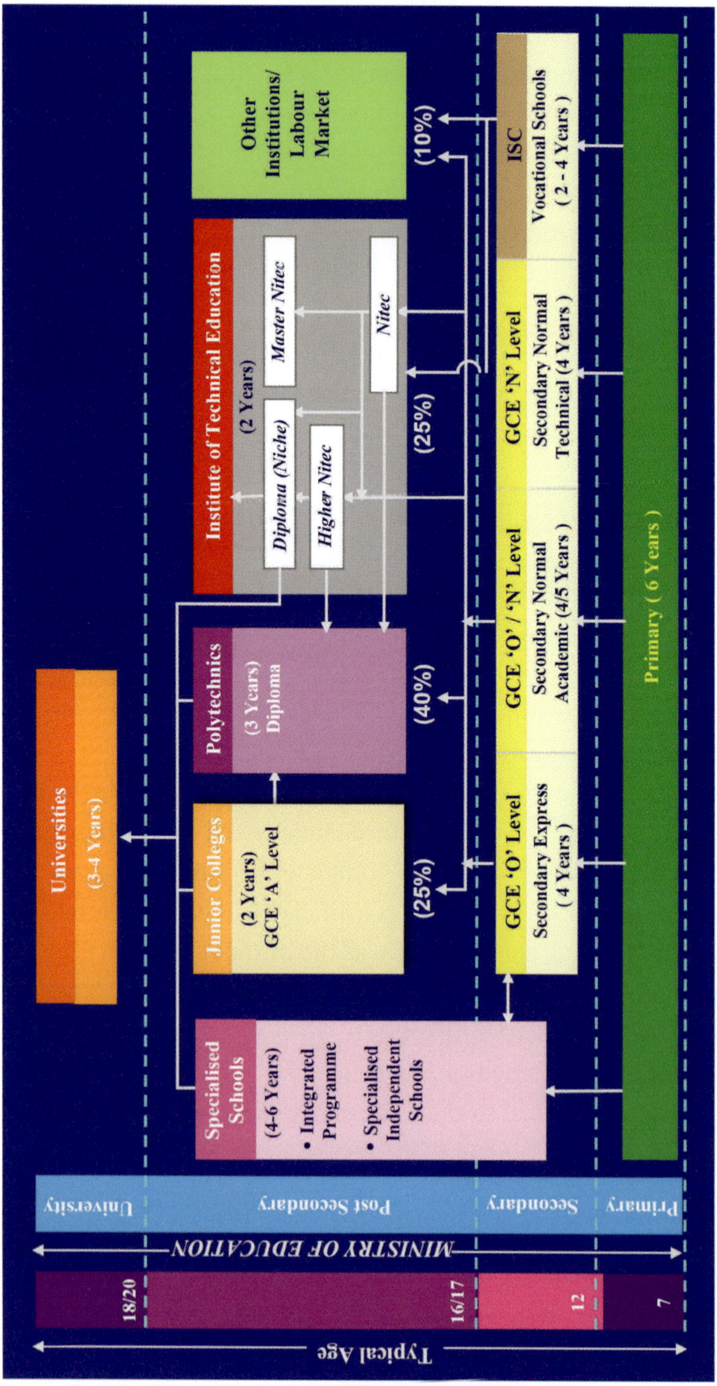

Figure A.1 Singapore's education system

a school cohort in preparation for a university education. Presently, there are four government-funded universities — National University of Singapore (NUS), Nanyang Technological University (NTU), Singapore Management University (SMU) and Singapore University of Technology and Design (SUTD) — and the privately funded SIM University (UniSIM). At his National Day Rally Speech on 26 August 2012, Prime Minister Lee Hsien Loong announced that the Singapore Institute of Technology (SIT) and UniSIM would be Singapore's fifth and sixth universities. This will increase the university participation rate of each cohort from the current 27 per cent to 40 per cent by 2020. Focusing on more applied and co-operative education programmes, they will create additional pathways and opportunities for a university education and upgrading within the total education system. The next 40 per cent of school leavers would enter the polytechnic for a wide range of practice-oriented three-year diploma courses. All funded by the government, there are five polytechnics (Nanyang Polytechnic, Ngee Ann Polytechnic, Republic Polytechnic, Singapore Polytechnic and Temasek Polytechnic).

The fundamental difference between ITE and polytechnic courses is the extent of practical skills. ITE's courses are "hands-on" and competency-based. The skills competencies are derived according to industry standards. Eighty per cent of the total curriculum time is focused on the core modules that define the occupational areas of work. Typically, 70 per cent of the time for these core modules is practical training and 30 per cent theoretical lessons. In contrast, the three-year polytechnic diploma courses are on average 50 per cent practical in nature. ITE graduates are recruited as skilled personnel, technicians or associate professionals. Their job scope would include the use of skills competencies in production, installation or maintenance associated with operating equipment, processes and systems. Polytechnic graduates, on the other hand, would enter employment as technologists, supervisors and para-professionals.

Entrants to the ITE consist mainly of students from the Secondary Normal (Academic) and Secondary Normal (Technical). These students are generally less academically inclined and form the bulk of those in the lower quartile of each cohort based on tests scores taken at the GCE "O" and GCE "N" level examinations. Those with higher scores are eligible for places in junior colleges or polytechnics. We cannot take for granted that those with lower scores will progress to vocational training in ITE. While ITE offers an attractive educational pathway for secondary school leavers, it is an opportunity that students must choose to pursue. Some of them may in fact prefer to enrol in a private school or enter the job market. Collectively, the polytechnics and ITE train 65 per cent of a school cohort in the educational system. The figure is comparable to the 60 to 70 per cent of school leavers who enter the dual system of apprenticeship in Germany or Switzerland.

The Singapore ITE model of vocational training is full-time and institution-based. Operating under the "One ITE, Three Colleges" system with 100 courses in various programmes and schools, the total full-time student enrolment is 25,600. The three colleges (ITE College Central, ITE College East and ITE College West) offer common programmes in Business & Services, Engineering and Electronics & Info-Communication Technology as well as niche programmes in Design & Media, Applied & Health Sciences and Hospitality, which are specific to individual Colleges. Another 20,000 working adults undertake part-time Continuing Education and Training courses conducted by ITE each year.

The ITE system of skills certification is based on the award of the National ITE Certificate or Nitec. A Nitec is to the ITE what a diploma is to the polytechnic and a degree is to the university. There are three levels of skills certification: the Nitec, Higher Nitec and Master Nitec. The minimum entry requirement for ITE courses is a completion of 10 years of school education. The Nitec is aligned with the needs of those with the Singapore-Cambridge General Certificate of Education (Normal) or GCE "N" level qualification. Those with the GCE "O" level are eligible for the Higher Nitec. The Master Nitec, modelled after Germany's "Meister" qualification, is designed for Nitec graduates who have the relevant work experience.

A SYSTEM WITH MULTIPLE PATHWAYS

Singapore's education system is designed with multiple pathways and built-in "ladders and bridges" to address the wide range of talents and aptitudes by offering different approaches to learning. Within the ITE system of certification, students who have done well at one level of training may progress to the next higher level. Beyond ITE, there is formal articulation for progression from ITE to the polytechnic and polytechnic to the university. The basic principle of progression is based on merit performance and the potential to do well. More recently, new pathways have been introduced to add flexibility and diversity. For example, ITE, in collaboration with world-renowned institutions, have started to offer "niche" diploma courses in areas not available in the local polytechnics. The first two Technical Engineer diploma courses in Machine Technology and Automotive Engineering were introduced in 2008 and 2010, respectively, in partnership with the Ministry of Education, Youth & Sports of Baden-Württemberg, Germany. The third Technical Diploma in Culinary Arts was offered in collaboration with the prestigious French culinary school Institut Paul Bocuse, in 2010.

The top 5 per cent of a cohort who enrol in the "Integrated Programme" in schools can skip the GCE "O" Level examination and pursue directly the Singapore-Cambridge General Certificate of Education (Advanced) or GCE "A", or the International Baccalaureate. There are also specialised schools for the talented in mathematics and science, music, arts and sports. The academically weaker students are not forgotten either. Students with good GCE "N" (Academic) results who prefer a more practical "hands-on" approach in learning may fast-track to the Higher Nitec in ITE without having to spend an additional year pursuing the GCE "O" Level. Students who have failed the Primary School Leaving Examination (PSLE) may opt to enrol in specialised vocational schools: the NorthLight School (2009) and Assumption Pathway School. These two schools provide an innovative and customised programme in basic education and vocational skills. The three to four-year curriculum is well supported by the creative use of pedagogic approaches and highly dedicated teachers from regular schools who volunteer their services (NorthLight School 2009). Those who graduate with an ITE Skills Certificate may continue their training in ITE. Under another pathway, two specialised secondary schools have been built for Secondary Normal (Technical) students. Providing a more customised and "hands-on" curriculum, students do both the GCE Normal (Technical) and the ITE Skills Certificate. The first school, Crest Secondary School, opened in January 2013 followed by Spectra Secondary School in January 2014.

About the Institute of Policy Studies (IPS)

The Institute of Policy Studies (IPS) was established in 1988 as an independent think-tank to study and generate public policy ideas in Singapore. IPS became an autonomous research centre of the Lee Kuan Yew School of Public Policy at the National University of Singapore in 2008. Today, IPS continues to analyse public policy, build bridges between thought leaders, and communicate its findings to a wide audience. The Institute examines issues of critical national interest across a variety of fields, and studies the attitudes and aspirations of Singaporeans through surveys of public perception. It adopts a multi-disciplinary approach in its analysis and takes the long-term view in its strategic deliberation and research. For more information about IPS, visit www.lkyspp.nus.edu.sg/ips/

Index